D0519899

K-9 Soldiers

Vietnam and After

Paul B. Morgan

Major, U.S. Army, Retired

To A Dog Lover

From A Dog Lover

Hellgate Press

Central Point, OR

K-9 Soldiers: *Vietnam and After*

© 1999 by Paul B. Morgan
Published by Hellgate Press

Hellgate Press
a division of PSI Research
P.O. Box 3727
Central Point, OR 97502-0032

(541) 479-9464
(541) 476-1479 fax
info@psi-research.com e-mail

Editor: Janelle Davidson
Book designer: Constance C. Dickinson
Compositor: Jan O. Olsson
Cover designer and illustrator: Steven Burns

Morgan, Paul B., 1936–
    K-9 soldiers : Vietnam and after / Paul B. Morgan.
        p. cm.
    "Hellgate memories. Vietnam."
    Includes index.
    ISBN 1-55571-495-1 (paper)
    1. Dogs—United States—War use—History—20th century.
2. Vietnamese Conflict, 1961–1975—Biography. 3. Morgan, Paul B.,
1936–   4. Soldiers—United States—Biography. 5. United States.
Army—Military police—Biography.   I. Title.
UH100.M67 1999
355.4'24—dc21   98-55569

Printed and bound in the United States of America
First edition 10 9 8 7 6 5 4 3

 Printed on recycled paper when available.

This book is dedicated to my grandchildren,
Matthew Stevens, Mary Clare, and James Morgan.

Certainly there is no hunting like the hunting of men and those who have hunted armed men long enough and liked it never really care for anything else thereafter. You will meet them doing various things with resolve but their interest rarely holds because after the other thing ordinary life is flat as the taste of wine when the taste buds have been burned off your tongue.

ERNEST HEMINGWAY

Contents

Preface

My father grew up during the period of World War I (1914–1918). He wanted to be a soldier like his older brother, John, who had been in the trenches of France with the U.S. Expeditionary Force. The fighting in Europe ended on November 11, 1918, the day my father, seventeen years old, was issued his uniform in basic training. My father never went Over There.

I grew up during World War II (1939–1945) and the Korean War (1950–1953). I was seventeen in 1953, also too young to experience the horrors of combat, but I wanted to be a soldier nonetheless. At nineteen years of age, after two years of college, I enlisted in the U.S. Army. I had been to a military high school and had joined the R.O.T.C. in college. It was an exhilarating experience to be a real soldier, not just a cadet.

Unlike many of my classmates in high school and college who wanted to make lots of money in the business world working in an office, I was dedicated to service to country. I was often asked, "Why did you join the Army?" and "Why don't you get a real job?"

I finished college and became an officer after five years of service, still dedicated to duty, honor, and country. An airborne ranger, Special Forces soldier, I went off to Vietnam in 1965.

But my liberal arts education and my conventional military training fell short in preparing me for guerrilla warfare in the jungles and rice paddies ten thousand miles from home. With training in special warfare and with the help of my patrol dog, Suzie, I did adjust, however, and served a second year Over There.

When I retired from the service at thirty-nine years of age, the world was a different place. Veterans were looked down upon. They were not heroes as were the veterans of 1945. Our service in southeast Asia was considered a national disgrace. The nation was divided. Many Vietnam veterans were discriminated against in the job market. Vilified in the press and in television news coverage, many of us denied our military service, quietly blending back into society, lest we be labeled baby killers and drug addicts.

I organized a K-9 security business, making a good living for my family for many years. It also provided jobs for other veterans who couldn't find work, and it provided the comradeship we experienced Over There. I gave a job to one buddy of mine who was absolutely determined to commit suicide. We worked side by side for over a year, talking about Vietnam. "K-9 patrol is the best therapy for him," one VA counselor commented. That veteran is still around today, working hard, raising his family.

Things turned around in the 1980s when Ronald Reagan was elected to office. The Vietnam Veterans' Memorial in Washington, D.C., was constructed with funds donated by veterans, many celebrities including Bob Hope, and hundreds of businessmen. Vietnam veterans were finally thanked for their service with parades and special ceremonies throughout the country. The black granite wall near the Lincoln Memorial, engraved with the names of over 58,000 servicemen and women killed Over There, is one of the most visited monuments in our nation's capital.

In 1995, my daughter and grandson began to ask questions about Vietnam and after. This book has been written to sort out my experiences and to answer those questions. I have written about Suzie, my patrol dog in 1965, whom I credit with saving my life on more than one occasion. I have also written about other K-9 soldiers, my buddies after Vietnam, who kept me sane with their companionship, their loyalty, their devotion to duty, and their unconditional love on those long dark nights on patrol.

I owe them all a debt of gratitude.

Introduction

As America celebrated the fiftieth anniversary of victory in World War II, there were many TV news programs about the final campaigns, the Battle of the Bulge, Okinawa, and the dropping of the atomic bomb. At Christmastime, 1995, my grandson, Matthew, who had just turned five years old, asked me a very simple question. "What was it like in the war, Grandpa?" I told him World War II raged from 1939 to 1945, claiming over 49 million lives, but I had not served in the Army back then. "I was just your age when the war started," I told him.

It was hard to explain to him that I was in the cold war and had served in Vietnam, a war America is still trying to forget. It's not easy to explain to a five-year-old what is was like, so I simply told him I was a paratrooper, that I hurt my back and broke my left leg.

My daughter grew up during Vietnam, watched the combat each night on the television evening news, and for the two years I was over there asked, "When is Daddy coming home?" As Matthew's mom, thirty years later, Maureen told me in no uncertain terms to write about Vietnam so she would know what my thoughts were and what I had experienced.

I started this work on December 26, 1995, writing individual stories. Soon after, I purchased a personal computer to efficiently record this memoir. I have written about uncles, buddies, officers, NCOs, partners, and, of course, my dogs. These stories cover the period 1957 through 1997.

Contained herein are many human interest accounts of my life in the U.S. Army, training as an airborne soldier in the '50s, surviving combat in the '60s, and surviving on the street in the '70s and '80s as a K-9 security cop. The information in each story is as true and as accurate as I can remember. Numerous letters, citations, newspaper clippings, personal papers, and duty logs were used to put this whole thing together.

I want to give a special thanks to all those buddies and relatives who served in the United States Armed Forces and, of course, all the K-9 soldiers, especially: Bear, Luger, Rommel, Wolf, King, Chinook, Suzie, Styx, Matt Dillon, Teddy Bear, Kenny, Sampson, Wolfgang, Danny Boy, Polar Bear, Buffalo, Bonnie, Simon, Duke, Little Bear, Max, and my special buddy, Cody Bear.

Another special thanks goes to my wife, Eileen, who has put up with me and those dirty dogs for over thirty-five years, and my daughter, Maureen, and her son, Matthew, who asked me to write this book.

The central theme in *K-9 Soldiers*, a memoir, is survival.

Chapter 1

Survival

1966

Suzie

Terrorism in Saigon

A few minutes after 4 A.M. on April 1, 1966, a commando team of twelve Viet Cong from Bien Hoa loaded into two gray vans and rolled out of a small villa compound in Cholon, the Chinese sector of Saigon. They headed east on Tran Hung Dao Street, armed with AK-47 assault rifles, Chinese K-5 pistols, and plastique explosives.

I was asleep in a small Navy officers' billet, dead tired after a twelve-hour shift on military police duty in the city. I had come off duty at midnight after briefing the duty officer, Lieutenant Chester Lee, Commander, C Company, 716th Military Police (MP) Battalion. I was a captain, in command of Company B's 200 military policemen.

I had only been asleep since 2 A.M. when I had arrived exhausted and hit the sack in my dirty, stinking, soaking-wet fatigue uniform after quietly placing my boots under my cot. My roommate was a U.S. Navy patrol boat commander with a bad temper. He slept with a .45 caliber pistol under his pillow. I didn't want to wake him up. He had warned me more than once, "Don't make any noise when you come into the room. I don't trust anybody over here. If I ask you who you are, you had better tell me quick or I'll draw down on you." I didn't take a shower and didn't want to make any noise at all with a roommate like that. I planned to shave and shower in the morning after four hours of sleep.

Since I had to be back on duty in five hours, I didn't turn in my M-14 rifle, ammunition, or .45 caliber automatic to the company arms room. I placed them under my cot and fell into a deep sleep with my pistol belt, holster, canteens, grenades, and ammo pouches at my side.

Saigon was a scary place to work. Military police duty was a lot tougher than I had thought it would be after coming in from the field and six months' combat duty with the 30th Ranger Battalion, Army of the Republic of Vietnam (ARVN). Out there I had my patrol dog, Suzie. She went with me everywhere. She was my constant companion. Out in the field, Suzie slept with me every night, tied to my wrist by twelve feet of parachute cord. I could rest in the field. With a lunatic for a roommate and terrorists on the streets of Saigon, I had to sleep with one eye open.

The squad of Viet Cong commandos in Cholon were joined by four so-called Saigon cowboys, local terrorists on Honda motorbikes, who guided them up Tran Hung Dao Street toward three possible targets, the Victoria Hotel, the U.S. Military Assistance Command, Vietnam, headquarters compound (called MACV II), and the Military Police station. At the Victoria Hotel, some two hundred junior staff officers and advisors lay sleeping in a hundred small, cramped rooms.

I had been in Vietnam for ten months and, due to go home on June 1, was worried about my survival. I was certain the Victoria was going to get blasted as had the Brinks Hotel, the U.S. Embassy, and the Metropole Hotel over the past fifteen months. We had received an intelligence summary stating that a major target for terrorists with a car bomb was the Victoria, a pie-shaped hotel with nine stories, but few officers really believed all the warnings about terrorist objectives.

At the Brinks Hotel on December 24, 1964, terrorists had killed 2 people and wounded 107 others with a truck bomb. At the U.S. Embassy on March 30, 1965, the Viet Cong (VC) had killed 22 people and wounded 190 others when a car bomb exploded. At the Metropole Hotel on Tran Hung Dao Street on December 4, 1965, 3 were killed and more than 100 were wounded after another truck bomb attack. One of the military policemen in my unit, Specialist Four Bill Seippel, was wounded in that bombing. He received a Bronze Star for Valor and a Purple Heart after taking on a Viet Cong squad all by himself. Saigon was a scary place. Bombings of U.S. facilities were great victories for the unseen enemy.

The VC from Bien Hoa didn't know the Saigon streets well. The Saigon cowboys guided and directed their operation. At 4:15 A.M., the two terrorist trucks split up, merging into farmers' market traffic on Tran Hung Dao. The first truck was a get-away vehicle. The second was a quarter-ton bomb headed for the Victoria Hotel at 4:30 A.M. As well as being guides, the Saigon cowboys acted as security teams, sealing off the target and preventing police reinforcements from entering the area.

At 4:25 A.M., the terrorists in the lead vehicle opened fire on the MP station and on MACV II guards across from the Victoria. Nearby in a jeep was the officer who had just taken over for me, Lieutenant Lee, who immediately ordered his driver, Specialist Michael T. Mulvaney, to step on the gas and head for MP headquarters to report.

Private First Class Patrick J. Brems, on duty at the Victoria, returned enemy fire. Armed with only a shotgun, he was overwhelmed by AK-47 automatic weapon fire and hand grenades. He quickly warned others in the hotel of the terrorist attack. The bomb vehicle halted in front of the hotel, while the VC on board opened fire on Brems and his Vietnamese policeman partner, Pham Van Ngoc, who was killed instantly.

Disregarding his personal safety, Brems pushed the truck away from the hotel out into the street. It exploded into thousands of pieces of shrapnel, leaving a gaping hole in the middle of Tran Hung Dao. The facade of the Victoria Hotel crumbled into a pile of dust on the street below. Most of the occupants, dazed and bleeding, began to evacuate the burning building, fearing it could collapse in minutes. Some officers in their underwear, some naked, fired their weapons onto Tran Hung Dao, scattering the terrorists in front of the hotel. Two Saigon cowboys, hiding behind the Moulin Rouge night club next to the Victoria, opened fire on Lee and Mulvaney with an AK-47 as the two MPs responded to the terrorist attack.

Three blocks away, I was thrown out of my bed by the enormous blast. My roommate landed on the floor next to me. He scrambled for his automatic, cursing and screaming, "Let's get the hell out of here before this whole place goes up in smoke."

My boots were on in a flash. I picked up my M-14 and jammed my automatic into its holster. Out of my room with helmet and flak jacket in hand, I bounded down the steps four floors to the street below, tripping over my bootlaces twice, crashing on to the sidewalk in front of the Navy officers' billet. I felt naked without my patrol dog. If she were with me, I could stop to tie my bootlaces while she would watch for terrorists. Sweat poured down into my eyes. I was rattled without Suzie. My roommate joined me on the street dressed in khaki shorts and sneakers, stripped to the waist. He was unarmed.

"Where's your weapon, man?" I asked him.

"God damn it, I lost the son of a bitch on the stairs," he cursed.

"Go back and get it and get your flak jacket too," I shouted.

"My jacket's on the boat," he yelled as he darted back into the hotel for his weapon.

Twenty officers from the Army and Navy armed with submachine guns, automatic pistols, and rifles were on the street searching for terrorists. Machine gun fire, bursts from other automatic weapons, and pistol shots could be heard the next block over. The streets were black. Power had gone out with the blast from the truck bomb. Since nobody was shooting at me, I tied my bootlaces, squatting down next to a crumbling concrete wall, and waited for something to happen.

I was in a complete daze. Exhausted from long hours on duty, lack of sleep, and ten months in the combat zone, I knew my thinking was slow and uncoordinated. I heard the siren of an MP jeep, saw the red lights, and watched as it pulled up to my billet. I recognized the driver, Specialist Four Lassiter, from my unit. The MP jeep was one of Company B's patrol vehicles. Lassiter said in his southern drawl, "They hit the Victoria, sir."

My executive officer, First Lieutenant Robert Zins, a cop from Youngstown, Ohio, came out of the shadows. "Ready to go, sir," he shouted.

"Yeah, let's go," I replied.

We jumped into the jeep and with lights out rolled cautiously towards Tran Hung Dao. I kept looking in the back seat for Suzie. I vowed never to be without a patrol dog again.

We didn't talk. With our eyes accustomed to the darkness, we scanned left and right looking for movement on the streets. There was none. Not a soul could be seen, but we knew we were being watched. We were sitting ducks rolling down the street on the way to the crime scene knowing full well terrorists would be escaping from the area, most probably running directly at us.

One block from the Victoria we stopped, dismounted, and went forward on foot. Lieutenant Zins disappeared back into the shadows. Lassiter and I crept forward towards a series of fires, smoke billowing up from a thousand holes in the street, and devastation resembling the London blitz of 1940. An entire city block had been reduced to a pile of smoking rubble. I expected to see Suzie walking out front, but she wasn't there. We were on our own.

A Honda motorbike came at us from the alley behind the Moulin Rouge before we could scatter for cover. It crashed into our jeep in the middle of the road. Two terrorists in black shirts carrying K-5 pistols were pinned under the vehicle. They aimed their weapons at us. I fired off a full magazine of M-14 tracer ammo, twenty rounds, cutting both in half in less than five seconds. I wasn't going to check to see if they were dead.

Lassiter rushed up, telling me, "MPs are in front of us. There's a jeep up there, sir."

Lieutenant Zins and Captain Bill Hollenbeck, my former boss from the 30th Rangers, were standing next to an MP jeep. The driver, Mike Mulvaney, was dead. Lieutenant Lee, the duty officer I had briefed at midnight, lay dying next to him, hit three times in the chest by an AK-47. Chet Lee wasn't wearing his flak jacket. His .45 caliber automatic in his right hand was empty. Lee and Mulvaney had been ambushed by the two terrorists I had just killed.

The two dead Saigon cowboys had discarded their AK-47 on Tran Hung Dao as they escaped from the area. Lassiter picked it up. I cleared it of ammunition and gave it to Captain Mike Harvey, the 716th MP Battalion intelligence officer, himself wounded by the blast.

I had been trained in mass casualty first aid before Vietnam but never really knew what it was all about. I had always thought mass casualties would occur after a plane crash or a train wreck. I was not prepared for a bombing in a city. This April Fools Day, I had 165 casualties to handle as the senior officer on this crime scene at 5 A.M. There were no ambulances, no medics, just the moans and groans of wounded and dying people. In the deep darkness before dawn, Vietnamese civilian dead and wounded lay everywhere I turned. Walking wounded, half naked survivors from the Victoria, stumbled about in the street heading for cover at MACV II or the MP station. I was powerless to help anybody. There was nothing Lassiter or I could do. I wondered if I would see my wife and daughter again.

I ordered every MP who reported to me to secure the crime scene. "Don't let anybody in or out. Kill any civilian with a weapon or anybody who runs from this area." Next we had to look for a second bomb. The terrorist always plants a second bomb to kill off the rescue workers arriving on the scene. We had to wait until daylight, 6:30 to 7:00 A.M., to conduct a proper search. We had too much time on our hands, too much time to think.

Captain Hollenbeck stripped to the waist and covered Mulvaney's face with his shirt. Mike had been hit in the face and had died instantly. Lee's vehicle, hit by AK-47 fire, wouldn't start. We tenderly carried Lee to our jeep to transport him to the U.S. Navy hospital half a mile away. His eyes were open as he gasped for breath. I held him in my arms as best I could.

"Why weren't you wearing your flak jacket?" I shouted, angry that he had been ambushed. Then I told him, "You'll make it!" But I knew he would die soon. I asked him a thousand questions about the bombing.

Lassiter cautioned me, "Take it easy on him, sir. He can't talk." There was no answer, just a gasp of air. His eyes closed.

I carried Chet Lee into the hospital emergency room. The Navy staff was waiting and well prepared after their mass casualties experience on December 4 at the Metropole bombing. Chief Medical Corpsman Ed Wilson took Lee from me, placing him on the floor next to a door. He covered Lee with a sheet.

I saw an Army sergeant with a nasty four-inch slash wound on his right forearm being sewn up by other corpsmen. I told Wilson, "Lee has been hit pretty bad, a lot worse than that guy. Can't you do something?" I insisted Lee be treated for his chest wounds.

"He's dead, sir. Go back to your unit," the chief ordered, pushing me towards the door.

I just couldn't believe it, I had been talking to him all the way to the hospital. He had died in my arms.

As daylight broke, about 6:30 A.M., I could see the contents of almost every room in the entire Victoria structure with the front of the building blasted away. Littering the street below were furniture, blood-stained bedding, wall lockers, mirrors, bathroom fixtures, hallway doors, and small refrigerators.

When briefing my company about this terrorist act on April Fool's Day, I lost emotional control for the first time in my nine-year military career. I simply could not handle the stress. I had to stop talking when explaining what had happened on Tran Hung Dao Street that morning. I got so choked up in front of the 200 military policemen of Company B that First Sergeant Campany took over. Lieutenant Zins walked me back to my office and said, "Get some sleep, sir. It's been a long day."

I looked at my watch. It was just 8 A.M.

Lieutenant Chester L. Lee from El Dorado, Arkansas, was posthumously awarded the Silver Star for gallantry and the Purple Heart for wounds received in action. For Patrick Brem, the soldier who had pushed the bomb truck into the street away from the Victoria Hotel, his parents received a Distinguished Service Cross for his extraordinary heroism and a Purple Heart for mortal wounds received that day.

My Patrol Dog, Suzie

Suzie's real name was Xa Xi, sarsaparilla, because she loved to drink that carbonated soda. Xa Xi was a favorite drink of the Vietnamese. Suzie was not an item of Army issue. She belonged to Father Nguyen Cong Tu, the village priest in Cau Xang.

Suzie kept Father Tu alive for several years by alerting on any person who came near the priest. The Viet Cong placed a handsome price on his head since he was both a spiritual leader and a guerrilla fighter. Suzie guarded him day and night. Suzie could be vicious and would attack any person who threatened her owner.

I received Suzie from Father Tu as a present after I gave him a .38 caliber pistol and a sterling silver set of rosary beads. Suzie slept next to me every night, tied to my wrist with parachute cord. She was responsible for saving my life on many occasions. As a military advisor, I also had a price on my head, but Suzie made sure nobody harmed me. She was the perfect German shepherd, obedient, faithful, devoted, and always at my side. I never took Suzie for granted.

In December 1965, I returned Suzie to Father Tu when I left my ranger battalion unit, for a military police assignment in Saigon.

In 1983, while a professional dog handler and K-9 security specialist, I bought another German shepherd, Bonnie, just because she looked like Suzie. Bonnie and Suzie were so much alike that even today I often cannot tell them apart when I see their photos in my K-9 files.

Xa Xi, alias Suzie

Photo by author, 1965

Chapter 2

Ranger

1957–58

Bear

Joining Up

I was born in New York City in 1936, and after twenty years in the Bronx, I was bored with city life. So I joined the U.S. Army seeking fun, travel, and adventure. Back in the 1950s, after World War II and the Korean War, all we heard from our neighbors who were veterans was, "Join up." It was considered the responsibility of every young man who was able bodied to serve your country like your uncle or your dad or your brother did. Where I was raised, if you didn't serve your country, you couldn't get a job. Employers wouldn't hire anybody facing the draft. If you were not in the service, you weren't anything. Military service was the rite of passage to manhood.

All my relatives and neighbors had been in the infantry, the U.S. Marines, or the airborne, or at least it seemed that way. My Uncle Bill served with the 82d Airborne Division at Normandy and in the Battle of the Bulge. A big guy, 225 pounds and tough, wounded at Bastogne on December 24, 1944, he was a neighborhood hero. When the movie *Battleground* was in local theaters in the Bronx in 1948, so was I, along with my Uncle Bill and dozens of other tough guys who were airborne troopers. He knew all of them and they knew him. *Battleground* was the story of a platoon of infantrymen with the 101st Airborne at Bastogne. After the movie, I wanted to join up right then. Bill talked about Bastogne until he died of his wounds in 1959. His son, Billy, joined the airborne in 1964. He was killed in action with the 101st Airborne at nineteen years of age at Tuy Hoa,

Vietnam, in June 1965. I brought his body home and escorted his mother, Jean Kelly, to his funeral.

My Uncle John served in the 82d Infantry Division in World War I, before they had paratroopers, back in 1918. My Uncle Joe served in the U.S. Marines in World War II and was wounded in an island-hopping campaign in the South Pacific. My Uncle Matthew was a colonel in the U.S. Army in World War II. He didn't talk about it much.

Military service was in my blood. The 82d Airborne was the place to go. On January 7, 1957, I raised my right hand and started a most interesting career. Before I retired twenty years later, I had been to every place all my uncles had been to and one worse, Vietnam. I was a combat infantryman, a ranger, a paratrooper, a Special Forces officer, and a military policeman. I loved every bit of it, except for the blood, sweat, tears, separations from my family, and two injuries worse than a train wreck or a head-on collision.

Basic training at Fort Benning, Georgia, wasn't that tough for this rugged guy from the Bronx, except for the blood, sweat, tears, and — you got the message. I thought I was going to die. I started out in the infantry, and we walked everywhere, of course. When we didn't walk, we ran everywhere. We slept little and ate less, but we learned to survive.

I found out I was a good shot with the M-1 Gerand rifle of World War II and Korean War fame. I knew how to stuff a field pack full of clothes one doesn't need. We called them full-field packs, with three sets of rations, fatigues, underwear, and socks. I would have preferred to have been dirty and filthy rather than carry that much stuff around. After basic and advanced training, sixteen weeks in the rain and heat, crawling around in Georgia clay under Georgia pines, I found out it was better to carry two canteens of water than three changes of clothes.

In the infantry, I became a heavy weapons specialist. That designation was given to me after the sergeants figured out I could carry machine guns, ammunition, and mortars like a mule. That meant I had a weak mind and a strong back. I was too stupid to complain. Tired of being a beast of burden, I volunteered for patrolling. That meant you carried very few things, no packs, only ammunition and water, a compass, a rifle, and the clothes on your back.

Before long, I was assigned as the point-man, which means being the lead man fifty feet out front of the rest of the group. It wasn't dangerous to be a point-man in peacetime. You just walked out in front of the company and acted like a hunter in the woods. For a guy from the Bronx, that meant I got lost all the time. I loved the job but didn't know how to read a map or a compass. And you know how hard it must have been for a wise guy like me to ask for directions. I was like Moses in the Sinai, hopelessly lost but putting on a good show as I wandered around in circles.

I fooled the brass and the sergeants. They thought I was great out there, covering lots of ground in a short period of time, thrashing about in the woods. When I ended up in the rear of the column once, while I was supposedly scouting out front, I told Sergeant Johnson, a patrolling instructor, I was checking their flank security.

I wanted to go to Ranger School and really learn how to do that stuff. Ranger School was for officers and sergeants. They should have sent the privates. By the time one gets to be a sergeant, he doesn't get lost any more.

Sergeant Johnson liked my attitude. He told our patrolling class, "Teams survive. Individuals don't." I never forgot that.

One day he said he needed a "big dummy" to serve as an enemy soldier for his patrol dog class. I volunteered. All I had to do was run across the field in front of the bleachers full of students and shoot blanks from my M-1 rifle at a man-dog team. I did it, no sweat. What theater! "Die, you yankee pig!" I screamed and fired my rifle at the dog handler. The poor soldier got so scared he dropped his dog leash. The dog charged me like a grizzly and hit me like a freight train, tearing my jacket to shreds before they could pull him off. I thought I was going to die.

The dog's name was Bear. He was old then, seven, and slow but a great school dog. He had won an unofficial Bronze Star and a Purple Heart in Korea. His handler won the awards and gave them to Bear, the military establishment being opposed to awarding medals to dogs. I loved that dog, even though he almost dismembered me in front of my rifle company. I laughed about it and swallowed Army aspirin for the next two weeks, trying to recover from the aches and pains.

Bear's handler was Sergeant Molnar, another Korean War veteran. I asked the sergeant how I could become a dog handler. He told me, "Just volunteer, son."

When basic training was over in the spring of 1957 at Fort Benning, my next assignment was to be the 82d Airborne Division at Fort Bragg, North Carolina. I was told to "wait for written orders to move to Fort Bragg and jump school." For three weeks I pulled guard duty, and still no orders came. I was bored. I met Sergeant Molnar at the post exchange and told him my tale of woe. He said, "I need somebody like you at the patrolling committee. I'll talk to Sergeant Johnson."

They needed an administrative assistant for the patrol dog committee at Fort Benning. That meant I would be cleaning out kennels, feeding the dogs, giving demonstrations, and taking hits from Bear. The patrol dog course was three weeks long, mostly for reservist non-commissioned officers (NCOs). I couldn't attend since I wasn't an NCO, a sergeant, but I could be on the committee and learn how to read a map, follow a compass, lead patrols, and handle a dog. I didn't care about jump school now. I had found my niche in the U.S. Army. I wanted to be a K-9 handler.

After talking to Sergeant Molnar, my first sergeant, Sergeant Stull, ordered me to report to the barracks. He said it was not customary in the service to seek other employment after signing a paper at the recruiting station. I was going to jump school and the 82d Airborne Division. I also was ordered to stop thinking about changing things. I convinced my first sergeant, whom we called God, that I could be detailed to the K-9 committee as a guard since I was pulling guard duty anyway. That night I was feeding dogs. It helped that Sergeant Johnson, Sergeant Molnar, and First Sergeant Stull were drinking buddies.

Upon my arrival at the kennels, Sergeant Molnar ordered me to "Learn Bear." I misunderstood, asking the sergeant what he wanted me to teach the dog. "You can't teach him nothin', boy. Bear knows everything. Get to know *him*. Learn Bear!"

Walking with The Bear

During the spring of 1957, I was assigned to Fort Benning's infantry school patrol dog committee as a guard. This was a temporary job for me while awaiting written orders to the 82d Airborne Division at Fort Bragg, North Carolina. My major duty was to feed the German shepherds, clean out their kennels, and take care of the unit area after hours. I ate with the dogs, slept with the dogs, played with the dogs, and worked with the dogs seven days a week. We had eight dogs in the kennels, and I knew every one of them well. They all liked me because I fed them, talked to them, and played with them.

These dogs had been through a sort of basic training after they had been accepted into the military. They were given basic obedience training. Then it was up to the handler to do any further training and fine-tuning after he got the dog. Over time, the handler and the dog together become a six-legged soldier.

Our patrol dog committee trained dog handlers to read maps, read the military compass, and work as point men. The dog-handler course was a three-week exercise, attended mostly by reservists from Georgia, Alabama, the Carolinas, Kentucky, and Tennessee. Military police and reserve infantry outfits sent sergeants to this course while on active duty for training. Virtually all of the students were Korean War veterans, policemen back home in small towns working the night shift. In many rural areas in the south, a police department consisted of four people, a chief and three patrolmen, and a patrol dog. A man-dog team kept the peace from midnight until 8 A.M. A man-dog team was better than two officers on night duty for two reasons. Most small town budgets couldn't afford two officers on night duty, and according to one officer, "Dogs have a way of keeping the peace on the night shift."

I sat in on all the classes and acted as a gofer, or errand boy. The sergeants would need something while conducting a class, and I would go for whatever they needed, whether chalk, maps, grease pencils, flashlights, or dogs. Map and compass work took up much of the first two weeks of training. I was good in the classroom reading a map but got lost in the field. These combat veterans were hunters and outdoorsmen with great night vision and tracking skills. No flash-lights were allowed at night in the field. They taught me how to use my night vision, and soon I was able to see at night as well as these sergeants from the back woods. A man has to see well at night to be a good hunter, to survive in combat, and do good police work, they told me.

One veteran, Sergeant Robert Thompson, liked to work at night with his dog, Bo. Thompson was a great fan of Ernest Hemingway. He gave me two paperback books written by Hemingway, *The Sun Also Rises* and *A Farewell to Arms*. He told me Ernest Hemingway was a hunter, an outdoorsman who loved dogs, and a veteran of World War I, the Spanish Civil War, and World War II. Hemingway also suffered from depression and what is today diagnosed as post traumatic stress disorder. Hemingway wrote about the hunting of armed men and about night vision and survival in very difficult situations. Sergeant Thompson told me, "Read Hemingway and you will be better prepared psychologically for combat." I followed his advice.

Night vision requires off-center scanning from left to right. One doesn't look directly at his target because if he does, it will disappear like a dot in a black hole. By scanning, the target can be seen. A night fighter cannot use a flashlight or strike a match. If he does, he will immediately lose his visual purple, the tech-nical term for night vision. My Uncle John told me a story about night vision and how one can die on the battlefield violating light and sound discipline.

Three soldiers on the western front in 1918 decided to light up cigarettes to escape the boredom of life in the trenches. All from the same town back home, they talked about their girlfriends and families. Our dough boys were notorious for talking, laughing, singing, and smoking cigarettes in the trenches. That had been the custom in the Civil War, 1861–1865, when there was an undeclared truce at night. On the western front in France, things were different. German snipers, hidden in trenches one hundred yards away, were scanning for Yanks. These three infantrymen from the 42d Division gathered together, sitting down on ammunition boxes. The first soldier struck a stick match against his wooden seat. A bright light was seen. The soldier lit his cigarette and that of the man to his right. An older man, a sergeant, bent over to light up on the same match. The crack of a Mauser rifle was heard. The first soldier holding the match was shot between the eyes. The second Yank was hit by another sniper. The third soldier died of a heart attack. The story is called Three on a Match.

In class, students were asked, "What good is a point man, scouting out front, providing security for the main body of troops, if he gives his position away?" Students would respond loudly, "No good! No damn good at all, sir!"

We were told not to smoke or talk while handling dogs because it would hamper their magnificent God-given senses of smell and hearing. The dogs were trained to be quiet, too, and all commands to the dogs were given silently. Arm and hand signals were taught. One could snap his fingers or make some animal sounds to get the dog to respond, but no talking was the rule. The most the dog would be allowed was to growl or flash his teeth. The main lessons we were taught were to keep quiet and to watch the dog's ears. "Learn Bear," Sergeant Molnar's order, meant something now.

While most of the students drank beer at the NCO club at night, I stayed back at the kennels working with Bear in the moonlight. As a guard, I was required to make rounds, and I did, but playing with The Bear took up most of my time. My favorite game was to sneak up on the sergeant of the guard or the officer of the day sent out to check on me while on guard duty. I would hide in the shadows and move with great slowness up to my target. When I startled one lieutenant about 2 A.M. on one such occasion, the officer completely lost his ability to speak. Lieutenant Ryan told me the next day, "You and that dog behind me last night rattled my cage so bad that I'll never forget it!"

As part of our duty assignment, we were attached to the Army Ranger School as scouts for combat patrols in the surrounding rural area. The Ranger Course was nine weeks long with three weeks spent at Fort Benning before the students went on patrol in the mountains of North Georgia and the swamps of Florida. The third week at Fort Benning was very tough, with four patrols in five days. The final week of our dog handler course was spent with these rangers, orienting them on the use of scout dogs.

My training really paid off for me during the third week of the course. I was in my element now. I got out of my jeep at the Ranger School and immediately felt at home, strutting around with Bear. I was dressed in camouflage, and with all the green and black grease on my baby face, nobody could distinguish me from anybody else. One of the instructors, seeing me with Bear, called me Sergeant. Boy, I felt good! My performance was pure theater once again.

I was assigned to a platoon of officers, recent graduates of West Point and of college Reserve Officers' Training Corps (R.O.T.C.) programs. They were joking around, laughing, smoking cigarettes, and having a great time, until I arrived. I had heard drill sergeants "chew butt," so I tried my hand at it.

"Knock off the talking and cigarettes! Don't smoke around my dog! Let's get serious! What you learn tonight might even save your life in combat," I shouted, like an old combat veteran. If anybody had looked past the black and green camouflage on my face, they would have seen that I didn't even shave as yet.

Their tactical officer, a captain, joined me. "You heard the sergeant. Knock off the cigarettes and the talking. Get serious. Move out!"

The patrol went into single file, and I was motioned to take the point. Out front with another scout, a military academy graduate, I was treated like an equal. Twenty-six ranger students got deadly serious as we crossed through friendly front lines into so-called enemy territory. The training area looked like the no-man's-land of World War I in France with open spaces, lots of shadows, and barbed wire. The moon had gone behind the clouds. We couldn't see ten feet until night vision kicked in after a while.

A lot of prestige goes along with the gold and black Ranger patch. Nobody wants to attend the course and fail a patrol. Even if a ranger student completes the training, he may not receive the Ranger tab if given a poor patrol evaluation. I'm sure the students were acting as if they were in combat so they would pass the course. I was there to learn all I could for I thought I might make the Army my career and possibly see combat some day.

The patrol moved at a snail's pace for two hours in thickly wooded areas and swamps in the Georgia boondocks. The aggressors, our opposing force, were trying to make contact with us, waiting in ambush. The 29th Infantry from Fort Benning made up the aggressor unit that night. They were dressed in green uniforms with helmets with a ridge down the middle that looked like French issue from World War I.

I couldn't see far in the dense terrain. There was no moonlight. I just watched Bear's ears as he moved along in the lead. Suddenly without warning, an officer signaled that the first phase of the training was over. We stopped for a few minutes, and a new patrol leader was picked from the students in the unit. The tactical officers change patrol leaders every so often so that each ranger student gets a chance to lead at least ten patrols in nine weeks of Ranger training. The tactical officer tells the first patrol leader, "You're dead." He lies there on the ground as if he were killed by a sniper. The assistant patrol leader then takes over, reorganizes the patrol, and orders the men to move out. The training is very realistic and challenging.

The new patrol leader, from Clemson University R.O.T.C., told me to continue as lead. "No changes, sergeant. Walk on." We were creeping down a dried out creek bed when Bear stopped and dropped flat down on the ground. I could not see a thing, but Bear did. He also heard something. I watched his ears. He flashed his teeth. The patrol leader crawled up and asked me if we had made contact with the enemy. I put my finger across my lips and pointed to the front. I thought that was the right thing to do — that's what they do in the movies.

Bear began a low growl. I could feel it through his collar. I scanned left and right. Directly in front of us, twenty feet away, aggressors were making a map check. They had a flashlight. I covered my eyes before losing my night vision. The wind had drowned out their talking until they began arguing with each other. They were lost. I never again felt lost after that training exercise. I knew exactly where I was, since I had kept a mental record of everything I did on that first of many patrols in my military career. I had the confidence of a veteran, and I didn't even shave as yet.

Our patrol leader told me to stay in place and organize a blocking force. No enemy movement forward would be allowed. I would be joined by a machine gun team. The ranger patrol would flank the aggressors on their left. With a creek on their right, the aggressors would be trapped. The machine gun team joined me just as the aggressors detected us. Bear growled and barked when the enemy soldiers pressed forward. I opened fire with my M-1 rifle, the machine gun opened fire, flares went up turning night into day, and I could see everything. If it had been real ammunition, our machine gun would have destroyed the entire enemy force as they bunched up and tried to scramble out of the stream bed. It was all over, as it is in combat, in a few brief seconds.

"Cease fire! Clear all weapons," the umpires ordered. Umpires are sergeants who accompany tactical units and account for everybody. They assess casualties and tell leaders who won and who lost. Sergeant First Class Barrow was the chief umpire. A veteran of World War II and Korea, he was very professional. An old guy about thirty-five, he had spent fifteen years in the Army. He was to see combat again, in Vietnam.

I'll never forget Sergeant Barrow's critique that hot, humid night at Fort Benning: "You men were doing fine until you started relying on that map instead of your own senses. While you were deciding where you where, instead of where the rangers were, you got ambushed. That dog started you in a panic! Load up, rapidly, K-9 up front. Let's go home and get some sleep."

The ranger students returned to friendly front lines. In their after-action report, they credited themselves with a job well done. They critiqued their teamwork and leadership ability and decided they were magnificent.

Their tactical officer returned their report with three questions to be answered: Who was the point man? Did he have a scout dog? What missions were assigned to the lead element?

They had forgotten about Bear. He was one of those unknown K-9 soldiers who never got credit for his work. He had found the enemy and fixed him in position. Without the Bear's contribution, things would have ended differently that night.

Sergeant Preston

When I was growing up in the '40s and '50s before television invaded the living room, we listened to stories on the radio after school. There was *Superman, Archie, The Lone Ranger*, and my favorite, *Sergeant Preston of the Yukon*. Sergeant Preston was a Royal Canadian Mounted Policeman with a patrol dog, King. The dog was instrumental in solving every crime and finding every lost person. Sergeant Preston was my hero. He had a horse and a dog, and he was a cop. I wanted to be like him and tell my dog, "Well, King, I guess this case is closed."

I learned how to be a dog handler while on the guard detail at the infantry school at Fort Benning, attending classes every day when the courses were given. I was fascinated with being a dog handler, working with a map and compass, going on patrol. It was outdoor stuff. I couldn't imagine working at a job indoors, in an office with no fresh air. At nights, I secured the kennels, cleaned them out, and fed the dogs. It was a temporary job with the fancy title of administrative assistant to the kennel master.

I enjoyed the job with the infantry school patrol dog committee. One day I would play the fearless point man, tracking the enemy with a patrol dog. The next day I was an enemy soldier, begging for mercy, caught behind the lines by a patrol dog working with the military police. The infantry lieutenants attending officers' basic training laughed themselves out of the bleachers when I was mauled by scout dogs at our classes. I was great at physical comedy, falling down, screaming, and suffering.

Then as luck would have it, I got the chance to go on a real mission just before Christmas 1957. It was a search and rescue job. I would have an opportunity to become Sergeant Preston.

A sergeant and his wife, living off post in rural Georgia, reported their child had been kidnapped, calling the local police for assistance. A K-9 man-dog team was needed to track the kidnapper, but no man-dog teams were available. The military was asked to provide a team since the two citizens requesting assistance were a soldier and his wife.

Out on patrol, checking ranges, ammunition holding areas, and back roads in my jeep on guard duty, I was called on the radio and told to report to post headquarters at midnight. I had my favorite infantry scout dog, Bear, with me. Of the eight patrol dogs used by our committee, Bear was the best. He was a Korean War veteran with a Bronze Star and a Purple Heart presented to him by his handler who had been officially awarded the citations.

The local sheriff arrived at Fort Benning a short time later and transported Bear and me to the area off post where we would begin our search. It was a cold, windy night, and no moon was visible with heavy cloud cover. The sergeant and his wife told investigators that they had gone out for a walk, leaving their five-year-old boy in his pajamas sleeping on the couch. When they returned, the child was missing. They searched the back yard, as did the police. The nearest neighbors were several hundred yards down the road. They didn't want to disturb them. They said that the neighbor was a hunter with many guns and he didn't like this sergeant. The neighbor's wife got along well with the sergeant's wife because the neighbors had a seven-year-old boy and their boys often played together.

The sergeant and his wife were in terrible shape, crying and feeling guilty they had left their child home alone. I went into the boy's room with Bear, and he picked up the child's scent in short order. With the boy's blanket in my hand, Bear and I headed out the back door. It was so dark outside that I had to wait several minutes to gain some night vision. Bear dragged me into the woods behind the residence without hesitation. I was not armed and wondered what would happen if I ran into a kidnapper who was armed.

For more than half an hour Bear dragged me through thick underbrush at the end of his twenty-foot lead. We circled around several times, and I became very disoriented. The boy must have wandered the same pattern. I knew we would find him because the scent was strong and fresh. I hoped he hadn't been killed and buried out there. Bear continued on the track. We entered an open field. There was a structure in the distance. We were back in some kind of civilization. Bear stopped for a moment, alerting on a noise. I could hear nothing but the wind.

Scanning left to right, I noticed a vehicle on a road near the structure. Two men were next to the car, smoking cigarettes. I thought I would approach them, asking them what they were doing out there at 3 A.M., but I changed my mind, remembering I was unarmed. Besides, they might be involved with the boy's disappearance. I had no radio to call for assistance and racked my brain for some way out of the situation.

Seconds later I heard some radio traffic, possibly a police unit. I began to think these men were game poachers armed with shotguns, monitoring police or forest ranger calls.

"Unit one hundred, this is base, over," the radio crackled.

"This is one hundred, go ahead."

"What's your situation, over?"

"We're still on site. K-9 team from Fort Benning is still out, over."

These men were two sheriffs I had met earlier. Bear and I were the K-9 team. I suddenly realized I had been traveling in a big circle in the woods following the dog. They had not detected me, and I felt good about that. Had they been poachers, I might have been shot if they had discovered me. I walked up to the two deputies.

"Anything new, sheriff?" I asked.

Both of them jumped as if they had seen a ghost. They tried to be cool, but I could see they were embarrassed. "Nothing yet," they replied.

"I'm going to check out the neighbor's house. His lights are on," I added.

"He's a hunter and a trapper. Game wardens would like to catch him at it, but he's crazy. Watch yourself," they warned.

Bear and I approached the house. I knocked on the back door since the light was on in the kitchen and I would be able to see any person inside. The door flew open and a large man in hunting clothes stepped outside. He came out the door so fast, with a shotgun in his hands, that I thought I was going to die.

"Freeze!" I ordered. "Drop the shotgun!" Bear growled and barked, terrifying the man.

The hunter complied, slowly placing his shotgun on the ground and raising his hands over his head. "This is my home. What do you want?" he asked.

I told him I was with the sheriff's department looking for a lost child.

He replied, "You're no sheriff. I know all of them. They don't have dogs."

"I'm from Fort Benning," I replied and quickly added "military police" so he would think I was armed.

"You all lookin' for that boy next door?" the hunter asked.

I had a sick feeling in my stomach. This man knew about the missing child. Was he the kidnapper? I almost panicked, thinking the hunter had killed the child and now he would kill me. What would I do next?

At that moment the hunter's wife stepped out the door. "What's the problem, officer? He's not been poachin'," she said in his defense.

I told her I was looking for the boy next door. She replied, "He's here, as usual. Whenever they go out, he comes over here to play with my boy."

The sergeant and his wife had filed a false police report. They had not been out for a short walk. They had left their son home alone, sleeping on the couch, at 6 P.M. while they went to a drive-in movie and then to a road house for a few beers, arriving home at midnight. I'm not sure what happened to the couple after that, but I know Bear and I could have saved their child's life. Had the boy gotten lost in the woods, Bear would have found him. I was absolutely confident of that fact.

I had my chance to be Sergeant Preston, but I didn't get the opportunity to tell Bear, "I guess this case is closed." He fell asleep in my arms, and I just hugged him on the way back to Fort Benning in the back seat of the patrol car.

Chapter 3

Airborne

1958–59

Luger, Rommel, Bear, Wolf,
King, Polar Bear, Chinook

Luger

While still at Fort Benning, Georgia, awaiting orders for the 82d Airborne Division at Fort Bragg, North Carolina, I was temporarily assigned as a guard at the 82d Airborne Division Headquarters during one of their field training exercises being held at Fort Gordon, Georgia. I was allowed to wear the airborne shoulder patch but no jump wings. Wings were awarded only after three weeks of hell called the basic airborne course, which included two weeks of ground training and five jumps in the third week of the course.

A field training exercise can be a lot of fun with jumping out of airplanes, flying in helicopters, playing war games, sneaking around with a green and black camouflaged face in the middle of the night, and playing commando. If one must see combat some day, field training exercises prepare the soldier for any possible situation. Excellent training with the 82d Airborne in the '50s kept me alive in Vietnam in the '60s.

While on guard duty I learned how military units function in the field. I was standing guard outside a circus-sized big-top tent. Inside the flaps, war raged on with radio messages, briefings, frantic reports from units in combat with enemy forces, messengers running back and forth to the front lines, and maps, maps, and more maps. Outside the tent you could hear nothing but generator engines providing electricity for the radios, the lights, and the kitchen at Division Headquarters. There were fifty players, officers and sergeants, in this war game. The division commander was a major general. I had seen this in the movies about World War II, but now I was experiencing war practice first hand.

According to the reports and map markings, our twelve thousand airborne soldiers had parachuted in small groups into a foreign country, actually Fort Gordon. Their mission was to disrupt, disorganize, and confuse the enemy, which was attacking another country friendly to NATO, the North Atlantic Treaty Organization. The other country was called the CSRA, the Central Savannah River Area. Our mission was to destroy enemy fuel and ammunition stores, thus preventing further aggression and possibly World War III. Although this was 1957, the 82d Airborne Division was training for a 1990s Desert Storm type war. Military police units from the army reserve were called up for these war games just as they were for the War in the Gulf when Saddam Hussein invaded Kuwait in 1990. As Joint Chiefs Chairman General Colin Powell had told Americans during Desert Storm, "Our strategy is quite simple. First we're going to cut off this army, and then we're going to kill it."

I thought my job was totally insignificant as a private first class dog handler. I was attached to a military police reserve squad of dog handlers from Georgia and North Carolina. These military policemen were Korean War veterans and professional dog handlers in civilian police departments. They knew their professions well and had brought their own dogs to Fort Gordon for the field training exercise. We guarded the headquarters, motor pool, communications center, and a prisoner of war (POW) compound.

My sergeant was a tough North Carolina good old boy who had two black and tan German shepherd dogs, Rommel and Luger. He worked with Rommel, and he assigned Luger to me. "Do what I do, the way I do it, and Luger will follow your orders," he told me, in no uncertain terms. The sergeant drove around the perimeter in a jeep with Rommel, and I walked with Luger every night from 6 P.M. to 6 A.M.

Luger was a real character. This dog weighed over one hundred pounds. Maximum for a large shepherd in good shape is ninety-five pounds. He didn't dash around or play ball or do anything but lie down and sleep. He was as lazy as lazy can be. He needed a bath, a good grooming, and some fitness training. I was ashamed of working with this dog. Whenever he was with me, the 82d Airborne MPs laughed at Luger, sleeping on duty at the command headquarters. The MP commander joked with me one night, saying, "Bury that dead dog before he stinks up this place."

I asked my sergeant, "Can I walk with Rommel on duty? They don't think Luger can do the job."

The sergeant got very angry with me. "Luger is a good dog, about seven years old and ready to retire, but he's a fine animal. You'll see. Wait until things get hot. Luger can be tough as nails. He's just bored now."

As the war game got into its third day, a so-called infiltrator in an 82d Airborne MP uniform was caught trying to blow up the communications vans connecting division headquarters with units in the field. There was a crackdown on security, and new passes were issued after screening of personnel was conducted. I didn't pass the screening. I was suspected of being an enemy agent, charged with being an infiltrator, and thrown into the POW compound to face many hours of prisoner of war interrogation.

My first sergeant's screening philosophy was simple: "Ask them questions only a trooper would know the answers to. If they hesitate giving you the answers, they're lying, so take 'em down." The questions they asked me included who was the division commander and name three bars in Fayetteville, North Carolina, the town outside of Fort Bragg. Wearing the 82d Airborne patch but with no jump wings and not knowing the division commander's name or where to hang out in Fayetteville caused me a lot of grief.

The first sergeant of the MP company had been with the 101st Airborne in the Battle of the Bulge in December 1944 when German SS troops in U.S. uniforms infiltrated friendly front lines, killing many American GIs. Some of those killed were buddies from my first sergeant's old outfit. The Germans were finally stopped after they couldn't satisfy guards asking them questions. Questions came from the *Stars and Stripes* newspaper comic strip characters like Dick Tracy and a gangster named Flattop known to American GIs in 1944. The Germans didn't read *Stars and Stripes*. When they couldn't answer questions about the comics, they were taken prisoner.

Since I couldn't answer questions about Fort Bragg, I was taken captive. The first sergeant had a tough, grim look on his face when he told me, "Your ass is grass, boy, and I'm the lawnmower!" I thought he was going to shoot me with his .45 caliber automatic. When he told me to move, I moved. He called me a "smart ass Kraut."

They kept me awake for forty-eight hours, harassing me like an enemy soldier. A spotlight continually blinded me, I received no food or water, and all I wanted to do was sleep. Every time I fell asleep, the guards woke me up and made me stand and sing the 82d Airborne battle song, "All American Soldier."

All my possessions, except for my wallet, were taken from me. The interrogation prisoner of war specialists, IPW, went through them and could find no reason for me to be wearing an 82d Airborne patch on my uniform. I explained to them that I was on temporary duty at Fort Gordon en route to Fort Bragg and jump school. They couldn't find any military orders to verify that information. I told them I was a dog handler at Fort Benning and had a letter of commendation to prove it. I produced the letter, which was in my wallet, and the last paragraph of it read, "Good luck with your future assignment at Fort Bragg." Only after they called the captain at Fort Benning who wrote the letter of commendation and he verified my identification was I released. I had learned some valuable security lessons in this training exercise, and I applied them throughout my military career.

After I returned to my guard duty assignment, I was issued Luger again. He was very glad to see me and was very affectionate after being left alone in a kennel for two days. An old dog, fat, slow, and lazy, he didn't get much love or attention. After a week of Army Reserve duty, he had lost a few pounds and seemed to enjoy my company. We were beginning to bond as dog and handler.

The MP commander at division headquarters inspected me on duty the sixth day of the field training exercise. He asked me if I would be interested in being an 82d Airborne MP after finishing jump school. His unit was going to have some vacancies, and there was a long waiting list to get into the military police. I must have made an impression on him holding up under POW interrogation for two days and nights. He said my letter of commendation from Fort Benning was an excellent reference and could possibly lead to an early promotion.

"Do you have a K-9 squad?" I inquired.

"No. The animal protection agencies won't let us jump with dogs," he answered.

I was crushed. I decided to stay in the infantry. I found out later that the guys in the airborne infantry jumped with their own security dogs, regardless of the agency rules. The animals were dubbed mascots, but they were trained as military working dogs and secured many field locations.

On the morning of day seven of the exercise, security began to get very lax. It was the last day in the field, and we were told that the war would be over that night at 6 P.M. We were dead tired from lack of sleep. Seven days in the field can wear anybody out. Once I got off duty at 6 A.M., I would be off for two days, I thought. As 5 A.M. rolled around, I was ready to hit the sack and sleep all day.

Suddenly things got very exciting. Enemy infiltrators had ambushed one of our convoys a short distance from division headquarters. Staff officers had been taken prisoner. The guard was doubled, and we would have to be on the alert for infiltrators in friendly uniforms. I would experience the war at last.

"Krauts did this to us at Bastogne," the first sergeant warned us. Again this six-foot, 225-pound NCO was flashing back to the Battle of the Bulge. "Check all identification regardless of rank. Nothing goes in or out of the headquarters without my approval!" he ordered. He was furious.

At 8 A.M. the alert was cancelled after three hours of quiet. No infiltrators, no rifle fire, no war, no fun, I thought. I was bored to death all over again. Luger had slept through it all. About to fall asleep on my feet after sixteen hours, I noticed a blue truck approach the compound. It was full of workers from the Georgia Power and Light Company (GPL). "We're here to make repairs on the telephone lines," the driver told me. Not thinking, I left my post to ask the first sergeant if these workers needed passes to get into the headquarters. The truck immediately took off past the gates into the compound. What the first sergeant said to me cannot be printed here. He was convinced once again that I was an enemy infiltrator helping the other side and he could no longer trust me. "Get outta my sight!" he commanded.

The first sergeant immediately alerted headquarters. A heavy fire fight started seconds later. Blanks, machine gun fire, and grenade simulators woke everybody up. The workers from Georgia Power and Light were not from GPL. They were infiltrators from the 77th Special Forces, green berets, there to blow up the communications center and kill off the general staff in the Big Top, the headquarters tent. They had penetrated the compound as civilian workers. In Vietnam years later, the same thing happened at U.S. installations too many times. Viet Cong soldiers dressed as civilian workers killed many American soldiers.

I cursed myself for being the weak link in the chain of security. The first sergeant would surely kill me. What could Luger and I do, I wondered, to redeem ourselves? The fighting was heavy now. More machine gun fire could be heard, and large artillery simulators were exploding. There was a lot of shouting, and then I saw the Georgia Power and Light truck rolling in my direction again. I had no vehicle to block the road. I needed to move fast, but I was so tired I couldn't think straight.

Luger had been tied to a log on the side of the road near my guard post at division headquarters. All the sentry dogs were secured outside the Big Top in that manner. He was still there, as he had been most of the night, but now he was all excited. Luger barked and growled and jumped up with all the shooting going on. He was starting to dislodge the log from its position. I rushed over to him and began to kick and drag the log across the road.

As the GPL truck rolled forward, the driver slowed down when he saw the log, trying to drive around it. However, the pine trees in the Georgia woods are so thick that driving off the road is nearly impossible. The truck crashed into a tree. I pulled my pistol and approached the right side of the truck, ordering the enemy soldiers to dismount. Luger went nuts, barking wildly, flashing his teeth, growling, and trying to attack the green berets. He was so strong I could hardly hold him back.

The infiltrators were terrified of Luger. They tried to get their truck on the road again, but the log was blocking their way. Luger and I held our ground. Two green berets, cursing at Luger, jumped from the truck and ran. They were immediately captured by the first sergeant and airborne military police who were swarming through the woods like a wolf pack moving in for the kill. Two MPs approached the GPL truck from the left side. I was with Luger on their right. The green berets were forced to surrender.

The infiltrators were taken into custody. The MP commander ordered me to search them and told his troopers, "Watch this soldier search with his dog. Nobody will try to run."

Luger had a great deal of experience searching prisoners as a civilian police dog. Six years of duty with a sheriff's department in North Carolina chasing moonshiners had turned this dog into a professional. He strutted back and forth, growled, sniffed, and pawed the prisoners with such power and confidence that even I was almost afraid of the animal.

Two of the prisoners turned out to be officers. One of them was a major. The other was a captain. I was credited with capturing four prisoners. Luger got none of the credit although I could not have done anything without him. The two officers were very upset their plan to destroy division headquarters had failed. They had never planned on a man-dog team at the headquarters compound. Luger had performed as his owner had said he would. His owner was very proud.

My job as a guard had not been so insignificant after all. It turned out to be one of the best training experiences I ever had. I had learned the value of teamwork. "Teams survive. Individuals do not," our instructor had told us at Fort Benning. Now I believed him.

The 82d MP first sergeant never mentioned my mistake of letting the GPL truck get past me. I was told, "When you get your wings, you've got a job with the 82d MPs, boy. You might not be able to jump with your patrol dog, but he can come to the field."

Luger went back to duty with his civilian police department. I was determined to get a dog like him some day, and I did.

Hollandia

Three decades before Saddam Hussein planned his invasion of Kuwait, bringing many nations to the brink of World War III, President Dwight D. Eisenhower had planned for this type of action.

In late 1958, the United States Strategic Army Command (STRAC) trained for the invasion of Middle Eastern oil fields by hostile forces in the belief that the Soviet Union would instigate such an action to destroy strategic NATO fuel reserves. The cold war was beginning to heat up after successful communist initiatives in China in 1949, Korea in 1950–1953, and southeast Asia in 1954. Russian troops and tanks were crushing revolts behind the iron curtain in Czechoslovakia and Hungary in 1954 and 1955. Many of the officers and NCOs in my unit had fought in World War II and Korea. They knew the threat was real.

"We live in dangerous times. Every five years the communists try something new," my father wrote to me in the service. "If the communists take over or destroy the oil fields in the Middle East, American, British, and French tanks will be out of gas on the sides of the roads in France and Germany. Russian tanks will overrun Europe quicker than the Germans did twenty years ago. NATO will be destroyed," he warned. Those were bad times, and our training would have to be tough, thorough, and very bold for a peacetime army on a restricted budget.

I was soon to have my introduction to what combat was going to be like as a paratrooper. I was twenty-one years old and a rifleman in the 82d Airborne Division stationed at Fort Bragg, North Carolina.

The 82d Airborne, the 101st Airborne, and many support troops made up STRAC forces which were to participate in Operation Oil Slick in the fall of 1958. The U.S. Air Force Strategic Air Command and the U.S. Military Air Lift Command would escort and carry us to the fictional country of Hollandia where we would stop the King of Hollandia cold in his tracks in the great desert. Hollandia was actually Holland Drop Zone at Fort Bragg, North Carolina, a few miles from Southern Pines, a beautiful resort. Thousands of troops were involved in this training exercise.

I was a private first class and could only imagine what it had been like for my Uncle Bill Kelly, a sergeant and a veteran of D day, June 6, 1944, fourteen years before. Uncle Bill was a forward observer on D day, and he told us about it many times, after having a few beers. Every Fourth of July, the family would gather around for a picnic in the park, and we would hear about the bunkers, the beaches, and the Germans. Bill would cry. At Christmas, he would talk about the Battle of the Bulge, December 1944. Christmas was not a happy time for Bill who was wounded at Bastogne in Belgium.

When I told my Uncle Bill about training for Operation Oil Slick, he gave me his cricket, an Army issue clicker used for signalling and identifying other multinational friendly forces. It looked like a whistle hanging around a traffic policeman's neck. When squeezed, it would screech like a cricket in the woods. There was no need for talking in any language.

Operation Oil Slick involved thousands of small units spread throughout the southeastern United States, each being graded on individual Army training tests. ATTs, as they were called, assessed unit combat readiness in the cold war. When Desert Shield and Desert Storm captured the headlines in 1991. I remembered Oil Slick as if it had taken place yesterday. President Eisenhower had been a strategic genius, preparing American forces for such a brush-fire war thirty-two years before it happened.

The King of Hollandia was a power-hungry man who had great wealth but wanted more. He would control the whole Middle East as Hitler had wanted to control all of Europe in 1936. History was repeating itself, but our leaders had read history and were prepared. As the King invaded El Sud Pinellas, or Southern Pines, North Carolina, the 82d Airborne would assault him from the rear and cut off his fuel. Without gas, the King's tanks would be stalled on the desert floor, an easy target for the fighter bombers of the U.S. Air Force.

Our platoon of thirty-eight airborne infantrymen would jump at dawn on D day. I was to be the first man out the door with a scout dog. It would be only my seventh jump alongside a group of tough guys who had seen combat in World War II, Korea, and Egypt. I had a lot to learn.

My platoon was worried about being captured as we parachuted into Holland Drop Zone but not me. With Bear, I needn't worry about being taken prisoner. My partner, Bear, was eighty pounds of black and tan German shepherd, an infantry tracker and a super dog. Highly intelligent, swift, and aggressive, he had been on many other jumps with other handlers. The dog had more experience than I could imagine. Everybody in the platoon had a healthy respect for Bear. He snarled at anybody who came near me. I was picked as his handler because he liked me. I walked and fed him every day and also cleaned up after him. His kennel was behind a Sergeant Jacobs' home off post because dogs were not regulation in the 82d Airborne in peacetime. They were unofficial unit mascots and pulled guard duty on field training exercises.

My squad was the point element for our infantry unit, E Company, 2d Airborne Battle Group, 503d Infantry. My squad leader was Sergeant John Reid, a former British paratrooper who had seen action in Egypt in 1956. Sergeant Reid hated dogs.

I did what John Reid told me to do, not only because it was my job to do so but also for a more import reason; he was a good leader. He could read a map and a compass, never got lost, always did the right thing, and looked out for his men. He never volunteered us for extra details, but when assigned those jobs, we did well. John Reid set the example. If he did it, we did it.

The company commander didn't like Sergeant Reid because he didn't take officers too seriously. Soldiering was his profession, but it was also an adventure for John Reid, who thought officers were too serious about everything, including mission, morale, supplies, and discipline. John was in the service to have fun and be with his buddies, whom he always toasted with a beer at the NCO club with, "To fun and games!" Reid always had beer in the field, regulation or not.

John Reid was a sky diver and a sports parachutist; he pumped iron, drove a motorcycle, and had traveled the world in his twenty-six years of life. He was as strong as a bull, could do 200 pushups after a few beers, and loved to arm wrestle and throw an ax and a knife. I could always get a rise of out him by talking like a British soldier, calling him "Sir!" with a British accent. John and I saw many of the now classic World War II movies about the British 8th Army, starring David Niven and Richard Burton. We learned tactics watching those movies together. John was the older brother I had never had.

At 11 P.M. on the day before our parachute assault into the Kingdom of Hollandia, we loaded aboard C-130 aircraft at Pope Air Force Base, North Carolina, carrying our parachutes, rifles, blank ammunition, training grenades, and field equipment. It would be a long flight to Holland Drop Zone. It was only a few miles down the road, but to simulate a ride from West Germany to Iraq, we were going to fly for six hours. We would get some sleep and then put on our parachutes, or chute up, on board. This can be very dangerous. Climbing into parachutes before loading on the aircraft was much easier, with jumpmasters checking each trooper's equipment. Chuting up on board requires much more effort and agility in cramped quarters, flying in formation with hundreds of other troop carrier aircraft, and with lights out. Putting on parachutes safely in the darkness while in flight would be the first difficult test of this training exercise. We were on our own. There would be no jumpmaster check.

Just as we lifted off at midnight in an enormous formation of C-130 Air Force troop carriers, Bear wanted to "go for a walk," which angered Sergeant Reid who said, "He'll have to hold it like the rest of us. Bloody dog. I hate dogs." In jest, John growled at Bear and flashed his teeth. Bear snapped back. The dog lifted his leg and let go on the rear loading ramp, gave Reid a nasty look, and then laid down at my feet. We had another smell to contend with on board. Lots of troopers had already been air sick.

John Reid commented, "It was like this at Port Said in 1956. Nobody jumped with a full stomach. The door was as slippery as if greased with dumped fuel." Reid was flashing back to the war in Egypt. He tried to be a tough guy, but he teared up talking about combat in the Suez Canal area two years before.

It was a cold, windy night, and the flight was very rough. The few who weren't air sick could sleep. Bear kept me awake wanting to play with his ball. In the field as a scout, I always carried a hard rubber ball. When I wanted Bear to search out to the front or to the flank off lead, I would throw out the ball like a hand grenade. He would charge after it and bring it back. If the woods were alive with enemy soldiers, I would soon find out. He would immediately alert, look at me, and growl if anybody was out there. Wherever the ball was thrown, that was Bear's turf.

"Damn dogs never sleep at night," Reid uttered in disgust.

Bear was dressed in what was called a B-4 parachute bag with holes for his legs and tail. The B-4 usually carries a rolled-up parachute, a reserve chute, and a helmet. Bear's B-4 jump suit was tailored for him by Sergeant Jacobs' wife. It was very snug. On the jump, Bear would be hanging below my reserve parachute, secured by two snap links to my parachute D rings. I would ride him to the ground like a horse. The landing would be tough since a trooper is required to land with his feet together to prevent a broken leg. I would have to land like a sky diver with my feet spread shoulder-width apart.

At 5 A.M. we got the word to chute up. Bear and I were up at the jump doors in the rear of the aircraft climbing into our equipment without too much fuss. But hooking up Bear under my reserve chute turned out be to a nightmare. He had done this too many times and suddenly decided he wasn't going on this trip. Reid and Sergeant Jacobs, the jumpmaster, finally got Bear hooked up to my parachute harness, but Bear fought us all the way. He barked, snapped, growled, and struggled until the red light came on, six minutes from drop time. We had to muzzle him to stop the barking and snapping. I was supposed to be standing in the door after our equipment check, but I was forced to kneel on both knees due to the dog's weight. I could not stand. I began to get very nervous.

Sergeant Jacobs sounded off the jump commands. "Get ready! Stand up! Hook up! Check static lines! Check equipment! Sound off for equipment check! Stand in the door!"

The static line is a thick, sturdy, yellow nylon tape fifteen-feet long, which is hooked to the aircraft and the back of a trooper's main chute. When the trooper leaves the aircraft, the static line pulls open his main parachute pack automatically. The main canopy opens up after a 150-foot fall below the jump aircraft. Since every trooper has a static line opening at the same time, the theory is that all personnel will ride down together and land together. Winds aloft change that, however.

Jumping at 1,250 feet in training is good. Jumping at 750 feet in combat conditions is very dangerous. At the 1,250-foot drop altitude, the trooper has time to check his parachute deployment, making sure everything is open. He may also pull his reserve parachute if the main chute fails. The ride down to the ground takes about fifty seconds, and troops get scattered about. At 750 feet, the chute opens and you're on the deck in thirty seconds, crashing to the ground in clusters. If the main parachute does not open, you're a dead man falling. When jumping below 1,000 feet, there are many injuries as troopers land on each other. There are some benefits, however. Enemy troops on the ground can't shoot paratroopers in the air when the drop is done at 750 feet, as long as nobody lands in the trees. At 1,250 feet, you're a swinging target for machine gunners on the ground, like ducks in a shooting gallery.

Because Operation Oil Slick was to be as close to combat as training could be, we would jump at 750 feet in the first assault wave. Bear was howling like a wolf at the moon as the night lights of Southern Pines, North Carolina, came into view. Hollandia, Holland Drop Zone, was dead ahead of us. We crossed over Little River and Manchester Road, the final check points before the drop. The aircraft slowed down to 110 miles an hour, and the green light came on.

Photo by the author, 1958

0600 hours on D day. We jumped into Hollandia with the purpose of seizing Objective Alpha.

Photo by the author, 1958

503rd Airborne troopers landing on Holland Drop Zone. Hundreds of troopers landed at Fort Bragg, North Carolina, the mythical Kingdom of Hollandia. This training was not too unrealistic considering Operation Desert Storm in 1991.

Go! Go! Go! The troopers shouted as we fell out the doors at 6 A.M. on D day. I could only imagine what it had been like for my uncle at Normandy. John Reid was with me in the air. "Just like the Nile. We're back in Suez," he shouted. The sand below seemed very bright as the planes flew off. I thought the sun was shining. Suddenly all became silent. Hundreds of us were riding to earth in that half minute together, yet hardly a sound could be heard with the aircraft off in the distance. Now, an hour before sunrise, the sky was dark blue, the silence was deafening, and I felt all alone.

Bear was wriggling around, fighting to get loose as we plummeted at a good rate of speed, at least thirty miles an hour. I pulled off his muzzle and placed his ball in his mouth. He dropped it, but at least he settled down and gave me a break from the struggling with him. I was comfortable, riding Bear to the ground, when all turned black. My helmet was pushed over my face by my parachute suspension lines twisted behind my neck. I was spinning in the air out of control driven by some wind gusts at tree-top level.

We slammed into the ground a second later. My heels hit first, then my butt, then my helmet crashed into the sand. As I rolled over, my helmet began scooping sand into my mouth as I was dragged face down by a good stiff wind. Bear began fighting to get out from under me, barking again. I was being pulled forward, face down, unable to stand with the dog under me. John Reid crashed onto my back, collapsed my chute, and got me to my feet.

"Shut the dog up!" he commanded. Egyptian dogs had given away the location of British paratroopers as they dropped in Suez in 1956. Machine guns then killed many of the British 6th Regiment before they were out of their equipment, I was later told. I understood John Reid's hatred of the dogs.

I cut Bear loose and he darted around, rolling over, trying to get out of his B-4 jump suit. Sergeant Jacobs collared Bear in a few seconds, wrestled him to the ground, and quickly calmed him down.

Company First Sergeant Tackle gathered up the unit quickly, leading us to the woods about two hundred yards away where we rolled up our parachutes, hiding them in a pile of pine needles. Commands were whispered by NCOs and officers as our company got organized at the end of the drop zone. Noses were counted, and almost everybody was accounted for in short order. Ten of our buddies from another platoon had been taken prisoner by military police of the aggressor force 300 yards away.

"Krauts," the first sergeant shouted. He had jumped into Normandy and Holland in World War II with the 82d Airborne. "Move it. Get moving," he ordered. He had flashed back to Normandy again. First Sergeant Tackle later told us, "This training was so real that I thought they were Germans!"

Photo by the author, 1958

Airborne troopers hustling off the drop zone to hide out in the woods
The King of Hollandia was furious, sending out tanks to annihilate the airborne forces.

Objective Alpha

We never found Bear's ball after assembling on the drop zone in Hollandia, so pine cones were used as his play toys for the rest of this combat training exercise. It was now about 7 A.M. The sun began to rise. We could hear trucks, jeeps, and tank engines. The King of Hollandia was sending his armor out to kill off the invasion force. Unlike Hitler at Normandy, this commander sent his armor after the airborne forces had scattered about. Sergeant Tackle told me, "The Krauts at Normandy could have wiped us out on June 6 if their tanks hadn't been held in reserve." My Uncle Bill had told me the same thing. When I mentioned Bill's experience to Tackle, he commented, "I knew two troopers named Kelly. Both were killed before D day was over."

Enemy armor couldn't penetrate the pine forests, so we hid well off the drop zone and away from the roads, awaiting orders to move. Completely exhausted, we fell asleep in groups of ten to twenty, with half of the troops on guard duty. I slept with Bear in my arms. He was worn out after the jump. Reid tied him to my wrist by a parachute cord. If Bear alerted, I would be awake. No MPs would take me prisoner or surprise our unit. Seven years later in Vietnam, I slept with a German shepherd named Suzie tied to my wrist at night. What I learned from John Reid and Sergeant Jacobs in Hollandia kept me alive in 1965 in the rice paddies ten thousand miles from Fort Bragg.

At 11 A.M., we were told to get moving again as the sound of tanks could be heard nearby. Aggressor infantry, 500 U.S. paratroopers from another unit dressed in tan uniforms with different helmets, were moving into our sector of operations. They had found our parachutes and knew we were out there. They had trucks, tanks, and machine gun jeeps. We were on foot and had to make a run for it. They wanted to run us ragged and show us how tough they were. The enemy force, our aggressors, were from the 504th Airborne Infantry. Their barracks were next to our barracks back in the garrison area. It would be very embarrassing to get caught by the 504th as unit rivalry was very intense. Army training tests were set up this way. We knew who the enemy soldiers were, and they knew who we were. That's why they call them war games.

Called the "devils in baggy pants," the 504th Airborne got their nickname from the Germans in World War II. A dead German officer's diary found during the campaign in Sicily read, "American paratroopers, devils in baggy pants, are less than five meters from my lines .... They pop up everywhere ... there seems to be no way to stop them .... " World War II type paratrooper trousers, with their baggy pants and side pockets for grenades and rations, similar to the jungle fatigues we wore in Vietnam, are worn today by some teenagers as fashion statements.

Our battle group, the 503d, nicknamed the third herd, moved off into the woods and got organized about noon on D day. Our mission was to destroy ammunition and fuel supplies at dumps ten miles away. It was designated as Objective Alpha. The King of Hollandia had sent his armored columns into El Sud Pinellas, twenty miles away, to seize oil fields. He was furious we were in his rear. Now he had to fight a war on two fronts. Since we were no match for troops with armor, we had to hide in the daytime and fight at night. The devils from the 504th walked all over the Holland Drop Zone area all day long looking for us, but we were in no mood for a fight. Hiding out, we rested for ten hours, waiting for night to come again.

Bear pulled a lot of guard duty on D day between naps. The dog wouldn't sleep for more than twenty minutes. He was really hyper. The company commander took advantage of the situation and put him to work. "Morgan, get that dog out on the flank. Check our perimeter. He's a scout dog, so do some scouting."

John Reid organized a small combat patrol of ten men, and we began to move. Reid started to like the dog, once he saw how well he followed orders. Coming back from one patrol, John hid out on the flank. We knew where Reid was, but Bear didn't know we were testing him. As we passed within fifty feet of the sergeant, the dog alerted and I released him. Bear was fast, hitting Reid like a football lineman sacking a quarterback. Bear hit him from the rear, rolling him over before he had a chance to aim his rifle at the dog. Reid was down, taken prisoner in less than a minute. "Sneaky bastard," he commented.

As darkness fell over Hollandia, we were ready to get on with our first mission. An umpire was assigned to our platoon which was being graded on a combat patrol exercise. We would be the point element of a company-size combat patrol, about a hundred men. Our mission was to lead the unit to a tank fuel depot, Objective Alpha, on Manchester Road. It was manned by the devils from the 504th, MPs, and a unit of seventeen tanks, about thirty vehicles altogether. This was an elite reserve unit of the King's army, the Republican Guard, if you will. Our orders were to attack the depot at daylight, set it on fire, and draw out the enemy into the open. U.S. Air Force tactical fighter-bombers would do the rest. A forward air control team was also attached to us after the jump to direct the fighter-bombers. We were told we would be extracted by helicopter or C-130 troop carriers when the mission was completed. The troop carriers would land on Manchester Road, if the area was clear of tanks. This was a do-or-die mission.

In combat, there is no reward for failure, we were told. "If we don't do it right, we'll all be prisoners of war," Lieutenant Varner warned. In reality, the company would flunk the training test and have to do it all over again. That was considered a fate worse than death or being a POW. We would never be able to live down the humiliation of being retested at the hands of the devils from the 504th. We had to do it right.

The guy who would judge us was an umpire sergeant from the 504th. We felt the deck was stacked against us. We didn't know that an NCO from our outfit, the 503d, was grading the aggressor force.

Ten miles in the dark is not a long walk, but with MPs on the road, tanks with spotlights, and truck loads of devils in baggy pants out looking for you, ten miles is a long way to walk. We started our patrol at 10 P.M. and went single file along the wood line for the first few miles. Every twenty minutes we stopped, and after an hour or so, we looked good, I thought. Bear was in a tracking harness on a fifteen-foot lead out front. I was behind him carrying an M-1 rifle, a World War II semi-automatic weapon which fired eight rounds. Sergeant Reid was behind me, and the rest of our thirty-eight-man platoon followed with the guys about five-feet apart. Nobody talked. All one could hear was pine needles being kicked and the sound of tanks and trucks off in the distance. We were on radio silence. All communication was done by arm and hand signals. Messengers were used between large outfits. All radio traffic was cancelled until Objective Alpha was in our hands.

About midnight, Bear dropped his head and walked slowly, beginning to stalk as if there were prey out front. We were in thick woods, unable to see anything.

Next, Bear hunkered down and stopped. I laid down next to him and watched his ears. He flashed his teeth and growled. Sergeant Jacobs crawled up next to us and began to tell me what to do. Sergeant Reid placed his hand over Jacobs' mouth and told him, "Shut up. It's his turn to learn. Don't tell him what to do." I really didn't know what action I should take, so I laid there and listened, hoping somebody would give an order. Bear flashed his teeth, growling again. To our front I heard some talking.

"This food is cold, man!"

Some aggressors were directly in front of us, trying to cook their C rations. There were four of them next to an MP jeep with a machine gun.

The MPs were huge men. Their commander was almost seven-feet tall and weighed 250 pounds. These troopers, all over six-feet tall, were sharp soldiers and armed to the teeth. A confrontation with one of them was out of the question. They had their helmets on backwards and looked like German soldiers to some of the World War II veterans.

We were on Manchester Road, four miles from our objective in the middle of an aggressor patrol a few feet away. I expected to be taken prisoner at any moment. Things got very serious.

"Double Image, this is Six, over," the radio crackled.

Double Image was the military police commander, and he was calling his check points to see if any third herd patrols had made it to Manchester Road as yet. The aggressors knew that four different 503d airborne infantry companies were on this same training test, and they were waiting for us.

The MPs near us didn't answer their radio. Some others did, however, and we listened to their radio chatter. After a few minutes, the MPs to our front started talking.

"This is Double Image Three. Negative contact. Out." This was the third MP platoon.

"The poor bastards don't know we're here," John Reid whispered.

Lieutenant Varner told me to get on my feet and walk towards the MPs to see what they would do. "They'll kill 'em, sir!" Reid whispered. Lieutenant Varner wanted to play games with the MPs, but Reid and Jacobs didn't think his idea was very good. They were both flashing back to combat and took this training very seriously.

The 504th umpire, Sergeant House, was also up front and thought the lieutenant's idea was stupid. The umpire sergeant killed off Lieutenant Varner, telling him he was a casualty. "You stepped in a sink hole, Lieutenant. You're dead," he said. Then Sergeant House told me, "You're doing well, son. March on." He assigned Sergeant Jacobs as our new platoon leader. Lieutenant Varner was assigned as a rifleman walking in the rear. He was very upset. I think he would rather have stepped in a real sink hole filled with quicksand.

We had to do something. We had to keep moving with an attack due four miles away in six hours. It was too late to just sit there. Our inaction was getting Sergeant House very angry. The MPs suddenly jumped to their feet. "Patrol coming," one shouted. I thought they had detected us. Bear stood up and was ready to attack.

We heard a truck, and then I saw the night headlights, or cat eyes, of a jeep and a truck. A lieutenant was in the jeep. He jumped out and started chewing them out. The MPs were supposed to be on patrol. Instead, they were sitting down trying to cook supper. Seconds later, the MPs were in a jeep and moving out. Unknown to us, the truck in front of us was loaded with twenty paratroopers from the 504th. We were in trouble and bound to be caught.

To our left, about five hundred yards down the road, we heard a tank clanking along and then shots were fired. Machine guns began blazing away, flares lit up the sky, and the aggressors in front of us rapidly dismounted from their truck. I knew we were going to get caught. Bear remained cool and didn't bark, however. The aggressors still didn't know we were less than fifty feet away.

Aggressors ran down the road to our left, more shooting started, and then police sirens were heard. Truck and tank headlights turned on. There were dozens of trucks and tanks and MPs everywhere and hundreds of troops on the side of the road. We were in the middle of the whole damn Republican Guard. Fortunately for us, they never discovered our patrol while they took charge of some prisoners they had caught down the road. It seems that four civilian deer poachers were out in the woods and didn't know there was a maneuver in progress. They were arrested and charged with criminal trespass on federal property. The field training exercise stopped, but we didn't. Sergeant Jacobs gave quick orders. "Cross the road in teams of ten. Move out."

While the MPs and the tanks were headed down Manchester to our left, we dashed across the road like a series of offensive squads rushing for yardage at football practice. Our platoon and our Air Force forward air controllers made it to safety on the other side of Manchester. Sergeant House was amazed that we had not been discovered. He was upset that his 504th had missed an opportunity to capture elements of the third herd. "If it hadn't been for Bear," Sergeant House told us, "you would have been POW in custody of the devils in baggy pants."

Then Sergeant House began to chew out Sergeant Jacobs for indecisive action after we got across Manchester Road. He warned him to get his act together or our part of the training exercise would be over. Umpires can kill off an entire unit for failing to take decisive action. Our whole company would be in the doghouse, and they would blame it on us, I thought. The rest of our men were still across Manchester, and we faced a big problem getting back together.

The company commander, back on Manchester Road, was unaware of what had happened since we were on radio silence. Reid and I were sent back across the road to brief him and get the company together again. Reid had his act together and reported, giving the company commander an excellent overview of the situation. Who, what, when, where, and how were spelled out in plain, simple language.

Reid was sounding like Richard Burton in *Desert Rats*. In that movie, which John Reid and I had seen together, the British were fighting Rommel in the north African desert in 1943. British 8th Army patrols were cut off from their lines by German armor. Their situation was desperate. The Desert Rats faced certain death. Our situation was not so dissimilar. To us, flunking an Army training test was a fate worse than death.

Sergeant Reid told the captain, "Sir, we're across with the first platoon. Follow me and we'll all be across in short order." The officer nodded, and Reid briefed each squad leader, pushing each squad across Manchester like a high school football coach in fall training. The company was across in half an hour while everyone else was stalled with lights on down the road. The company commander was truly impressed, as was Sergeant House. Although Reid had never played American football, when given the radio code signal "coach," he was very pleased. To John Reid, football was "soccer to you Yanks."

After a quick briefing and a meeting of the officers and NCOs, we moved out again. It was 2 A.M., four hours to daylight, four hours to Objective Alpha. The whole patrol, about one hundred of us, was in one column, in thick woods, stumbling along at a snail's pace. I still had the lead, and Reid held the compass, guiding me first left, then right. Manchester was off to our left, black as pitch. There were no sounds, and we used hand signals, but every time Reid touched me, Bear turned on him. I had my hands full.

After two hours, we came upon a clearing. Ahead of us there were sounds of trucks and people talking. The depot was directly in front of us out in the open. We could see trucks, tanks, fuel barrels, and patrols driving by in jeeps. There were hundreds of people out there. We had no chance at all.

Sergeant House called the NCOs together and told them all the officers had been killed when artillery hit the column on the move. We hadn't heard any artillery, but that had been written into the training test so there could be a change of command under fire. First Sergeant Tackle was also dead, we were told. It was now our junior NCOs' chance to lead, conduct the attack, and organize the airborne extraction. The officers were still with us, as was the first sergeant, now evaluating their men and acting as riflemen. Sergeant Jacobs took over the first sergeant's job, and Reid became the platoon leader.

Reid briefed us. "This is the coach speaking. Now that the officers have all gotten themselves killed, poor dumb bastards, I'm in charge of the left flank and

Jake is running the company. Manchester is off to our left about four hundred feet that way. The Egyptians are directly to our front. You'll smell 'em after a while. Lay low and we'll give you a place to start shooting from, once we agree on how to do it. Morgan, come with me." Reid was back in Suez again. "We had an Objective Alpha there too," he whispered in my ear. "We took no prisoners, either," he added.

Reid placed Bear and me near Manchester Road, ordering me to watch for enemy patrols but not to give my position away. I was not to fire my rifle. I laid there with Bear, watching his ears and the direction he faced. Bear would alert every so often as sounds of voices could be heard. MP patrols in jeeps crawled by at five miles an hour. My night vision kicked into high gear, and I could see as if it were daylight. I could hear the crackle of rifle fire, then machine guns would open up. Patrol contacts were all about us as other units on this training test ran into MPs and the devils from the 504th on foot patrol. This was very similar to the combat I saw in Vietnam several years later. There was much confusion and random automatic weapons fire, and everybody was scared. John Reid called it a SNAFU: situation normal, all fouled up.

While I was the left flank guard, Reid and the other sergeants placed every trooper in our unit flat on the ground in an assault line 200 feet from Alpha. We were side by side, boot to boot. The enemy to our front never detected one of our troopers. As the morning began to break, I could see the guys on my right. Enemy patrols had disappeared. The suspense was making me nervous. Some guys went to sleep, but I was wide awake. This was serious stuff to me. I knew someday I would see combat, maybe in the Middle East, maybe in Iraq, and it might be like this.

Just when I thought the time of the attack would never come, the word was passed down the line as one trooper whispered to another, "Stand by for assault. This is it. Make it look good." When whistles were blown, we would rush the ammo dump. Suddenly, Bear alerted left just as I was getting on my feet. A foot patrol with a dog was approaching. The aggressor MPs had dogs, too! Bear growled, as did the MP patrol dog. The two MPs on the patrol ordered, "Stand up and move out so we can see you." Reid was ten feet away and signaled me to stay down. As the MPs moved closer, all hell broke loose.

Flares lit up the morning sky, whistles blew, rifle and machine gun fire roared. The MPs began running away as our company opened fire, yelling, screaming, and charging forward as fast as we could run. Explosions rocked the morning silence. I felt like I was in the middle of a Hollywood war movie. It was like the Washington Monument on the Fourth of July, a thousand rockets and explosions turning night into day. Because we couldn't fire live ammunition in this training exercise, the umpires set off demolitions to make it look like artillery and mortars were hitting the ammo dump. It sure looked real to me.

Photo by the author, 1958

Objective Alpha in Operation Oil Slick

The main objective of Operation Oil Slick in 1958 was to jump into the enemy rear to seize tanks, trucks, fuel, and all ammunition stores, which would be needed by the King of Hollandia in his conquest of El Sud Pinellas. We were also out to destroy his reserves.

In 1991, a similar attack was conducted in operation Desert Storm that destroyed many elements of Saddam Hussein's strategic reserves, his republican guard. In Desert Storm, the strike behind enemy lines was done with helicopters carrying airborne troops who linked up with armored forces making an end run around Saddam's right flank on the desert floor.

In seconds, our assault line troopers overran the compound, screaming like commandos led by John Wayne. Bear pulled me so fast I could hardly keep my balance. I fell flat on my face more than once.

Enemy patrols had been removed from the area to allow us to overrun the compound without any physical contact. This was a safety feature of the training. They didn't want any of the 504th troopers inside and the 503d troopers outside to get involved in hand-to-hand combat.

As we hit objective Alpha, two other companies from the 503d assaulted the same motor pool from different angles. Three of our rifle companies had succeeded in their missions, while another company had been caught in an ambush on Manchester Road. The unit that had been ambushed didn't have a scout dog. Aggressor MPs with German shepherds had detected them as they attempted to cross Manchester Road, catching them in a terrible cross-fire. Their riflemen scattered in the darkness, and the outfit could not get reorganized until daybreak.

Dawn broke, and out of the sun came the Air Force fighter-bombers. What a magnificent air show! We pulled back from Objective Alpha when the forward air controllers told us the bombers were on the way. The coordination was perfect. We certainly didn't want any friendly-fire casualties as there had been in Korea and World War II.

Lessons I learned in Hollandia were not forgotten in Vietnam ten years later, where on many occasions I directed artillery, helicopter gunships, and tactical fighters to less than 100 feet from where I was standing.

We secured Manchester Road and waited for the C-130s to pick us up. But they never arrived to take us back as the written plan specified for after the attack. No C-130s were on the way. It was 8 A.M., and we found ourselves back in the real world. We were told we would be walking the twenty miles back to garrison that day. There would be no welcome home parade for us when we returned. More patrol duty was the order of the day. It's no wonder Bear had decided he didn't want to go on this trip. He had been through it all too many times before.

They fed us a quick breakfast from the company mess-hall-on-wheels. Bear wolfed down left-over eggs and bread donated by the rest of the platoon. Then I heard, "Morgan, take the point," and "Move out" followed as I finished a cup of hot coffee. As I stumbled along the road, trying to stay awake, John Reid was at my side, his arm around my shoulders. He offered me a sip of beer out of his canteen cup. It tasted awful.

"You're a good soldier, and so's that bloody dog," he said. Then he finished off the beer with a toast, "Here's to fun and games!"

Those Dirty Dogs

In January 1959, just after Alaska became the forty-ninth state, I was ordered to move there for two months with my unit, the 503d Airborne, part of the 82d Airborne Division from Fort Bragg, North Carolina. It was to be a rugged winter expedition in Alaska, eight weeks of cold weather training. I viewed it as the adventure of a lifetime and felt that volunteering for duty as a paratrooper with the 82d Airborne was the best decision I had ever made.

The purpose of this cold weather training was to see if troops accustomed to mild winters, hot summers, and desert warfare conditions could move to a frigid climate and perform as well in combat missions. Back at Fort Bragg in the previous November and December, we had learned how to ski on straw, and on one of those rare days when it snows in North Carolina, we traveled all over post on our new toys, cross-country skis.

Photo by Louis Petzold, 1959

The author in Alaska

We had numerous casualties training for Alaska. Troopers who jumped out of Air Force troop carriers and Army helicopters at 1,250 feet and slammed into the ground at thirty-four miles an hour without injury, guys who could run five miles each morning in extreme heat, young men in great physical condition, all had more broken arms and legs falling down on skis than anyone could imagine. When the 503d Airborne left Fort Bragg for Alaska, several troopers remained back at Womack Army Hospital, out of action from ski training.

Flying to Anchorage and Fort Richardson by way of North Dakota and Fort Lewis, Washington, in C-124 U.S. Air Force Globemasters, we ate box lunches, sang songs, and laughed a lot. We all had cameras to record our campaign in the northland and to send photos home to Mom and Dad. When we stepped off the plane in Alaska, it was thirty-three degrees below zero. It was cold! We were transported by trucks to Camp Denali outside of Fort Richardson, settling down in Quonset huts left over from cold weather training during World War II. Some of our non-commissioned officers, who to me seemed like real old guys in their thirties, had been through the winter of 1944–1945 in Europe. They were veterans of the Battle of the Bulge, Christmas 1944, and warned us, "The weather will be your worst enemy here. This is what Bastogne was like." They had grim looks on their faces, flashing back fifteen years in time.

After two weeks of additional ski training, one parachute jump with combat equipment into six feet of powdered snow, and many more injuries, we were off

Photo by the author, 1959

Our platoon in Alaska in front of an old Quonset hut

on Exercise Caribou Creek. Our platoon of forty men, minus the base camp personnel, most of them in plaster casts, was given the mission of patrolling the western edge of the maneuver area, from the town of Willow in the south to the settlement of Talkeetna fifty miles to the north. We were to patrol the railroad tracks along the Sisitna River looking for lost personnel.

Troops on this maneuver exercise were given instructions to ski west if they got lost: "Ski towards Mount McKinley, stop at the railroad tracks, and wait there for pickup." The only landmark we could recognize was Mount McKinley, 20,230 feet high and eighty miles to the northwest. However, it was daylight only from 10 A.M. to 3 P.M.

At night, you couldn't see this landmark. If it was snowing, you couldn't see it either. The whole area looked the same to us, foothills and mountains, Mount Foraker, Mount Dall, Mount Gerdine, and the Talkeetna Mountains. We might as well have been sent to the moon.

Our opposing force was the 23d United States Infantry, stationed at Fort Richardson, Alaska. The 23d Infantry played the role of militant renegade Russians who wanted Alaska back. They were upset that the United States had bought Alaska from Russia in 1867 before the Russians had developed the timber and fishing industries and oil resources. The Russians were mostly mountain men, trappers, and hunters who invaded our forty-ninth state, wanting to start a new life in their old country, Russian America.

Post Card

Picture of Mount McKinley sent home to Mom in 1959

The first two weeks of the maneuver were uneventful. The 23d Infantry had tanks and personnel carriers with warm heaters and had years of experience in cold weather training. We entered the maneuver area in three columns on skis looking for them. They had a base camp in the maneuver area, but we couldn't find any trace of the enemy.

Each 503d Airborne trooper on this exercise carried a sixty-pound pack with a double sleeping bag, three changes of clothes, six boxes of C rations, two canteens of water, skis, ski poles, rifle, and ammunition. We were soaked from sweat cross-country skiing while carrying this load, so we had to stop, establish base camps, and drop our gear or else suffer exhaustion. Frostbite was a major problem for those with military wool undershirts and wool socks. If these were soaked with sweat when we stopped for the night, a soldier could cool down so quickly that he would begin to chill and freeze. No fires were allowed for we were in combat conditions. We had no heated tanks or heated personnel carriers as did the enemy. Capturing enemy vehicles would be our priority if we were to survive.

Four of our patrols lucked out, as the saying goes. Since we had search-and-rescue missions, we were given civilian sled dog teams to assist us in carrying our gear and casualties. The sleds were about eight-feet long and could carry all our packs, extra rations, and one man. Four dogs pulled each rig. And because the dog teams knew the area well, we knew we could not get lost.

Post Card

An Alaskan sled dog team

All of our dogs had traditional names: Wolf, King, Polar Bear, and Chinook. Chinook, which means warm wind in the Native American tongue, was the smallest dog, about ninety pounds. He hadn't had a bath in two years. Wolf was the biggest, dirtiest, toughest, and strongest dog. He led the team at a fox trot. It was very difficult keeping up with the dogs on our cross-country skis, or the boards, as the guys called them. Those dirty dogs could run twenty miles a day.

As the third week of the exercise started, our outfit ran into the Russians, and combat patrols began to maneuver against each other. We could hear tank fire and rifle fire off to the east but saw no enemy soldiers. Our scout planes spotted enemy troops and were fired upon. We listened to the radio traffic, but then our radio batteries went dead. Even though we kept the batteries inside our shirts in special pouches to keep them warm, they didn't last more than two weeks on the maneuver. We were suddenly cut off from the rest of the 503d Airborne. And things got worse. A three-day blizzard shut down the maneuver.

The scout planes, troop-carrying helicopters, and U.S. Air Force troop carriers stopped flying. The wind gusted up to 100 miles an hour. Snow swirled about so that we couldn't see ten feet ahead of us. It was what meteorologists call a whiteout. Mount McKinley disappeared as did the railroad tracks. Snow drifted up to 50 feet, driven by the vicious wind. We were very lost and very cold.

Forced to hide in snow drifts to escape the wind, our patrols of four men settled down for the duration of the blizzard. Cooking food was impossible. We couldn't get our frozen canned combat rations heated with the tiny field stoves we were issued. The stoves wouldn't light, and the gas would pour out on one's hand and freeze it instantly. The water in both canteens was frozen. We ate snow to prevent dehydration. The best we could hope for was cold rations which were thawed by body heat. Cold canned fruit, bread, pound cake, and ham and lima beans were consumed as a last resort.

Then there was the cold. We crawled into our sleeping bags to wait out the blizzard. Two men in one patrol had to crawl into the same sleeping bag to stay warm the first night. I was too big to get into a bag with anybody else. The other trooper in our team was from Poland. He weighed more than 225 pounds. Louis Petzold didn't even seem to feel the cold. Things looked grim for me. Would I survive? I was a skinny, six-foot-two-inch, 175-pound kid with not an ounce of fat on me.

The dogs curled up in the snow and went to sleep after eating all the scraps of food left from our combat rations. Chinook hadn't settled down as yet when I called him over and offered him some of my second entree of the day, half-frozen beefsteak and potatoes. Army issue C ration beefsteak and potatoes looked like Alpo, tasted like Alpo, and I think it was Alpo. Chinook loved the stuff. I unzipped my double sleeping bag, snuggled up to this filthy wretch, and fed him my food. He fell asleep in my arms after he licked the can inside and

Louis Petzold on guard duty

Photo by the author, 1959

out, struggling with me for twenty minutes as I zipped up my bag so he couldn't escape. We slept for twelve hours, totally exhausted. I was warm and comfortable for the first time in two weeks.

After a two-day hibernation in our cave, eating snow and cold canned food, each of us eventually sleeping with a dirty dog, the wind stopped. The sun came out, and we crawled out of our bags. We were almost blind from the glare of the sun on the frozen icy mountain slopes. Mount McKinley reappeared to the northwest, and we could hear a helicopter. Over our wool uniforms and parkas we had white cotton camouflage suits called overwhites, so the helicopter crew looking for lost personnel couldn't find us in our camouflage. We stripped off our overwhites and signalled the bird to land. That was a mistake. Snow swirled under the rotor blades, and it was worse than the blizzard we had just survived.

When the aircraft landed, we were given two large tents, twenty gallons of gasoline, enormous amounts of fresh rations and water, and told how to set up a base camp. We were also directed to set up a bonfire to serve as a beacon for lost personnel. We weren't considered lost, however, because we were dead center on the railroad tracks, according to the maps. The dogs had done their jobs well.

The captain who flew the rescue aircraft was a Native American from the Alaska National Guard, an Eskimo born and raised in Anchorage. He showed us a break in the woods and explained to us, "That straight break is not natural.

Photo by the author, 1959

H-21 helicopter in Alaska

That's where they laid tracks fifty years ago. You're on the tracks, see." We agreed with him as he set up a fire for us with dead fallen trees, soaked them with gas, and set them ablaze.

The captain told us, "Lot's of troopers are lost. Stay here with a fire until ordered otherwise."

Large cans of food, called five-in-one rations, were issued to us. They were supposed to feed five men at one meal. We were so hungry we ate several cans in quick order, boiling hot off the bonfire. We set up our two large tents as more lost troopers wandered into our base camp, directed by the search-and-rescue helicopters. Hungry and half-starved, the soldiers ate hot rations faster than our dirty dogs, crawled into the tents, and slept for hours. Many had to be evacuated with frostbite. Two days later, the maneuver started up again. Well rested and seasoned cold-weather veterans, we were ready to resume our adventure.

On our first patrol, we heard tanks and saw enemy personnel coming towards us. It was about 3 P.M., just starting to get dark again. The enemy soldiers were Alaska National Guard scouts attached to the 23d U.S. Infantry for training, but Sergeant Jackson, flashing back to Bastogne, called them Krauts. They had two tanks and a squad of seven men on skis. They set up a base camp and secured their tanks, which kept running, putting out much warmth from their engines. Observing the enemy activity, the four of us laid out in the snow, frozen half to death.

Photo by the author, 1959

Those dirty dogs kept us warm, but they gave our positions away

We did not have military working dogs who could be trained to be silent in a tactical situation, and our dogs started barking. The Eskimo scouts came over to investigate. They spoke a Native American tongue to each other. Sergeant Jackson was the only man to be discovered. Taken into custody, he told them he was a fur trapper lost in the blizzard.

The Eskimo scouts knew all the trappers in the area and didn't believe him. He was dragged off to their base camp near the tanks. Their officer from the 23d Infantry interrogated Jackson. The sergeant played a game on them, first telling them he was lost, then pretending to have flashbacks and babbling that he had been wounded by the Germans and Patton was on the way with his tanks.

Their first sergeant asked Jackson about Bastogne, and Jackson told him all the details about the Battle of the Bulge fifteen years before. The first sergeant was also a Bastogne survivor. The first sergeant was nearly convinced Jackson was a civilian trapper as he called into his headquarters on his radio to report him as a lost person.

"Denali Six, this is Scout Twenty-six, over."

"Go ahead, Scout."

"This is Twenty-six. Got a lost trapper here with a dog team, a civilian dog team, not one of ours. What are your orders? Over."

"This is Denali Six. Check him out. He's probably with the 82d Airborne. They've got civilian dog teams. Watch your flanks, or you're gonna get ambushed. Over."

The first sergeant took off Jackson's parka and saw the 82d Airborne patch, sergeant stripes, jump wings, and Jackson's name tag on his wool shirt. He smiled at Jackson and asked him, "Where's your outfit, you dirty airborne bastard?"

The scouts all laughed until Jackson told them they were surrounded by a platoon of airborne troops in the woods. The 82d Airborne Division had a reputation for being tough guys after their World War II exploits.

"If we're surrounded, go get one of your officers and prove it," the first sergeant told Jackson. They took away his rifle and skis to make sure he would not run away. Off his skis, up to his waist in powdered snow, Jackson stumbled out to find the rest of the patrol. He located us quickly, giving each of us special instructions.

We put on a great show for the 23d Infantry. I became Lieutenant Morgan. My buddy, Andy Rabatin, was my platoon sergeant, and Louis Petzold was the rest of the platoon.

We strutted back with Jackson and reported in to the scouts. I saluted the 23d Infantry lieutenant and told him he was a prisoner. He sat down in the snow and gave me his carbine. His first sergeant was shocked and gave me his M-1 rifle. The scouts dropped their weapons in the snow, placing their hands over their heads.

Andy Rabatin had a heavy beard and looked like Sergeant Mike from the War comic books. He played the role. As our radio operator, Andy swaggered over to the lieutenant and told him to turn his radio to our radio frequency. Andy grabbed the radio handset and reported in to our commander, Lieutenant Colonel Blanchard.

"Gibraltar Six, this is Fox Trot Six, over."

The 503d Airborne Headquarters had no Fox Trot Six in its signal operating codes. The 503d operator responded, "Unknown station, this is Gibraltar Six. Please identify yourself correctly, over."

"This is Fox Trot Six with scout dogs on the tracks, on special assignment, over."

The radio operator knew Andy's voice. He also knew Andy was a corporal. So was I. The operator knew we were playing some sort of a desperate game, trying to talk our way out of a bad situation. "Go ahead, Fox Trot," the operator answered.

"This is Fox Trot. We've captured two tanks and seven scouts. What are your orders, over?"

After a brief wait and some tense moments for us, Colonel Blanchard got on the air and said, "This is Gibraltar Six. Shut down for the night. Safety is most important with this weather. Safeguard the prisoners in place, keep them warm, make sure they are fed. Umpire on the way, over."

The lieutenant knew Gibraltar Six was our commander, and he was prepared to follow orders. Rabatin and I told the lieutenant to stay in place until an umpire could arrive on the scene to determine his fate. We saluted him and walked away.

Umpires have the last say in war games for safety reasons. They determine what happens when troops engage in physical contact. Without umpires, as in baseball games, fist fights will break out. Our bench only had four men. Thank God we had an umpire on the way.

We went back out to join Louis Petzold in the snow. Sergeant Jackson also joined us, and we made lots of noise as if we were posting four squads of men and machine gun crews around the perimeter of the captured tanks and scouts. We had all sorts of conversations with troops who didn't exist. Sergeant Jackson called me "Lieutenant, sir" so often that I thought I was an officer for a while. We had them surrounded.

The next morning, 200 paratroopers from the 503d flew into the area by helicopter. Umpires informed the lieutenant, the first sergeant, two tank crews, and seven scouts that they had been surrounded all night by four men and four dogs. When the lieutenant found out I was just a corporal, he was furious. He was a West Point graduate who didn't lie, cheat, or steal or tolerate anyone who did. He believed in the honor code. He wanted to kill me! When he approached our sled to chew me out for lying to him, all our dogs barked viciously at him. He backed off.

I met that officer years later in Vietnam when I was a company commander. He was a major at that time. He never would forgive me for the tricks we played on him in Alaska.

Photo by the author, 1959

Two dirty dogs

The next two weeks of the maneuver were as uneventful for us as the first two weeks, although there was some furious combat going on elsewhere. Then this wonderful adventure of a life time was finally over.

Filthy dirty, weather beaten, dead tired, cold, and hungry, we flew back to Camp Denali eager for a hot meal, a shower, and a change of clothes. We hadn't washed or shaved for forty-two days. Since there wasn't enough hot water for every trooper to shower, we had to wait our turn.

So we ran sled races with the dogs, showing off to the rest of the infantry who had been on skis for the whole maneuver. They weren't impressed.

Then we went to the club for some hamburgers and a beer before we showered and changed our clothes. As Andy Rabatin, Louis Petzold, and I walked into the club, we were met at the door by a very angry sergeant at arms who shouted, "You can't come in here. You stink like filthy dogs."

"We're hungry, Sarge," we replied.

"Get out of here!" he yelled. "Go take a bath, shave, and burn those clothes. When's the last time you took a shower?"

"Six weeks ago. Why?" I shouted back.

The sergeant at arms rushed us with a broom in his hands as other troopers threw beer cans at us. We retreated outside. Out in the fresh air for six weeks, we hadn't realized how bad we must have smelled indoors. I guess we did, but we didn't care.

In later years, I made a career out of working with military patrol dogs in the Army and with a civilian security business. I never met a dirty dog I didn't like, and I never forgot my skiing vacation in Alaska.

Chapter 4

Special Forces

1962-65

Training for the Crusade

I left active duty as an enlisted man in January 1960, joining the U.S. Army Reserve and enrolling in an ROTC program at Fordham University, New York. In 1961, during the Berlin Crisis, I was recruited by the 11th Special Forces Group of the U.S. Army Reserve and asked to volunteer for active duty again. I declined the offer, finishing college and ROTC and receiving a regular army commission in June 1962. I returned to the 82d Airborne as an infantry officer.

A year later, I had completed the U.S. Army Ranger course and was a qualified jump master with five years' airborne experience. In June 1964, I was recruited for duty with the 6th Special Forces at Fort Bragg, North Carolina.

What was Special Forces all about? Barry Sadler, a Special Forces sergeant, had written a song which told the story. *The Ballad of the Green Berets* said it all. "Silver wings upon my chest / I know I'm one of America's best / One hundred men will test today / Only three will get the green beret." In a conventional war, Special Forces would work behind enemy lines to delay, disrupt, and disorganize enemy forces. They were commandos, sneaky petes, the dirty dozen, and dirty tricks squads all rolled into one. Their main jobs were reconnaissance and training of resistance forces.

In Vietnam, an unconventional war, Special Forces were counter-guerrillas. Our mission was to destroy enemy forces, to kill enemy soldiers; it was that simple.

Vietnam, 1960–1975, was not one of those conventional, twentieth-century wars as we knew in 1917–1918, 1941–1945, and 1950–1953. There were no battles for the high ground for which our troops had been trained. The enemy seldom wore a distinctive uniform. There were no front lines or towns to be liberated. Our operations were called search-and-destroy missions. We were vilified by the press for using that term. There would be no victory parades.

In my opinion, we were fighting the nineteenth-century Indian Wars all over again, chasing shadows, being surprised and frustrated by hit-and-run tactics. In Vietnam, as in the Indian Wars which dragged on until 1890, strategies and policy directed by Washington were unclear and redefined too many times, our frustrated troops became brutal in the field, war crimes became commonplace, alcohol and other drugs were abused, and discipline in the ranks deteriorated.

In airborne school where one earns those silver paratrooper's wings, the drop-out rate is about thirty-three percent. Most who are eliminated are injured making parachute landing falls after jumping from twelve-foot-high platforms or from an aircraft at 1,250 feet. Many are washed out in the physical training tests and runs. The drop-out rate in ranger school is about the same. Those who successfully finish their nine weeks of mountain operations, small boat training, and combat patrols earn a small black and gold Ranger tab worn on the left shoulder. According to Sadler's ballad, I was one of 3 men remaining who started out on day one trying to earn that green beret.

As soon as I arrived in the 6th Special Forces Group, I was assigned to an A team of twelve men. One B team usually controls four A teams in the field, or 200 to 500 soldiers. We began training in the Special Forces areas of expertise: light weapons, heavy weapons, medical aid, communications, and demolitions. We were in the field almost immediately training, training, training. There were long runs, long-range full-field-pack marches, and an introduction to the tunnels, thatched huts, and man-traps in the Vietnam Village at the Gabriel Training Center.

I attended the Special Forces Counterinsurgency Course, which lasted ten weeks. In our class, we had officers and non-commissioned officers from many free-world nations. Most had combat experience fighting terrorists at home. One British paratrooper who had fought against communist terrorists in Malaya told me, "There are only two types of guerrillas out there, the clever and the dead. Trust no man, woman, or child."

The biggest eliminator in special operations training was the injury rate. Those with broken bones from parachute jumps and jump training, rappelling from helicopters, hand-to-hand combat exercises, and obstacle course runs were forced out of the program and, in many cases, out of the Army. In bayonet training, the palm of my left hand was run clean through by my ranger buddy, Jimmy

Walker. I took his rifle away from him and dislocated his right shoulder. We both ignored our injuries, stayed in training, and survived two years in Vietnam. The training was very tough, but I am sure it was the chief factor in my surviving Vietnam. Attitude, a positive attitude, was another major factor.

The Special Forces' daily cross-country runs of two to five miles with weapons and combat gear wore out many troopers who had had no difficulty in jump school running without such equipment. Wearing combat boots and jungle fatigues while carrying an M-14 rifle, light field pack, three days' rations, an extra uniform, and three pairs of socks burned out a lot of guys on the sandy trails through the pine forests of Fort Bragg.

Tactical schooling was also a big eliminator on the road to earning that green beret. We always seemed to be on patrol somewhere, day and night. The helicopter was our lifeline to survival. We flew in UH-1B models from pickup zones to landing zones, jumping out of them or rappelling out of them down sixty-foot ropes above the ground. We also directed combat fire support from helicopter platforms 1,500 feet above insertion points on the ground. The airmobile training at Fort Bragg in 1964 and 1965, flying with combat experienced aviators, taught me so much about air operations that I was totally prepared for combat and survival in Vietnam where I flew as a fire support coordinator on 104 missions, getting forced down twice by ground fire.

Rappelling out of helicopters caused a lot of casualties. Many troopers slipped and fell off their ropes at forty to sixty feet above the ground. In July 1962, I fractured my lower back, falling sixty feet into a dry stream bed near Staunton, Virginia, on an airmobile exercise. It took me four months to get back on my feet, walking and running again. I fell a second time in Vietnam with a patrol dog strapped to my back. I walked around with a swollen left leg for two months after that accident.

Survival, escape, and evasion (E&E) training washed out a number of troopers who could not read maps, follow compasses, or negotiate tough cross-country courses back to their base camps. We were trained to live off the land but had no time to search for food, constantly moving toward our patrol objectives. Surviving two and three days on one day's rations was a great challenge.

My ranger school buddy, Jimmy Walker, once dropped a cookie from his C rations while on patrol. I saw it hit the mud and knew it would disappear in the knee-deep muck we were wading through. I picked it up and ate it right away. Jimmy stopped the patrol to make a map check and search for it. After a minute, we moved out again. I could see he was very upset, but I said nothing. In Vietnam three years later, while we were having dinner and a beer at the officers' club, I told him about my theft of his combat ration. Jimmy, who had been a Golden Gloves champ, jumped up, struck a boxer's stance, and shouted, "You dirty airborne bastard!" I pretended to pull a knife on him. We laughed so hard tears came to our eyes.

Navy and Air Force pilots trained with us in E&E in 1964. I met one of those officers in Vietnam in 1966. He had been forced down by ground fire and told me, "I survived because of that special operations training I received at Fort Bragg. There's no doubt about it."

Each Monday morning during those ten weeks of counterinsurgency training, fewer and fewer students showed up for classes. "Jones quit," "So did Brown," and "I thought they would make it" were typical comments as we rearranged chairs in our classrooms. Most of the troopers who quit were forced to do so after visiting the emergency room at Fort Bragg's Womack Army Hospital. They had broken bones, pulled tendons, and torn ligaments, or they were worn out and exhausted.

Writing papers on guerrilla warfare, giving presentations, writing patrol orders, and coordinating fire support plans and air operations were daily pressures which caused many to fail academically. I had read a great deal about Napoleon fighting what was called the small war, or *guerrilla*, in Spain, 1808–1813, against remnants of the defeated Spanish Army. Guerrilla warfare gets its name from that campaign almost two centuries ago. I had also read a great deal about Francis Marion, the Swamp Fox, whose exploits were instrumental in George Washington's victory over the British in the American Revolution. After a trip to Ireland in the summer of 1964, I wrote a report about the Irish Republican Army in 1916 and their campaigns against the British. All my presentations, orders, and briefings stressed the historical principles of surprise, expecting the unexpected, and trusting no man, woman, or child.

Getting ready for two years in Vietnam was also very tough psychologically. A captain who gave us a class on air operations one day told us, "Look at the man to your left, now to your right. One of you won't be coming back from Vietnam. Get used to that. Take this stuff seriously." He was killed two days later in an aircraft accident.

One good friend, Chris O'Sullivan, a buddy of mine in high school and college, a real tough guy and an airborne ranger, was killed on Memorial Day 1965 just as I was shipping overseas. His widow, Eleanor, and his two sons, Michael and Stephen, received his Distinguished Service Cross and Silver Star on August 11, 1965. I wondered if I would end up like Chris O'Sullivan.

Army Chain of Command Photo

After earning my green beret, I served two tours in Vietnam. My first assignment was with the 30th Ranger Battalion (ARVN) as an assistant battalion advisor. My second assignment was as Commander, Company B, 716th Military Police Battalion in Saigon.

Photo by U.S. Army, 1969

Cherokee Trail

On one field training exercise, code named Cherokee Trail, in September 1964, we were separated into several twelve-man A teams and ordered to recruit and train a guerrilla army to operate against two brigades of the 82d Airborne Division. We would have no helicopters on this assignment. We would have to live off the land. We would be terrorists, freedom fighters, the aggressor force.

Several towns in North and South Carolina were areas of operation on this exercise. Local newspapers in Lumberton, Dillon, and other small towns along the Little Pee Dee River carried accounts of the training scenario. Citizens could watch the exercise or be participants in the training, if they wished. They could become guerrillas or work with the 82d Airborne and hunt us down like criminals who had escaped from state prison. Local TV stations broadcast news of the upcoming invasion by the 82d Airborne Division. D day was coming soon.

At D minus three, three days before the invasion, my team parachuted onto a high school football field at 4 A.M. to be met by no less than sixty high school seniors who wanted to be guerrilla fighters. With deer season approaching, they had dressed as hunters. So did we, so that we could blend into the population for guerrillas wear no uniforms. The group was led by some tough-as-nails football players and their new coach, Mr. Thomas, recently hired at Central High. We were hidden out in a gym at the school, fed well, and treated like liberators. For two days, we briefed the students on the concept of the operation and became familiar with the local road network. As guerrillas, the students on the exercise would carry their own hunting rifles and shotguns, without live or blank ammunition.

It was arranged for one student's father who owned a gas station to hire us as temporary employees. The service station with its outside pay phone would be our team headquarters and a base camp. We rented two pickup trucks from local families and waited for the 82d Airborne to parachute into the town. We pumped gas, serviced cars, changed flat tires, and hung out at the station like a bunch of guys curious about the Army maneuver. From the gas station we could observe all movements of the 82d Airborne troopers and create havoc as required. It was the perfect opportunity to see how local terrorists or freedom fighters could effectively destroy and frustrate conventional uniformed military forces trying to operate on foreign soil.

On D day, the 82d Airborne Division parachuted into many small towns south of Fort Bragg to liberate the area. The football coach from Central High disappeared. Many of our Special Forces soldiers were taken into custody at the gas station. Most of us escaped, however. I suspected one of our guerrillas had sold us out to the other side. Then again, the coach who had disappeared was someone the students didn't know well. He had a new pickup truck and claimed he had no family, but he had the mark of a wedding band on his left ring finger. Remembering that "there are only two types of guerrillas out there, clever or dead," and "trust no man, woman, or child," I decided to check him out.

A buddy of mine whom I had known since 1957, a North Carolina state trooper, was assigned to this area south of Fort Bragg. I called him on the phone one night to find out who the coach really was. I gave him the coach's name and his truck license tag number. Trooper Gene Caldwell met me the next day, informing me the coach was an Army officer driving a rented pickup from Spring Lake, North Carolina. The officer also had a family in that town. I phoned the coach's wife, telling her I was her husband's new first sergeant but had not met him as yet. Apologizing for calling her at home, I asked her to contact her husband for some special instructions from his commander.

She spilled the beans. "He's down in Lumberton or some other small town on a special mission," she informed me. The coach was actually Captain Thomas Higgenbotham, an officer with the 82d Airborne's G2, or secret intelligence, section.

That night, Higgenbotham was arrested for driving under the influence of alcohol (DWI), empty beer cans having been found in his truck. Hauled into jail by the local police, Higgenbotham swore up and down that he had not been drinking. In truth, he hadn't touched a drop, but an anonymous phone call to the state patrol had reported him as drunk and disorderly and driving all over the road. He had to spend three days in jail before being sent back to Fort Bragg on D day plus four.

People in the community were very upset that an army officer on this maneuver had been arrested for DWI. It was in the local press and on TV. A phone call from our gas station to his G2 commander straightened out the whole mess. Without identifying myself, I told his boss the man had to be eliminated but that, of course, "we couldn't actually shoot him." Having been set up by the Special Forces, Higgenbotham was furious. The G2 then made a special effort to eliminate our team. Higgenbotham, the G2 staff, and the 82d Airborne Provost Marshall had a conference back at Fort Bragg.

Until this time, a few of us had hung around the gas station without any great difficulty. We had posed as helpful citizens while giving false information to military police and reconnaissance units, sending them on wild goose chases looking for Special Forces soldiers. We flattened tires on parked military vehicles, gave some officers watered down gas, and denied others gas because their government credit cards supposedly had expired. We also had given some troops beer on warm nights then reported them to officers who reacted violently to reports of troops drinking in the field.

Almost immediately after Higgenbotham had been eliminated, the military police staked out our gas station, preventing anyone from using the pay phone and watching our every move. An incoming phone call from another Special Forces soldier to coordinate an operation was intercepted by the Military Police. We faced off with the MPs, then scattered into the woods, hunted like animals by two infantry platoons, about eighty men total. Had the Military Police and the infantry been armed with live ammunition, our guerrilla force would have been put out of action. The MPs also seized our rented pickup trucks. We were on foot again.

Fugitives, we hid out for three days at a student's home. Glen Johnson's mother let us use her phone to coordinate operations. We contacted our boss, giving him our new phone number. Our boss, a lieutenant colonel B team commander whom we had never met, had a pay phone communications point at the other end of town near a national guard armory. He was also being watched by intelligence agents. On the way to brief us, he was taken prisoner by the 82d Military Police. The MPs showed up outside the Johnson's home an hour later, after they had found the Johnson's phone number written on the palm of the colonel's left hand. We scattered into the woods again, out of action for one more day.

At D day plus eight, the 82d Airborne was putting us out of business. They patrolled the roads, the neighborhoods, and the Central High School area, stopping anybody they pleased. If a person didn't have a local driver's license for identification, they became a guerrilla suspect. I called Fort Bragg for more instructions, now that my boss was out of action. I found out our A team was to be consolidated with another and we were assigned to another B team for command and control purposes.

Our new boss drove around in a radio-equipped Ryder cargo truck, delivering hay to horse barns, which served as safe houses for guerrilla teams. Operating on amateur radio frequencies, he was not monitored by the 82d Airborne. They didn't use amateur radios, so our communications were relatively safe. A local amateur radio club operated out of a farm and an airfield near town, and our boss worked with them quite successfully for the rest of the maneuver.

He sent me into town to find out what was going on, since radio traffic on the 82d Airborne communications nets was picking up. In civilian clothes, I slipped into Central High School, attending a press briefing as a reporter from the *Fayetteville Observer*. Posing as a newsman and photographer, in possession of a fraudulent press pass, I found out that two battalions of troops, 1,800 men, were due in our area of operations on D day plus nine. They were going to land at the small airfield outside of town. I called my boss at the amateur radio club headquarters and reported everything. An ambush was immediately planned. I was told to stick with the press corps and report what information I could.

I had no vehicle, so I walked along with 82d Airborne troops on patrol, interviewing them and taking many pictures. They trusted me and even fed me C rations. I received a great deal of information from them. My identification was never verified since I had a press pass. Also, because short hair was worn by most southerners at the time, my military haircut didn't give me away. I camped out with these troops that night. Then that evening, I had a problem I never planned on in all my adventures.

I ran into Lieutenant Colonel Tom Llewlyn, who recognized me from my assignment with the 503d Airborne Infantry in 1959 and Ranger School in 1963. He knew me well, but I played dumb, telling him he must be mistaken, saying, "I just look like that soldier you knew back then." For some reason, he let the whole thing go, but nevertheless, I knew he would turn me in to intelligence officers or the military police. I dropped out of sight but not before I had stolen signal operating instructions, which gave the call signs and unit designations for every 82d Airborne unit in the field.

In the middle of the afternoon on D plus nine, I walked back to the airfield and made contact with my B team commander. We pinpointed the time of the upcoming helicopter assault and the location by listening to 82d Airborne radio traffic. We monitored an airborne security team en route to the airfield who were lost and asking for directions from their headquarters. My boss sent me down there as a newspaper reporter to interview the team for a press release.

I hitched a ride to the area where the security force was parked on the side of the road in a ten-vehicle convoy. I began taking pictures and interviewed the team commander. He told me everything, including unit designations and commanders' names. Then I began to interview the troops, who were pleased to know their pictures would be in hometown newspapers along with a story about their part in the training exercise. What they didn't know is that my 35mm Retina camera had run out of film, but I kept snapping away with the empty camera.

The roar and popping of rotor blades was heard in the distance. The first elements of a battalion of airborne troops was on the way to the airfield in ten UH-1B helicopters. The commander told me he had to move out, and the convoy started up on the way to the airfield and an ambush. As the helicopters touched down, sixty Special Forces guerrillas jumped from my boss's Ryder truck, opening up on the airfield with machine guns and M-14 rifles. The security team was also ambushed. The 82d Airborne Division Commander, Major General Robert H. York, was very angry. I casually walked up to the airfield, playing press corps reporter to the hilt. Then Tom Llewlyn, who had known me from 1959 and 1963, stopped me dead in my tracks, aiming an automatic at my chest. Two MPs in a jeep arrived. My press pass was taken from me. My wallet was taken. My cover was blown. Cherokee Trail was over for me, now a prisoner of war.

Interviewed by several intelligence POW specialists, I told them nothing, not even my name. They threw me into a local jail cell along with other Special Forces soldiers I didn't know. None of us spoke to each other. An FBI agent interviewed me, since I was a civilian. At least he said he was an FBI agent, but I didn't trust any man, woman, or child. I told them I was a newsman and had the wrong identification. It was a mistake but "certainly not a crime," I said. They went through my wallet and found my military ID, and soon I was on the way back to Fort Bragg, out of action.

I earned my green beret on April 3, 1965, my daughter's second birthday. I also received orders for Vietnam, with a departure date of June 19. I didn't have to go to Vietnam since my military obligation was completed on June 13, but my wife told me, "Now is when your country needs you."

While clearing post, closing out my bank account, and other affairs at Fort Bragg, I met Captain Higgenbotham in the post exchange parking lot. He came up to me, saying, "Hey, Morgan. Remember me, the coach from Central High? You wouldn't believe what happened to me. I got set up on Cherokee Trail and got arrested for DWI. Would you believe it?" "Yes, sir, I would," was my reply.

As I got into my car, he shouted at me, "You dirty airborne bastard! It was you, wasn't it?"

I met Higgenbotham in Vietnam in 1970. He was a lieutenant colonel on the joint general staff in the J2 intelligence section at that time. He was still mad at me.

Chapter 5

Vietnam, 1st Tour

1965

Suzie, Styx

The Nature of Terrorism

At 11 A.M. on March 30, 1965, four days before I received my green beret back in the States, a cream and blue Peugeot taxi pulled up to the U.S. embassy in Saigon. Some news reports insisted the vehicle was a black Citroen. There were no passengers. When a Vietnamese National Policeman approached the vehicle to question the driver about his purpose for being at the embassy, the driver stepped out. Some eyewitnesses say the driver ran towards the Bank of China, across from the embassy. Others say a Honda motorbike zipped by and picked up the driver trying to escape. Before the Vietnamese policeman could react, the vehicle exploded.

Two Americans and twenty Vietnamese were killed, and 190 others, most of them Vietnamese, were wounded. Deputy U.S. Ambassador U. Alexis Johnson was among the Americans injured by flying glass. The street in front of the embassy appeared to have been bombed from the air. There was a large crater where the vehicle had been parked. Dead and wounded civilians lay among bits and pieces of buildings, vehicles, and unrecognizable, charred remains of other human beings. Rescue workers from the U.S. Navy Station Hospital in Saigon arriving on the scene were totally unprepared for what they encountered.

"We just went through the motions, trying to help out anybody and everybody who streamed out to us," Chief Navy Corpsman Ed Wilson told me several months later. "I had seen this before in the movies, in the railroad yard scene from *Gone with the Wind*. I couldn't handle it. What could we really do for all those people?"

At Fort Bragg we were learning: trust no man, woman, or child. The military police in Saigon believed that every taxi driver, truck driver, Vietnamese civilian, and, unfortunately, every Vietnamese soldier was a threat to personal survival. Soon all U.S. compounds added concrete barriers to their defenses. The military police posted behind those one-ton barrels would shoot to kill anything that moved towards them. The psychological weapon of terrorism had been properly employed. There was an atmosphere of fear. An attitude of hopelessness and frustration overwhelmed many soldiers who served in Vietnam combat. They were fighting an unseen enemy.

At Fort Bragg in the ten-week course on counterinsurgency operations, we learned the philosophy of terrorism, the tools of the trade, and ways to counter the terrorist. Of course, I had studied terrorism and guerrilla warfare in other courses, but this training was oriented on Vietnam where I would soon be assigned. If I failed to follow the lessons in this course of instruction, I would be coming home in a body bag. I would have to be clever or I would be a dead man.

We learned, to start with, that terrorists are not soldiers in uniform. They don't have the guts to face another soldier or a policeman in uniform. They are criminals, and there would be no mercy for them in Vietnam. Surprise is the terrorist's best weapon. Terrorists have many limitations. They are not trained in tactics, do not have strength in numbers, and are not familiar with their weapons. Most of their weapons and vehicles are stolen.

Disciplined counterterrorists, well trained and equipped, can eliminate these adversaries in short order. Efficient police work, good communications, and attention to detail are the best weapons for security forces. Gathering of intelligence is the first matter of business. Security of installations, vehicles, weapons, and personnel are major additional priorities for government forces.

A British officer, Major Michael Bury of the 6th Parachute Regiment, who had served in Malaya fighting communist terrorists (CTs), told me, "More CTs starved out in the jungle than were killed by gunfire because we cut them off from the people."

Mao Tse-tung wrote, "The guerrilla is like a fish. He must swim in the sea of the people. But he is not one of them. He can be identified and eliminated."

Our job was to catch the fish and hang him out to dry.

On June 25, 1965, I stepped off the plane in hot, humid Saigon, met at Ton Son Nhut Air Base by a military police officer who escorted me to my temporary quarters in Saigon. Dressed in khakis, wearing my green beret, I was directed to change into civilian clothes. Another advisor, an army aviator, was my new roommate. He invited me to go downtown to eat at a Chinese restaurant.

As we approached the My Canh floating restaurant on the Saigon River waterfront, we were stopped by military police who questioned us about our destination. We told them we were going to the My Canh. "Not tonight, sir," one MP told us. "They just blew it all to hell with a claymore mine."

We rushed down to the scene to assist rescue personnel. The crime scene at the My Canh was pure horror for me. "Welcome to Saigon," my roommate said to me as we assisted wounded civilians to ambulances. What Major Michael Bury told me was true, but I could only think how hopeless it was to catch the fish who had blown up the U.S. embassy or the My Canh restaurant. Where would somebody like myself, with all my education, training, and dedication, begin? I was the fish out of water. The Viet Cong were going to hang me and my buddies out to dry.

I was assigned to Advisory Team 100, after in-processing at the Military Assistance Command compound, MACV II. Old friends from Fort Bragg, the 82d Airborne, and Special Forces were in every briefing I attended. We had all arrived in Vietnam just days apart, and we were as green as our new jungle fatigues.

At lunch one day, I met my old platoon sergeant from the 503d Airborne, C. Q. Williams. He was now a second lieutenant assigned to the Special Forces. Wounded several times, C. Q. had just survived a horrific battle at a place called Dong Xoai. One year later, President Johnson would present him with the Medal of Honor. C. Q. Williams told me, "Get out in the field somewhere and get your feet wet in some rice paddy, or you'll die here with dry socks in Saigon."

C. Q. told me all about terrorists. "They're cowards, criminals, sneaky bastards. They run the restaurants, drive taxis, do your wash, shine your shoes, and throw grenades in the back seat of your jeep. You can't shoot them because you can't find them. The only way to kill terrorists is to kill everybody. This is Indian Country. The only good Indian is a dead Indian. C. Q. Williams had been my platoon sergeant in the 82d Airborne for over a year. I had trusted him in 1959, believing every word he told me. I trusted him again in 1965.

Efficient police work, good communications, and attention to detail were the best weapons for the security forces, according to the instructors at Fort Bragg. But in a city of 3 million people crammed into a metropolitan area designed for 500,000 inhabitants, there was no efficient police work.

The best soldiers in the South Vietnamese Army were in the Special Forces, the Marines, the Airborne Brigade, and the Ranger Command. The Vietnamese National Police were, at best, average performers with low pay, little education, and virtually no training. Armed only with .38 caliber pistols and no rifles or shotguns, they were no match for well armed terrorists with AK-47 assault rifles.

Because they wore white cotton uniforms and scattered in the face of overwhelming odds, they were given the nickname white mice.

I took C. Q. Williams' advice and found myself a job with the 30th Ranger Battalion as an assistant battalion advisor. My classmate in college, Dan Garde, who had been out in the field with the 30th Rangers for over six months, was ready to rotate back to a staff job at team headquarters in Gia Dinh Province. I volunteered to be his replacement.

The Bridge

I was assigned to the 30th ARVN Ranger Battalion as an advisor and fire support coordinator. We were out in the rice paddies and pineapple fields thirty miles west of Saigon, sitting squarely on the major terrorist infiltration routes from Cambodia. There were canals running north and south, east and west, tunnels everywhere, and one major road. The place was called Cau Xang.

Cau Xang, in Gia Dinh Province, was a small village, a hub of local market activity since the east-west road intersected a major north-south canal system. I was stationed there from June to December 1965.

Spanning the canal complex was a rusted-out steel bridge, built by the French in 1950. It had been hit by artillery so many times that we expected it to

Photo by the author, 1965

The bridge over the canal at Cau Xang

collapse at any moment. Busses, taxis, ox carts, and motorcycles used the bridge from 6 A.M. to 6 P.M., seven days a week. We closed down the structure with an A-frame barrier from dusk until dawn.

I served as an advisor to rangers with the Army of the Republic of Vietnam (ARVN) and to Vietnam National Police (VN) at a checkpoint on the bridge. Our mission was to inspect every bus, taxi, ox cart, and motorcycle for terrorists, arms, or ammunition. Our major challenge was to identify cowboys, terrorists on motorcycles who attacked outposts and terrorized civilians with grenades. An American military police advisor had been killed by a grenade thrown from a motorcycle at nearby Binh Chanh bridge on August 10, 1965. Five days later, we were shot at by terrorists on a motorcycle. Operating the checkpoint was a very dangerous job. The civilians caught in the cross fire hated the police and the rangers. In return, any hostility from civilians could trigger a harsh response from government officials at the outpost.

Photo by the author, 1965

Viet Cong on an ox cart loaded with ammunition

The purpose of the grenade attacks was to create panic and a diversion, according to intelligence reports. As busses or taxis loaded with Viet Cong soldiers, arms, and ammunition approached checkpoints, cowboys would throw a grenade or fire pistols at police and run through the road block. Other vehicles following would also rush the barrier and race through the outpost without an inspection. Police and rangers could not stop the panic once the shooting started or a grenade exploded.

My partner on the Cau Xang bridge was a female named Suzie, a forty-five pound German shepherd. She could smell out explosives, detect drugs, and identify Viet Cong in seconds, according to rumors. Since she was a police dog, many assumptions were made about her training and abilities. Once she helped apprehend a Viet Cong suspect who jumped from a taxi and ran from rangers. Suzie and I had prices on our heads for those bold enough to attempt to kill us.

When we closed down the bridge at dusk on August 15, 1965, an assassination squad moved in on the bridge. Two cowboys, dressed as regional soldiers, approached the bridge from the west asking for passage. They said they were on the way to Binh Chanh. Meanwhile, the VC were told to wait on the west bank and to take cover in an abandoned sugar mill until it was safe to travel at dawn.

Photo by the author, 1965

The sugar mill

They disappeared as the shift on the bridge changed at midnight. They had scouted out our positions, counted our numbers, and at 1 A.M. attacked us from the mill. Four other VC, hiding in the sugar mill, reinforced the two cowboys we had watched for six hours on the road. From three sides, we were fired upon by AK-47 rifles, B-40 rockets, and a 57mm recoilless rifle, a World War II antitank weapon.

The ten rangers on the bridge at midnight scrambled for cover when the first B-40 rocket hit the A-frame barrier dead center. Two rangers were wounded. Suzie and I headed for cover on the south side of the bridge, hiding in an abandoned, mud-filled fighting position across the canal from the sugar mill. Four rangers joined me, and we watched for enemy activity. Rangers on the bridge fired down the road with a machine gun, and we sent up flares to detect any movement.

Suzie alerted left, and we scanned left to right but saw nothing. Next we heard the splashing of water and the clank of metal. The two VC with the 57mm recoilless rifle were somewhere in front of us, but we could not see them, blind from firing our weapons in the darkness. When we finally saw the VC in the dancing shadows of a parachute flare landing in the canal, we fired at them. They fired at the bridge but missed. The antitank round shot over the village. Our bursts of automatic weapons fire had wounded the gunner and killed his ammunition bearer. The bridge at Cau Xang had survived another attack.

At 2 A.M., we heard the sounds of a motorbike west of the bridge. We fired off more flares, and rangers swept the road with more machine gun fire. We also fired a claymore mine, which is like shooting twenty shotgun shells down the road. Hundreds of shotgun pellets are fired with one blast of a claymore. All was quiet once again.

At 6 A.M., we sent out patrols checking for battle damage. The two cowboys were dead on the road next to a motorbike. The recoilless rifle team was dead on the banks of the canal near the sugar mill. No enemy weapons were found. Other VC had taken them away in the darkness before dawn.

The next morning, I wrote an after-action report, fighting off sleep, trying to make sense of this enemy contact. Four enemy soldiers died attacking an old bridge which had no military significance. What was the purpose of their sacrifice? I gave Suzie credit for detecting the enemy in the canal. Had we not fired there, the bridge would have been destroyed. The action was reduced to a two-line entry at Military Assistance Vietnam Headquarters: "0115, 16 Aug 65, contact at Cau Xang, 30th ARVN Ranger BN, 4VC, KIA, 2 ARVN, WIA, no weapons recovered."

Baptism of Fire

September 29, 1965, was the date on the calendar. I had been in Vietnam for three months, had been shot at a few times on those long walks in the hot sun, but had not seen any real combat. My companion most every day was a young lady, Suzie, my German shepherd patrol dog. Suzie was tied to my wrist by a parachute cord at night so I could sleep. You never knew who the enemy was in Vietnam. I surely expected to be killed by an unseen enemy on some ill-defined battlefield in this undeclared war. I usually slept with an M-14 rifle, and as I was not one of those country boys who could run in my bare feet, I wore boots in the daytime and sneakers at night.

Photo by a Cau Xang villager, 1965

Captain Bill Hollenbeck, Suzie, Father Tu, and the author
Taken following the ceremony in which I exchanged a set of rosary beads and a .38 caliber pistol for the patrol dog, Suzie.

We were at Ton Son Nhut air base, just outside Saigon, on convoy detail getting ready to carry pierced steel planking, sand bags, and large supplies of 60mm mortar, 81mm mortar, and M-60 machine gun ammunition to our ranger outpost at Cau Xang, twenty miles west of Saigon on the border of Hau Nghia Province. I was a first lieutenant, an advisor to the 30th Ranger Battalion (ARVN), and one of four advisors in a combat assistance team out with 900 ARVN rangers.

Twelve rangers were on the detail this day. We had four trucks and three jeeps. Sergeant Nhan was the squad leader. His troopers were armed with World War II .30 caliber M-1 carbines. All the ARVN soldiers' gear was in my trailer. We had loaded up all the ammunition on September 28, and the rangers went home for the night to see their families at Ton Son Nhut. I guarded the convoy overnight with Suzie, waiting for the rangers to return at dawn.

Sergeant Nhan reported in first at 7 A.M., and the rest of the detail showed up an hour later. As we drank coffee and smoked Vietnamese cigarettes, Ruby Queens, one trooper tumbled out of a taxi with red eyes. He was drunk or had been smoking pot. Red Eyes was well built, physically strong, and very mean spirited. Suzie growled at him and flashed her teeth when he reported in for duty. Most of the rangers appeared to be intimidated by Red Eyes.

At 9 A.M., we rolled out of Ton Son Nhut on the road to Cau Xang. As we drove through one small village after another, I couldn't help thinking how many VC were watching us. We had some precious cargo with all that ammunition. Especially needed by the VC were our 81mm mortar ammo and 81mm mortar parachute flares. One flare could turn night into day, making a VC attack an instant surprise. We used the parachute flares to spot patrols or large formations of enemy troops and to guide helicopter gunships.

We kept rolling at 20 miles an hour, when we could, to prevent an ambush. Stop a convoy and loose the convoy was the general rule. In Special Warfare School at Fort Bragg, North Carolina, British officers who had served in Malaya fighting communist terrorists warned us, "Stopping for logs across roads, a broken-down cart, or some other obstacle or for someone asking for help on the side of the road can spell disaster. If one stops, he will be killed by a sniper and the convoy will be attacked."

As we approached the village of Ba Hom, about fifteen miles west of Saigon, Suzie sat straight up and began scanning the road. Corporal Phung, my driver, had a worried look on his face. My heart began pounding, and I was as thirsty as a dog on a hot day. Just as we left the village, shots were fired at the rear of our convoy. "I knew it! An ambush," I thought.

We turned on our headlights and picked up speed, racing down the road lined with rice paddies on both sides. Cau Xang was five miles ahead, and we were in no-man's-land with no villages, only open country. There were water buffalo in the rice paddies, but the boys tending them, whom we called Buffalo Bills, were hiding. The VC were out there. I knew I was a dead man and started reciting my Catholic prayers, waiting for a command-detonated mine to blow up the road in front of me. Nothing happened. No machine gun fire, no mines, no mortar shells, no snipers. I couldn't figure it out.

Gun fire continued from the rear, but we weren't hit. Fifteen minutes later, we rolled into base camp, and I was sweating like a race horse. We hadn't lost a truck or a jeep or any rangers. The battalion commander, Captain Tot, a former French Legionnaire, was furious. He began chewing me out in French and Vietnamese. Suzie stood behind me, glued to my left leg, ready to tear up the captain. Sergeant Nhan caught it next, standing at attention in the hot sun, sweat running down his face and neck. Next, Captain Tot lined up the twelve-man squad, looking each man in the face. Suddenly, he attacked one soldier with a bamboo walking stick. Red Eyes was beaten to the ground, disarmed, and kicked brutally. I couldn't believe what I was seeing.

This soldier had been firing his weapon at the water buffalo and the boys tending the beasts. I also found out he was not on the detail, he was absent without leave (AWOL), having been classified as a deserter in August 1965. He returned to the battalion without authorization. Issuing him an M-1 carbine, ammunition, and another soldier's equipment was my mistake. Sergeant Nhan was under the gun for allowing this man on the detail. Another soldier must have been left behind at Ton Son Nhut. This man had been doing all the firing in the rear. Red Eyes was signalling the VC that we had ammunition in the convoy, according to Sergeant Nhan.

The ARVN NCO was sure this ranger was a VC in our ranks. Nhan told me he had been AWOL for two months, probably operating with a main force VC unit. "Now he returns to our battalion to recruit more rangers and steal arms, ammunition, grenades, medical supplies, and uniforms. He will probably turn on us in a fight and kill you advisors and many officers in the battalion," Nhan warned me in confidence. Sergeant Nhan also told me the ranger left behind had most probably been killed by Red Eyes, unless he was also a VC who traded places with him.

Photo by the author, 1965

Water buffalo and their herders, called Buffalo Bills. The delirious Red Eyes started shooting at them.

This AWOL soldier was placed in a prisoner-of-war tiger cage to roast in the sun. The cage was three feet high, three feet wide, and three feet deep, too short to stand in and too small to lie down in. Out in the open, there was no protection from the sun or rain. The prisoner was stripped to his shorts, not given any water, and bound hand and foot all day. United States soldiers were treated in the same fashion when taken prisoner by the Viet Cong. I couldn't stand to look at this inhumane treatment, nor could I do anything to help the soldier. "There would be hell to pay for this," I thought. Captain Tot was in serious trouble.

The ammunition was distributed to all the bunkers and emplacements in the ranger battalion, and I reported to my post at battalion headquarters, exhausted. This had been a long day for me. I had not slept the night before, guarding the ammunition trucks. I needed some rest. After four hours of sleep during the heat of the day, I was on my feet again and very tired. Troops filled sand bags throughout the day and reinforced their bunkers with the pierced steel planking our convoy had carried from Ton Son Nhut. Red Eyes was still in the tiger cage. I checked on him. He had not been given any water or food since his arrival at battalion. I thought he might die in the tiger cage, but Captain Tot didn't seem to care.

As the battalion advisors and the battalion staff sat down to dinner in Captain Tot's office that night, Red Eyes was released from the tiger cage after nine hours of confinement. As he was being fed, he overpowered his guards, seized a grenade, and headed for battalion headquarters. We heard a great deal of noise outside, looking up from our meal of rice and fish. Red Eyes was standing there with an activated grenade in his hand. The pin had been pulled, and he told Captain Tot he was going to die. We were all going to die! Unarmed, we stared him down as three other rangers jumped the soldier and got the grenade from him, replacing the pin. The man was dragged away and thrown into the tiger cage again.

Dinner at the officers' mess was over. I was rattled, as were the other advisors. Captain Tot strutted around, smoking a cigar, being cool. I sat down to smoke a cigar with him, but I was too nervous to relax. The battalion commander assured me Red Eyes would be going back to Saigon in the morning, in chains, to prison. I wasn't so sure.

Photo by the author, 1965

Captain Nguyen Chi Tot, 30th ARVN Ranger Battalion Company

At 9 P.M., I made radio checks with higher headquarters, adjusting artillery fire on probable enemy approaches into the village. I wanted to make sure our artillery support was ready if we were attacked that night. An hour later, we were hit on both flanks by a main force Viet Cong battalion. Claymore mines, spitting out hundreds of shotgun pellets, along with machine guns and rifle fire destroyed the silence on the outpost. Our battalion senior advisor was with Captain Tot at the time of the attack. He ordered me to direct helicopter gunships on to attacking enemy formations. I had never seen the VC in the open before. This was my baptism of fire. I was on the air instantly, directing helicopter gunships on station, making a few mistakes in fire direction but getting the job done with the help of experienced combat aviators.

As the NCO advisors in our team began coordinating with ranger companies in enemy contact, the situation became very confusing. Our mortars were lighting up the sky with their illuminating rounds and parachute flares. White phosphorous grenades marked our front and flanks. Gunships passed across our front engaging Viet Cong formations, and enemy mortar fire landed in our positions. The village was catching fire. Civilians were running for the aid station. Casualties began coming in, and I was trying to be cool.

Lieutenant Paul Morgan,
Assistant Battalion Advisor

Photo by Sergeant First Class James Des Verney, 1965

Red Eyes was released from his cage when an incoming mortar shell wounded him. He was furious, crazed, turning into a wild animal. Red Eyes killed two rangers, took their clothing and equipment, and attacked the mortar position with grenades, silencing it immediately.

The village defensive positions were being infiltrated on both flanks, and we could no longer see the enemy in the open without our parachute flares. Without them assisting our forward elements, helicopter gunships could not fire on enemy ranks. The team commander ordered me to get the mortars running again. I didn't know what had happened at the mortar pit, but I was prepared for the worst.

Photo by the author, 1965

The mortar pit

With Suzie at my side, I began creeping through the blacked out village, radio on my back and M-14 rifle in my hand. My magazine was loaded with twenty armor-piercing 7.62mm tracer rounds to direct fire. I was talking to my NCO advisors out with ranger companies on the flanks in heavy contact. It looked like the VC would overrun the village without fire support from our artillery and gunships. Sergeant Nhan joined me, along with Corporal Phung. It seemed like an eternity had passed before we found our mortar pit. One member of the crew was dead, torn to shreds from grenades. Three rangers were seriously wounded.

75

Placing my M-14 down for an instant, I tried to help the wounded rangers. They had to be cleared from the pit so we could start firing again. Sergeant Nhan and Corporal Phung pulled the dead ranger from the position, and we readied the gun for firing. Corporal Phung gave me two rounds of illuminating ammunition, and I dropped them down the tube one after the other. We had "flares on the way," I reported on the radio.

A moment later, Sergeant Nhan shouted, "Look out!" I turned, and Suzie began barking viciously.

A VC wearing a ranger uniform was standing behind us with another grenade. Sergeant Nhan fired my M-14 full auto into this soldier wearing our uniform as he tried to throw his grenade at us. Corporal Phung jumped on the grenade. I emptied my .45 caliber pistol into the VC as he dropped to the ground. Stepping back, I tripped over Suzie and fell into the mortar pit. Corporal Phung was killed by the grenade. He had saved Sergeant Nhan, Suzie, and me from certain death. Sergeant Nhan was wounded by grenade fragments in the right arm. I survived without a scratch. The VC had the top of his head blown off. His right arm was missing at the elbow. He stared up at us in death with the same vicious look we had seen at daybreak. It was Red Eyes. I guess he knew he was going to die that day.

Sergeant Nhan later told me that Suzie had alerted on the enemy first, warning him that Red Eyes was behind us. In my after-action report, I gave Suzie all the credit for saving us, but the entire incident was reduced to a few lines in the battalion duty log that night. "2215, 29 Sept 65, 506th VC Bn (Main Force) attacked

Photo by the author, 1965

A U.S. medevac helicopter lifts off from our base camp after taking out our wounded rangers

Cau Xang. Infiltrators attacked mortar crews, killing four and wounding three ARVN. Main force unit withdrew when gunship support arrived on station. Enemy casualties unknown." Red Eyes was counted as an ARVN soldier, and Suzie received no credit for her actions.

I received an Army Commendation Medal for surviving my baptism of fire. In the commendation report, there was no mention of Red Eyes as an enemy soldier. He was officially described as a "delirious soldier" and as a "deranged individual who indiscriminately fired his weapon in all directions and threatened the unit with an activated hand grenade."

```
                              HEADQUARTERS
              UNITED STATES MILITARY ASSISTANCE COMMAND, VIETNAM
                          APO San Francisco 96243

GENERAL ORDERS                                       15 December 1965
NUMBER   2591

              AWARD OF THE ARMY COMMENDATION MEDAL


1.  TC 320 The following AWARD is announced.

MORGAN, PAUL B.  095061 1ST LT MPC USA Adv Tm 100 CMD APO 96243
   Awarded:  Army Commendation Medal
   Date of Service:  29 September 1965
   Theater:  Republic of Vietnam
   Authority:  By direction of the Secretary of the Army under the provisions
              of AR 672-5-1, and Department of the Army Message 941895, dated
              22 October 1963
   Reason:    For distinguishing himself by exceptionally meritorious achieve-
              ment on 29 September 1965 while serving as advisor to the 30th
              Ranger Battalion, Army of the Republic of Vietnam.  During the
              early evening a delirious soldier ran through the area indiscrim-
              inately firing his weapon in all directions and threatening the
              unit with an activated hand grenade.  Disregarding his personal
              safety, Lieutenant Morgan continued to maintain vital communications
              and direct air support for an element of the battalion that was
              engaged in combat some distance away.  Approximately five hours
              later the deranged individual accidentally detonated the hand
              grenade, killing himself and another soldier and seriously injuring
              three others.  Lieutenant Morgan then assisted in directing a
              medical evacuation helicopter to the area and organized security
              around the landing zone from which the dead and wounded were
              evacuated.  Lieutenant Morgan's meritorious achievements were in
              keeping with the highest traditions of the United States Army and
              reflect great credit upon himself and the military service.

FOR THE COMMANDER:


                              W.B. ROSSON
                              Major General, USA
                              Chief of Staff



OFFICIAL

L.M. HARRIS
Colonel, AGC
Adjutant General
```

I had heard many tales from Special Forces soldiers who claimed ARVN units were full of VC who turned against their comrades under fire. It appears Sergeant Nhan was correct.

I slept soundly each night, when I could, after September 29, 1965 because I had my German shepherd, Suzie, tied to my wrist with a parachute cord, an M-14 rifle at my side, and sneakers on my feet.

The French Villa

On the canal complex west of Saigon, built by the French for commercial purposes in the early twentieth century, there were many decaying monuments to the French Indo-China empire. Among them was a beautiful, spacious white villa with expensive orange-tiled roof. It had been designed and modeled after a villa on the Azure Coast of France. Now the perimeter walls were sandbagged and crumbling. The front lawn was criss-crossed with trenches. The main house was pock-marked from small arms fire, and rain leaked through the roof. The carriage house had been destroyed by fire.

The villa was frequently used as a Viet Cong headquarters and hospital. No VC were ever captured when the villa was raided every so often. Rice and bicycles were found on many occasions, however. We suspected the VC were local rice farmers by day and terrorists by night.

One sunny day in September 1965, a formation of helicopters descended on the villa. Rangers from the 30th ARVN Battalion hit the ground running and overran the grounds in less than a minute. Hot rice, four bicycles, an AK-47 rifle, some plastique explosives, and some AK ammunition were discovered. I accompanied the rangers with my patrol dog, Suzie, directing combat support for the ARVN soldiers. No VC could be found. There were some rice farmers in the field. We knew they were the Viet Cong.

Patrols searched the fields around the villa. Farmers were interrogated, as were boys tending herds of water buffalo. One farmer on crutches warned us about mines on the paddy dikes and paths which criss-crossed the area. After six hours of patrolling in the hot sun, two Vietnamese Navy boats picked up half the rangers, while the rest of us remained behind on an ambush detail. I was one nervous advisor, keeping Suzie tied to my wrist with a twenty-foot parachute cord while we settled in for the night. Sergeant Nhan, the squad leader, told me I could rest in the main house, but I remained on the canal in a fighting position. My M-14 rifle was off safety, and I could not rest.

I didn't think we had fooled the VC, leaving an ambush patrol behind, and we didn't. One of their four-man patrols checked us out at 1 A.M. We held our

Photo by the author, 1965

A company of Vietnamese rangers assigned to the 30th ARVN Ranger Battalion

fire, but they knew we were there. We had booby-trapped their bicycles with a claymore mine. One blast, well aimed, would shower the enemy with the several hundred shotgun pellets. No one could escape alive from a claymore explosion.

While we watched the silent shadows 100 feet away, Suzie growled and flashed her teeth. With one burst of fire from my M-14, I could have taken out the VC to our front, but our orders were to hold our fire and report enemy activity. It was hard to watch the enemy, not being allowed to shoot.

An hour later, another patrol visited the villa. This bunch was noisy, six of them, and they never stopped talking. They even had flashlights. We watched and they left, unaware we were there. At 3 A.M., the canal was alive with sampans and more VC. I called in their location on my radio, and soon the air was filled with the sound of rotor blades and machine gun fire. Our fireflies, as we called them, UH1D helicopters with powerful flood lights, hosed down the canal with machine guns. Red tracers from above bounced all over the canal. There was a great deal of shouting and screaming as VC were trying to hide from the gunships. We couldn't see a thing, just heard the noises.

At first light we sent out a patrol to assess battle damage. Suzie led the way along the canal. She did not alert on any VC. We didn't find a trace of the enemy. No sampans, no dead bodies, no blood trails could be found. They had just vanished from sight. When we returned to the French villa, we found the four VC bicycles were also gone. The clever little devils had disconnected the claymore booby-trap and taken it, along with their transportation. We also found missing from our supplies were more mines and trip wire. They had disconnected four booby-trapped mines and carted them off, too.

As we lifted off from the area by helicopter later in the day, rice farmers in the field waved at us with smiles on their faces. I remembered my grandmother's stories from the troubles in Ireland, how the IRA gunners were friendly farmers by day and IRA soldiers who fought the British at night. The British soldiers had a saying about them: "Anyone that friendly is too sweet to be sound."

Photo by the author, 1965

Farmers in rice paddies of Cau Xang, west of Saigon
I took this photo while on patrol in the vicinity of the French villa. The rice farmers smiled and waved at my patrol as we passed by the paddies. They seemed friendly enough. Were they the Viet Cong at night and friendlies by day?

Prayer on the Battlefield

In October 1965, I was still serving as an advisor to the 30th ARVN Ranger Battalion at Cau Xang, thirty miles west of Saigon, astride several infiltration routes from Cambodia to the capitol of South Vietnam.

Cau Xang was a Catholic community headed by a very tough anti-communist priest, Father Nguyen Cong Tu. He had spent several years in jail after the country was divided in 1954. Father Tu spoke French but no English. My French was poor, but we could communicate. His bodyguard and house aide, Brother Hugh De Puy, spoke some English. Both Father Tu and Hugh taught me some

Father Nguyen Cong Tu and the author

Photo by Brother Hugh De Puy

Vietnamese, but they didn't care what I spoke as long as I directed U.S. fire support and kept the Viet Cong at bay.

I was a Catholic, and I went to mass every day. My patrol dog, Suzie, accompanied me, and the priest blessed Suzie every day. The military chaplains issued us green cord rosaries for field duty. Many Catholic soldiers wore these items of issue around their necks. Metal rosaries, as we had in the States, rusted with sweat and the high humidity in Vietnam. Most of the Vietnamese rangers in our battalion were Catholic soldiers, so they too wore the green ropes, as they were called.

From our base, we sent out reconnaissance patrols every day. They were usually four-man squads with little ammunition. Their mission was not to engage the enemy directly but to report enemy activity. The U.S. advisors would direct fire support on the enemy. We coordinated artillery and helicopter gunships almost every day. We also controlled medical evacuation, or medevac, helicopters extracting casualties from the field. The flying ambulances were collectively called Dustoff.

Photo by Sergeant Nguyen Chi Nhan, 1965

The "Dustoff" (medevac helicopter) Playboy

On October 20, one of our reconnaissance patrols was ambushed 500 meters from the village. The ranger patrol had triggered two booby traps, and radio communications ceased. At daybreak, about 7 A.M., we still had no radio contact. We feared all the rangers had been killed or seriously wounded. A rescue mission was mounted. I knew the area well, having lived four months in the village. I volunteered to accompany the rescue force. Well prepared, I had an M-14 rifle, 200 rounds of ammunition, two canteens of water, a first-aid kit, extra rations, four grenades, a radio, and my patrol dog, Suzie. Father Tu blessed the four of us and our dog at mass that morning as we set out on our patrol.

Suzie was a personal dog, not Army issue. I had gotten her from Father Tu. A beautiful German shepherd, Suzie understood French and had lots of combat scouting experience. She was devoted to me. Father Tu and Hugh told me that God protects dogs from the knowledge of death so they will be brave and serve their fellow man. Because of their unconditional love, devotion, humility, and honesty, all dogs are rewarded in the afterlife with the equivalent of heaven.

Three hundred yards from Cau Xang, as we crossed over a rice paddy dike, I heard the crack of a rifle. A rifle bullet sliced across my left forearm, cutting it open four inches above my wrist. It looked like I had been slashed with a razor. The blood poured down my arm onto my radio handset. I was rattled and nervous and stumbled into a canal. Sweating and shaking uncontrollably, I called in on the radio, requesting artillery support.

"Base, this is Cabbage Chops. I'm hit. Let's have gunship support, over."

The medic with our patrol, pulling me out of the canal, took a second sniper round in the chest and died instantly. We were in serious trouble. Any unit with fifty percent casualties is combat ineffective. Two rangers out of four were down a few minutes after crossing the line of departure on this operation.

Gunships in the area called me on the radio. "Cabbage Chops, this is Gatling One-Six, over."

I answered, "This is Chops. We've got one Line One and one Line Two and a good sniper out there, over."

Line One was the duty log reporting terminology for our honored dead killed in action, KIA. Line Two designated wounded. Gatling One-Six was a scout leader with four gunships carrying modern versions of Richard Gatling's Civil War machine gun. Helicopter gunships made our small squads powerful fighting machines. Each gunship carried two gatling guns, a grenade launcher, and some rockets.

With gatlings on the way, I felt better. Binding my wound with a field dressing, I was ready to move out again. Suzie licked my arm, washing away the blood. She also watched over the dead medic, floating in the canal near us. The two rangers with me had a great deal of combat experience, and they were not as anxious to move out as I was. The sniper had done his job well. Four men were missing, and now four more were stopped dead in their tracks. I expected mortar rounds to start hitting us and told the guys we had to move out or die in place.

Another sniper round hit the paddy dike. I returned fire with my M-14 rifle. My rangers also returned fire, and then we charged forward with Suzie in the lead. I called in to the gunships. "Gatling One-Six, this is Chops. We're south of the village. Do you see us? Over."

"Chops, we can't see you, but we worked that area yesterday and took some ground fire. I think you've hit some VC supply unit. Maybe you're in over your head. Watch your butt, over."

I replied, "One-Six, this is Chops. Thanks for the advice. I'm ready to guide you when you're ready to shoot. I think our sniper may be going underground now with you flying overhead. This might be a supply cache, over."

Two figures darted across our front. I couldn't see them clearly with the sweat in my eyes. It was hard to concentrate with the throbbing in my left arm. The gunships made a pass at the rice paddy dike to our front. Their gatlings could tear up a football field in five seconds. Suzie was in front of us, and the gunships were so close that I prayed out loud, "Lord help us, don't let Suzie get hit."

The dog saw the gunships coming and retreated back across an open rice paddy. I was sure the sniper would kill her. She looked at us, hunkered down, and wagged her tail. That meant she had a live find. We followed her and discovered our missing men, although two were dead and two were wounded. The two figures we had seen were Viet Cong who had shot our rangers a second time, taking their weapons and ammunition, and leaving them for dead.

Medevac was calling me. "Chops, are you the guys we're looking for? Over."

"Roger," I replied. "We've got three Ones and three Twos in pretty sad shape, over. Thank God you're here."

"Chops, this is Dustoff. Keep prayin', son. It ain't over yet."

Photo by Sergeant First Class James Webb, 1965

"Chops, this is Dustoff. Keep prayin son. It ain't over yet."

While the birds circled overhead, ready to touch down, I spoke to one of the survivors, our patrol squad leader. He was twenty-two years old, a sergeant with three years' combat experience. His face and arms were in terrible shape from fragment wounds. He told me that the first man across the canal had picked up an AK-47 rifle, triggering one booby trap. He was killed instantly. While crawling for cover, they triggered a second booby trap, and another ranger was killed. The Viet Cong came next and shot every man, taking their weapons, leaving them for dead.

The squad leader passed out after giving his report, and I turned to the other ranger. His legs were just about ripped off and he had lost a great deal of blood.

This man had his green cord rosary in his hands, praying. When I bent down to help him, he stopped and looked at me with great concern, more worried about me than himself. I must have looked pretty bad. My nerves were shot, and I was shaking and sweating, hardly able to talk on the radio.

"Dustoff, we're ready with two Line Twos and two Line Ones, over."

"Chops, I can only take your Line Twos. Logbird will take the Ones," he replied.

Logbirds are logistical helicopters that bring in food and ammunition and carry out the dead. Medevacs are supposed to carry wounded only, but if they have space, they take out the dead for morale purposes. Units in combat are reluctant to move, leaving their casualties behind. The Viet Cong were the same way, always carrying away their dead and wounded when they could. This medevac already had two wounded aboard. His space was limited. In the heat and humidity of Vietnam, our helicopters had limited lift-off power when trying to fly straight up from the battlefield.

The wounded ranger with the rosary held my left arm with both hands, pressing the cross on my wound. I knew he was praying for me as he looked into my eyes. He smiled as I picked him up and started to carry him to the medevac bird. I was shocked when he died in my arms without warning, dropping his green rope to the ground. His wounded sergeant, stumbling to the aircraft, picked up the fallen rosary and placed it around his buddy's neck. Then he closed the man's eyes.

Our sniper crawled out of his hole again and began blasting away at us. We couldn't fire back while caring for the wounded. The rangers tried to drag me aboard, but no dogs were allowed on the medevac ship. I stayed behind with Suzie and our dead, waiting for the logbird. The medevac lifted off immediately, leaving us alone out there.

Logbird called me and gave me an order. "Chops, move it now. Leave the Ones behind, over."

In a minute, the logbird was on the deck, and I scrambled aboard with Suzie. We were off in a flash, and gunships strafed the suspected enemy positions.

Our dead were left behind in two locations but were recovered the next day with a company-size combat patrol, about one hundred men. They discovered that we had stumbled into an enemy cache while on patrol. Several days' rations, bicycles, a small field hospital, our lost weapons, and some ammunition were recovered. The enemy had withdrawn someplace, as usual. He had taken casualties, however. There were blood trails in three locations.

I was treated and released back to duty the following day. As I wrote my after-action report and a long letter to my wife, I thanked God that Suzie and I had survived. I carried my green rope through twenty-four months of combat in Vietnam, acknowledging that there was great power in prayer on the battlefield. The medevac helicopter was a large and easy target. I could never figure out why a sniper, who hit me and killed our medic from 200 yards away, missed a helicopter ambulance at point blank range.

I still have my green Army-issue rosary today. At the Vietnam Veterans Memorial in 1984, I tried to leave that rope behind for whatever reasons things are left at that wall in Washington, D.C. I just couldn't give it up.

Mayday! Mayday! I'm Going Down!

It was just about 4 A.M. on November 9, 1965. My patrol dog, Suzie, woke me up gently, touching my left ear with her cold nose. She put her right paw on my chest, crawled up on top of me, shivering as if she were cold or very frightened. Forty-five pounds of German shepherd, Suzie was protecting me, guarding me from some unknown danger.

Something was wrong. Things were too quiet. I crawled out of my sandbagged bunker and felt the heat of the day long before sunrise. Humidity was high. I was soaking wet. Off in the distance, I heard the sound of helicopter gunships patrolling the canals south of Cau Xang. The birds were firing M-60 machine guns into canal banks on reconnaissance-by-fire missions. They were looking for antiaircraft positions which had fired on friendly aircraft the night before. One of every five rounds in our machine gun belts was a red tracer which guided gunners on to their targets. The enemy had green tracers. Machine gun fire from our helicopters off in the distance could have been mistaken for lightening. I turned on the radio and listened to the pilots talking to their ground control.

"Base, this is Playboy Six, over."

"Go ahead, Playboy."

"This is Six, gettin' ready to pack it in. Dry run, over."

"Roger, Six. Come on home. Hot coffee and pound cake in the hooch."

After a brief pause in the radio conversation, Playboy was on the air again. "Base, this is Six. Got some green tracers coming up at us. Looks like we made somebody mad, over."

"Watch yourself, Playboy. We took some hits there yesterday."

"Roger, Base. This is Playboy, clear."

A heartbeat later, Playboy was back on the air. "Base, I'm hit! Mayday! Mayday! I'm going down!"

I couldn't believe it. Right in front of me, two miles away, we lost a bird. I didn't hear the aircraft hit, but I saw the glow of the fire on the ground. They had crashed and burned. A crew of four was down. I got on the air right away.

"Playboy, this is Cabbage Chops, just north of you, over." There was no answer. It was 0441, nineteen minutes before 5 A.M., and it was dark. We could not see anything but the fire on the ground south of us.

Base came back on the air. "Cabbage Chops, this is Base. Do you hear our aircraft? Over."

"Negative, over," I replied.

"There are four of them out there. Can you see anything? Over."

"Negative, over," I replied again.

"Cabbage Chops, this is Red Baron, over." The vibrating sound of another aviator's voice came on the air. In the background, I heard the popping sound of helicopter rotor blades and more M-60 machine gun fire. The Playboy platoon had scattered when Playboy Six went down. Another unit, the Flying Circus, was on the way to the rescue.

"Go ahead, Red Baron," I answered.

"Where are you, Chops? Over."

"North of the burning aircraft, two clicks. Over."

"Who are you? Over."

"Lone Rangers, Sneaky Petes, over," I replied. Special Forces soldiers were called Sneaky Petes and U.S. advisors to ARVN rangers were called Lone Rangers. I was both.

Red Baron wanted my help. "Got anybody to go out there and pick up my buddy? Playboy Six is down. We've got Playboy's crew, but he's still back there, over." Captain Donald R. Clark, age thirty, a cavalry officer, was missing in action.

"Standing by. Two six-packs ready to rock and roll, over," I assured him.

We lived by a code back then. Never let a fallen comrade fall into the hands of the enemy. We had two six-man squads of ARVN rangers ready to help. Six rangers would fly as passengers in each troop-carrier helicopter, Bell UHID models, the work horse of Vietnam. We called them slicks.

Out of the night sky, I suddenly heard the sound of four helicopters buzzing our outpost. It was the Red Baron and his Flying Circus, named after Baron Manfred von Richthofen's World War I flying aces. Our Red Baron was an American of German ancestry, a chunky man with a red, handlebar mustache. I got on the air again.

"Red Baron, you just passed over me with four birds. Break to your left, and I'll show you where we are. Whiskey Poppa on the deck, over." I threw out a white phosphorus grenade marking our position. Red Baron saw the glow of the white heat and circled our position.

"We're breaking for POL and bullets. We'll be back," Red Baron informed me.

POL was short for petroleum, oil, and lubricants. His flight was out of fuel and ammunition. The Flying Circus was just about to finish patrol when Playboy Six called in his Mayday. Their four helicopters had to leave the contact area to reload after rescuing three members of the downed Playboy Six crew.

We sat on the landing zone, planning the rescue attempt, waiting for the Flying Circus to return. Two of their aircraft had been hit. Their crews were changing helicopters and getting additional personnel, waiting for clearance for the rescue mission.

I watched the glow of the downed aircraft die out as daybreak approached. I wondered what it must be like to be left behind. I had been on many four man patrols, LRRPs, long-range reconnaissance patrols, but never had been left behind. I had also been hit but never seriously wounded. After being shot down, the captain was probably badly injured. I worried about him. Suddenly Suzie jumped up, cocking her head. The popping of rotor blades could be heard in the distance. Flying Circus was returning to our location.

"Cabbage Chops, this is the Red Baron, over."

"Go ahead, Red Baron," I responded.

"Are you guys loaded for Bear? Over."

"Roger, standing by," I replied. Each ranger had 200 rounds of ammunition and four grenades. We were also very nervous, knowing the VC were waiting for us. They knew we would be coming back to pick up Captain Clark.

A new radio signal interrupted our conversation. "Cabbage Chops, this is the Headmaster, over." I knew the voice, but not the radio call sign.

"Go ahead, this school boy is listening, over."

It was our team commander, Colonel Shedd. He had monitored the whole operation and warned me, "Don't throw good after bad. If it's too hot down there, abort, abort, over."

I had the choice to scrub the mission or go in. What a decision to make!

Two UH-1D slicks landed on our pickup zone as I cleared the air with Colonel Shedd. I looked at the pilots' faces. Then Red Baron and I exchanged a quick glance. There was no decision to make. When that Army Ranger tab is awarded after nine weeks of training in the Infantry School at Fort Benning, Georgia, a ranger knows that he must never let a fallen comrade fall into the hands of the enemy.

We loaded up on the aircraft without hesitation. Suzie jumped in first, and then we scrambled aboard. I called Colonel Shedd on the radio. "Headmaster, this is Chops. We're en route. I'll advise further if things get too hot, over."

"Chops, this is Headmaster. Clear. Good luck! God bless you," he replied.

Photo by Captain Otis Skinner, USAF

Two UH-1D helicopters on the rescue mission
I flew in the the lead helicopter with Sergeant Chi Nhan and four ARVN rangers. Sergeant First Class James Des Verney and five other rangers flew in the second bird.

We lifted off with four aircraft altogether. Two were gunships with rocket pods, 40mm grenade launchers, and M-60 machine guns. They flew ahead of us, immediately opening fire on suspected enemy positions as we headed to the landing zone looking for Captain Clark. Our two slicks had machine guns, one in each door, and a 40mm grenade launcher in the nose of the aircraft. Even with all that firepower, we were still sitting ducks flying over the rice paddies.

I flew in the lead slick with four ARVN rangers led by Sergeant Nguyen Chi Nhan. Sergeant James Des Verney, another U.S. advisor, flew in the second aircraft with five ARVN rangers. We could see the two gunships ahead of us attacking the canal dikes bordering the rice paddies where the captain's ship had crashed and burned. How would we find him down there, I wondered.

The door gunners on our slicks began firing their M-60 machine guns as we headed for the canal dikes. The radio traffic, popping of rotor blades, machine gun fire, and grenade launchers distracted me so badly that I didn't know we had landed until Suzie jumped out.

My patrol dog had much more combat experience than I, scrambling out of the helicopter on touch down. She turned and looked at me as I off-loaded, heading for cover. Suzie led the way to the first objective, an antiaircraft bunker on the canal bank. There were seven bunkers on the dike and every one of them was firing at the gunships.

Photo by Sergeant Nguyen Chi Nhan, 1965

Bunker on the canal dike
Every one of the bunkers on the paddy dike was firing at us.

Sergeant Nhan led the attack on the first bunker. He threw in two grenades, and we all fired into the openings. One VC wearing black pajamas appeared for a brief second, falling dead in front of us. Suzie moved forward, checked out the enemy soldier, and returned to my side. Sergeant Des Verney and his crew destroyed the second antiaircraft position. No enemy soldiers survived.

As we approached the third bunker, Suzie flattened down, hiding behind some vegetation. I threw in a hand grenade. The blast shattered my hearing. Two VC lay dead in the doorway. The four rangers with me did not fire. Suzie checked on the dead enemy soldiers. We moved on to the next position.

Sergeant Des Verney led the charge on the fourth position. No enemy soldiers survived our overwhelming firepower. As we headed to the next three bunkers, I was stopped dead in my tracks by the sight of the downed aircraft.

I had seen burned cars and charred human remains at highway accident scenes, but nothing I had ever seen before prepared me for this. The fallen gunship was all ashes and scrap, and sitting in the middle of this black pile of twisted wreckage was Playboy Six. His legs had been blown off. The top of his head was missing as if he had been scalped. Captain Clark's eyes and mouth were open. He must have died a horrible death, burned beyond recognition. The captain's arms were curled up in front of his chest as if he were praying. His Seiko watch on his left wrist had stopped at 0441, 9 Nov 65. In his right hand was his .45 caliber automatic. It was still loaded. The hand grips had been burned away. I could see the ammunition in the magazine. Four bullets had expanded from the heat.

Sergeant Des Verney tried to help me pull the captain's body from the aircraft. I gave him my M-14 rifle, pushing him aside. "I'll do it. Cover me," I ordered. Putting my arms around his body, I lifted Donald Clark from the helicopter's left seat. All the fluid from his head poured over my face and down my neck. Without his legs, the officer weighed less than fifty pounds. He was easy to carry. I laid him down on my poncho and secured his remains with great care.

Suddenly Sergeant Des Verney and Suzie looked at me strangely. Something was terribly wrong. Then I realized I couldn't move. I couldn't hear anything either. I felt completely exhausted, psychologically devastated. Our mission had failed, and I wasn't prepared for that.

Sergeant Nhan ran over to our position and viewed the situation. Then he shouted at me, "Move out, Lieutenant! We're running out of ammunition! This place is crawling with VC! Call for an extraction! Let's get the hell out of here!"

Rudyard Kipling had written in his *Barrack-Room Ballads*, "There's nothing better than a sergeant." He was right.

I was pumped up again, on the radio in two seconds. "Red Baron, this is Chops. Let's go. Pick us up, now. Move it!" I ordered.

"Be cool, ranger. On the way," he shouted at me.

The slick ships approached the landing zone through a hail of small arms fire as the VC tried to knock down another helicopter. All of us on the ground fired at the enemy positions less than 100 feet away. We also threw grenades and began screaming like wild, vicious beasts.

Red Baron got on the air. "Knock off the grenades. You'll blow us out of the air, goddamn it!"

Concussion of hand grenades can knock down a helicopter close to the ground. We didn't need that. We were not thinking clearly, throwing hand grenades while waiting for an extraction. We were desperate.

As the slicks approached the pickup zone, Suzie guarded the captain's body, sitting on it. She held down the poncho flaps as rotor blades stirred up the dust, blowing debris in all directions. Suzie was calm and cool, apparently aware of the situation.

The rest of the patrol got ready to lift off. I turned to Suzie, hugging her while pushing her off the poncho with the captain's remains. Then I picked up Captain Clark, heading for the first slick ship. I placed Playboy Six up forward, next to the aircraft console and his fellow aviators. Both pilots turned around and gave me a thumbs up signal. I off-loaded again, picking up Suzie and placing her in the aircraft next to the captain's body. Both slicks were loaded by this time, and we lifted off once again.

Our escort gunships plastered the VC positions with rocket fire as we gained altitude, heading back to Cau Xang. Our door gunners fired on suspected positions as we laid low in the aircraft, hoping to survive this extraction. We were out of ammunition and grenades. If we went down, we would be in serious trouble.

In less than ten minutes, we were back at Cau Xang, off loading the slicks while the gunships circled overhead. As I left the first aircraft, the pilots turned in their seats and lifted their sun visors. "Thanks, rangers. That was above and beyond," they whispered over the radio. I saluted them, stumbling away with Suzie at my side. Captain Clark was back with his crew again. As our patrol slowly shuffled back to our base camp, all twelve of us were amazed and thankful to God we hadn't lost a man. I was especially grateful Suzie had come through this without a scratch. She was my constant companion.

As the Flying Circus circled over head, the door gunners waved at us. We saluted the pilots as the Red Baron reported his mission status on the air. "Base, this is Circus Six. This show is over. On the way to the barn. Nobody was left behind. Clear."

Operation Juan Valdez

In between my two Vietnam tours, I returned to the States where I was assigned as the Army operations officer for the Armed Forces Police in New York City. From 1967 through 1968, I had the responsibility of coordinating AWOL apprehensions in the greater New York City area. There were many GIs charged as absent without leave during the Vietnam War, and in many cases, families assisted soldiers, sailors, marines, and airmen in evading their service obligations. Most service personnel who deserted did so when given orders for Vietnam.

One patriotic father, who had been in the U.S. Marine Corps (USMC) in World War II, called me on the phone at my duty station, the 18th Precinct, New

York Police Department (NYPD). He wouldn't identify himself, but he told me his son had deserted the Marines in 1965 when ordered to Vietnam. The AWOL suspect was allegedly working at a small, family-owned grocery store near the 72d Precinct Station in Brooklyn. He gave me a description of his son, whose nickname was none other than Semper Fi. How an AWOL Marine could call himself Semper Fidelis (always faithful) after deserting the Marines dumbfounded me.

Not knowing the man's name, I followed the tip anyway and went to the grocery store with my partner, a sergeant who was also a Brooklyn native. We talked to the manager, asking him if he had an employee who was a former Marine. "Yeah, Semper Fi works here as a stock clerk. Got wounded in Vietnam in the Rungsat special zone. Never talks about it much, except to other Marines."

Some USMC operations in the Rungsat had been conducted in 1966. We checked out Semper Fi's real name and social security number, which the store manager had furnished. Our AWOL hadn't seen any combat in Vietnam and was reported absent in October 1965, as his father had stated. Now to find him. The man worked at night, stocking the shelves for the next day's business.

After warning the manager not to tell Semper Fi we were looking for him, we left the store, returning later in the evening with two FBI agents who had a federal fugitive warrant. The Marine deserter was observed working in canned goods, stacking coffee cans and vegetables. As we approached him, he spotted us and took off in a flash. We suspected the store manager had warned Semper Fi. He denied it, of course, saying, "He knew you were looking for him. Other employees told him, not me." Then he warned us, "He's into dealing hard stuff, has a gun, and runs with some bad people. He's real dangerous."

His car parked on the street was impounded. Then we inspected the man's locker in the back of the store and cleaned it out. We found three empty 2.7-pound red coffee cans in his wall unit along with two changes of clothes. Dark grains were found on his clothes and in nearby trash barrels. We suspected he distributed drugs in these containers. After the store closed at 10 P.M., we searched the area where he was working, hitting paydirt within half an hour. Three more red cans were found to be empty of coffee, opened at the bottom, and packed with heroin and considerable cash. The white plastic lids which are usually on can tops were on the bottoms of these containers. Now all we had to do was to connect the drugs and cash to Semper Fi.

When we called for instructions from the Brooklyn District Attorney's office, we got chewed out pretty badly for conducting a search without a warrant. No matter what we said in our defense, we were in a no-win situation. We were ordered, "Let the stuff go, wait until Semper Fi picks up the contraband, and then arrest him." We knew he wouldn't return to the store ever again, unless he was really stupid. He was.

My partner and one FBI agent staked out the store all night, making sure the drugs didn't disappear. The next morning, the sergeant and I pretended to shop in the store, waiting for Semper Fi to return. The place was crowded. We were sure he wouldn't spot us.

A joint task force of FBI, uniformed, and undercover NYPD officers were on the street sealing off the store and any escape routes. Two cops, dressed as New York City sanitation workers, were cleaning up the streets with a steel garbage can and brooms. Three cops in Coca-Cola uniforms were unloading soft drinks from a truck near the front door.

My partner, who lived a few blocks from the store, was very innovative that morning, deciding to dress as an unsighted person to make sure Semper Fi wouldn't suspect him. The sergeant even brought along his large, solid-black German shepherd dog, Styx. Wearing a black overcoat, hat, and sunglasses and carrying a red and white walking stick, my partner fumbled about, filling up a grocery cart with canned goods and dry dog food.

Semper Fi entered the store at 10 A.M., heading straight for the office. He had two other rough looking thugs with him. Things looked very bad for us. My partner and I stuck together. Then an FBI agent entered the store and told us, "This place is too crowded. If this clown decides to shoot it out, we'll have a blood bath. Seize the drugs now and get them outside to the painted GMC van on the corner." The GMC camper was a field headquarters with three agents and was loaded with communications gear and cameras.

We moved quickly, seizing the drugs and cash, and going through the check-out stand with our food purchases. The check-out clerk couldn't believe his eyes as we walked up with the cans of coffee. He was in with Semper Fi on the drug sales and knew the containers were full of heroin and cash. The clerk started to make a phone call in the middle of the check-out procedure. My partner told him, "Don't even think about it!" Styx growled and flashed his teeth, getting ready to jump up on the counter. The man at the register was frozen in place.

Once on the street, we started walking fast. The clerk from the store charged down the street after us, trying to slow us down, screaming, "You forgot your change!" We almost broke into a run when Styx turned on the clerk, who beat a hasty retreat back into the store. The federal agents in the GMC van jumped out with pistols drawn and took our groceries, telling us, "Get lost." The sergeant and his K-9 partner disappeared into an alleyway and went home. I watched the store from across the street.

Semper Fi lost control of himself when he found out we had seized his drugs and money. He burst out onto the street, cursing and arguing with the store clerk. The FBI tried to arrest Semper Fi, but he bowled over two agents, darting into traffic like a frightened deer. I couldn't keep track of him. We had temporarily lost our man, but things worked out for the best. He raced home to his mother's house where he was taken into custody by NYPD detectives.

My partner joined me on the street again after changing his clothes. What happened next was pure theater. The man who ran this drug operation arrived in a big, black Lincoln sedan, violent and ready to kill. A short, fat man in an expensive, blue pin-striped suit, wearing a black homburg hat, Main Man waved his arms as if he were directing a symphony orchestra. Cursing and screaming, he threatened the check-out clerk whom he tried to strangle, "You gave the stuff away, Stole my stuff, you bastard! You're a dead man!"

A motorcycle cop on a three-wheeler arrived, ticketing the black Lincoln parked at the bus stop in front of the store. The traffic cop was unaware of our operation. Main Man's driver got into a confrontation with the officer and was arrested after offering him a bribe. When searched, he was found to be armed with a .45 caliber blue steel automatic without a pistol permit in his possession. Main Man tried to keep his driver out of harm's way, arguing with the traffic cop and two other uniformed officers walking their beats near the store. They patted down the thug in the pin-striped suit and found he was also carrying a concealed weapon.

A brawl started on the street between the three uniformed officers and the two thugs near the black Lincoln sedan. That's when the two sanitation workers joined in the scuffle, as did the three detectives in Coca-Cola uniforms, all identifying themselves as police officers.

Blind with rage and sweating after an attempt to break away from the police, Main Man finally surrendered, throwing his hands up, screaming, "Isn't anybody who he is?" It seemed that every person on the street that morning was a cop out to get him. He even asked some other people passing the store, "Are you cops, too?" I couldn't keep a straight face and began laughing so hard that tears came to my eyes.

I left to report in to the Armed Forces Police that Semper Fi had been taken into custody by the NYPD. Semper Fi's other friends were also arrested when found hiding behind the grocery store in a pile of cardboard boxes. The black Lincoln sedan was impounded. After a search warrant was issued, the car was torn down piece-by-piece by federal officers. More drugs, cash, and weapons were found in the search.

We had stumbled into some mess out there in the 72d Precinct, trying to arrest an AWOL. We never did get our man, since the FBI and NYPD took jurisdiction. Nevertheless, the operation was declared a success. For our reports, I named it Operation Juan Valdez. While this drug bust was not of the magnitude of a French Connection, we did at least have a coffee connection.

Chapter 6

Vietnam, 2nd Tour

1970

Polar Bear

Polar Bear

In early 1970, I was stationed in Vietnam at a fire base in Tay Ninh Province. Like other fire bases, Fire Base Diana was a little outpost manned by a 900-man infantry battalion with a battery of artillery to support the patrols that were sent out.

Near Cambodia on Fire Base Diana, the area was honeycombed with tunnels used by the Viet Cong for headquarters elements, troop barracks, and hospitals. Infantry scout dogs worked this area with platoons of infantry, digging up enemy supplies in large caches. Seldom was the enemy confronted face to face. We knew we were in enemy territory because of the mines, booby traps, and enemy supplies found daily.

As a major at the time, I was a fire support coordinator directing U.S. artillery, gunships, and high performance aircraft, jet fighter-bombers. Attached to the first brigade, 1st Cavalry Division, I flew about the area of operations directing fire support for both Vietnamese and U.S. units.

One morning as I stepped off the helicopter at Tay Ninh base to receive new signal operating instructions, I met Polar Bear. A truly handsome white German shepherd patrol dog, he had been wounded in the face and left shoulder by small-arms fire. His handler had been killed in action. Polar Bear had turned on every soldier who tried to help him, including two sergeants who fed him scraps from the mess hall. His water bucket was turned over, and he paced back and forth where he had been staked out at a command bunker. He had been left there for security duty, and he behaved like a trained, vicious sentry dog, allowing no person to pass.

Having been a dog handler ten years before as an enlisted man, I wasn't afraid of Polar Bear. He tried to attack me, breaking his lead, charging me head on, but I knew he was wounded and I had compassion for him. I stood my ground and ordered him, "Out," then "Sit and stay." I was ready to shoot him with my M-16 rifle if he tried to attack me again. He knew that, too.

He followed my commands, although he was free to run off or stay with me. I took off my helmet, turned it over, and emptied my canteens into the steel pot, offering it to the dog. The water was cool and fresh from an iced bag at the brigade headquarters. Polar Bear growled at me, lapped at the water, wagged his tail, and then sat down to finish what I had poured out for him. I hunkered down with him, leaning against the sandbagged walls of the fire direction center.

Two NCOs appeared at the main entrance. "Watch that white dog, sir. He's a bad dude. His handler was killed in action two days ago," they warned. They told me Polar Bear's background and why he was at headquarters.

It seems that he had been wounded by the same small-arms fire that had killed his handler. Although they don't carry wounded dogs on medevac aircraft, they will carry them off the field in logbirds, supply aircraft that bring in rations and ammunition and carry out the dead. Their company commander had them both evacuated from the field on the same lift. But no handlers were available to take care of Polar Bear at that time. Expecting him to die from his wounds, they tied him to an artillery piece. When he survived, they placed him at the command center as a guard. Not properly fed, eating just scraps and garbage, and hurting from his wounds which were not cared for, the dog turned vicious.

A medic came forward and, while I held Polar Bear, cleaned his wounds. The medic was terrified of the animal who was growling, whining, and snapping in great pain.

The NCOs asked me to remove the dog from the area, and I complied. I found a piece of rope and turned it into a lead for my new companion. As I went about my business, picking up new orders, maps, and signal instructions and talking to Air Force forward air controllers, Polar Bear walked with me just as if I were his assigned handler. We became good buddies as I shared some meat with him. The dog was truly starved, eating bread and meat as fast as I could feed him.

At the brigade aid station, I found out some more information. Polar Bear was assigned to an infantry scout dog outfit. His platoon was flushing out VC from a bunker complex when the handler was killed by small-arms fire. The infantry scout dog unit had listed him as killed in action along with his handler.

One infantryman who saw me with Polar Bear asked me if I was his handler's brother. He assumed the dog and I got along well together because I looked so much like his previous handler. We had a very special bond.

I flew to the nearest scout dog unit to return Polar Bear to his home in the field. The vet technician was surprised the dog was still alive. He, too, confirmed that I looked like a twin to Polar Bear's handler. When I asked him what would happen to the dog, he replied, "He's salvage equipment, sir." Polar Bear was considered just a piece of junk, damaged equipment, worthless. They were going to put him down.

I turned away and started off with Polar Bear. The vet tech asked me what I was going to do with the dog. I replied, "I'm en route to Saigon, and I'll turn him in for you."

The vet tech got the message. He knew I wasn't going to Saigon. He went into the kennel area, returning with a water-proof bag. I thought he was giving me a body bag in which to place the dog's remains. Instead, it was full of dry meal, at least ten pounds of dog food. "You'll need this," he said. "Thanks," he added, turning away again.

I carried the dry meal and my other official paperwork in my backpack, boarding the next helicopter back to Tay Ninh. That afternoon, I landed back at Fire Base Diana, placing Polar Bear on guard duty at my bunker. He crawled under my cot at first. Later, he was found sprawled out on my bed, head on my pillow, snoring away. He was at home.

In a short period of time, he became accustomed to his new surroundings. He had his own cot, ate rice, bread, meat and dry meal, and drank water like a GI drinks beer. He was living like a king. No more patrols for Polar Bear, not just now. He was a buddy to every trooper who liked dogs. Everybody petted him. The medics cared for him, and in short order he looked good for a piece of Army surplus, junk, salvage equipment.

On January 25, 1970, our unit was almost overrun by a North Vietnamese regiment. Eight people were killed and twelve wounded. Among the wounded, I was evacuated to a field hospital in Saigon.

Two days later, Polar Bear was killed in action by mortar fire while wandering about the fire base looking for some new friends. For the two weeks we had him as a mascot on Fire Base Diana, he brought much joy, companionship, and love, as dogs have done for twelve thousand years serving man.

Lady Diana is in Trouble!

Dip. Dip. Dip. Incoming! Chinese 82mm mortars were on the way.

"When you can hear mortar rounds leaving their tubes, they are close, two hundred yards away," Sam Parsons told me. He was my assistant fire support coordinator at Fire Base Diana. It was 10:30 P.M., January 25, 1970. Lady Diana was in trouble. Fifteen hundred North Vietnamese Army troops (NVA) were on the way to overrun our battalion.

Fire Base Diana was an ARVN outpost on the Cambodian border down the road from the 7th U.S. Cavalry fire base, Jamie. The North Vietnamese wanted Diana. We had just received six new artillery pieces and several hundred rounds of 105mm ammunition. We had only two rifle companies on line, 300 men, just in from three days on patrol. These airborne troopers, although the best soldiers in the South Vietnamese Army, were dead tired. Our bunkers were half completed. Barbed wire had been in position for only three days. It was a new fire base and a thorn in the side of the 242d NVA Regiment operating against Tay Ninh Province, thirty miles west of Saigon.

Sixty 82mm mortar rounds splattered all over the fire base. They turned fighting positions without overhead cover into pits filled with wounded soldiers. Antenna that had linked our radios to helicopter gunships, flying to our rescue, lay on the ground. They had been blasted into short pieces of aluminum. Two of our six 105mm howitzers were out of action from direct hits. We had eight dead and twelve wounded in a matter of minutes.

Then came the gas. Tear gas covered this desperate little piece of ground, as did the CS vomit-agent gasses. Our CS booby traps had been set off by incoming mortar fire and the North Vietnamese had lobbed in several rounds of tear gas in the mortar attack. I was choking from the tear gas, stumbling around trying to get things organized, and calling headquarters on my backpack radio since the main command center and our long-range radios were out of action due to a direct hit.

"Sierra, this is Mike, over," I called out on the radio.

"Mike, this is Sierra. You're awful weak. Can't read you, over."

"This is Mike. NVA inside the wire. Lady Diana is in trouble. Over."

"Mike, this is Flying Circus. Hang in there, we're on the way." Captain Jones was calling me on the radio. He was leading a platoon of helicopter gunships out to help us.

"Standing by, Circus. Is the Red Baron up there?"

"Negative, Mike. He's gone home. Two years over here was enough, over."

My buddy, the Red Baron, had rotated home to the United States. I was going home in thirty-five days, "if I live through this," I thought out loud.

Our M-60 machine guns were firing from every bunker we had on Diana. We were firing our 81mm mortars back into the screaming ranks of the NVA assaulting us from the west side of our outpost, which was about to be overrun. Sergeant Conner, an advisor, aimed a 105mm howitzer directly at the enemy running at us, blasting a swarm of their soldiers tangled in the wire.

Flares lit up the sky. I could see NVA about two hundred feet away. M-60 machine gun fire ripped holes in their ranks, and riflemen were firing at individual targets now, not just shooting into the dark hoping to stop the massed troop formations we knew were there. Two NVA slipped through the wire and began working their way in my direction with satchel charges. While I watched them, three of our troopers fired on them with shotguns and an M-16 rifle from a bunker in front of me. The sappers collapsed twenty-five feet away, dismembered. They never had a chance. Their charges exploded harmlessly outside of the bunker line.

Sam Parsons and a radio operator, Rosario, were with me as we watched this Pickett's Charge on Diana. Attacks like this during the Civil War, World War I, and World War II never worked. It seemed their military commanders hadn't read history books. The slaughter of this frontal assault was pure horror.

My wounded patrol dog, Polar Bear, sat on my left foot, leaning against me. He had been hit two weeks before and was out of service, resting, gaining strength every day, sleeping twenty hours out of twenty-four on my cot, until this happened.

He had gained ten pounds each week, eating rice, fish, and C rations and drinking good water. He didn't care for the dog food issued by the Army. Polar Bear was scrap, damaged goods, salvage equipment, not going back to work any more. He was dead, as far as the U.S. Army quartermaster was concerned. Had he gone back to Saigon for care, they would have put him down. Out here he was a buddy for me, and he loved his retirement from active duty.

The gunships were coming on station and getting ready to fire marking rounds as they circled about Diana. Tracers from our machine guns marked our perimeter quite well from the air. We were in almost a perfect circle. Twelve of our M-60 machine guns were firing into enemy ranks west of the fire base where the main attack was directed against us. M-79 40mm grenades fired by soldiers in forward bunkers and white phosphorus grenades thrown by advisors clearly identified enemy targets in the close combat.

Captain Jones was on the air again. "Mike, are we on the right spot? Over."

"Roger, you're right over us. Our wagons are circled. Hostiles are massed west. Wilson Pickett is marking the place where they are coming through, over." Wilson Pickett was slang for white phosphorus grenades.

"Mike, button up, get your folks under cover. Here comes a marking round."

Two rockets hit the area where we thought the enemy was concentrated. Machine gun fire continued to cover that spot, while individual troopers were still taking aim at enemy soldiers clearly visible in the light of the flares.

"Circus, this is Mike. You're on target. Let her rip, over," I answered back.

Just when things looked like they were under control, Polar Bear got very excited. He alerted right, and Sam, Rosario, and I squatted down. There was a communications trench off to our right that led directly into the command bunker behind us. Polar Bear saw something or heard something we didn't. Then he jumped into the trench and began barking.

With all the fireworks our night vision was gone, and we needed flares to see anything. We couldn't fire flares, however, with gunships on missions overhead. I strained to see what Polar Bear was barking at, calling him back as Rosario fired into the darkness with his shotgun. I fired my M-16.

Flares were dropped from some support aircraft overhead a few minutes later, turning night into day for the Cobra gunships on strafing runs.

"Mike, this is Flying Circus. Watch your flanks. Looks like they are running around to your north side, over," Captain Jones warned me.

"Circus, this is Mike. Clear. Thank you," I replied.

As flares danced to our rear, I saw what Polar Bear had been barking at. Two NVA soldiers were dead in a trench thirty feet away. Rosario had killed them both with three blasts from his Winchester pump shotgun.

"Did you see them, Rosario?" I asked.

"No, sir. Just fired where the dog pointed me," he shouted back.

The NVA had paid too high a price for their frontal assault on Diana. Now they were running back into the jungle. It was about midnight, and their attack had failed. Forty-two dead NVA were left behind in our defensive wire. Blood trails were found the next day. They must have had a hundred casualties or more. Lord knows how many men they lost to our artillery and gunships out in the jungle.

We were satisfied that we had held, feeling very proud of our work, when more mortars began to drop on the fire base as the enemy withdrew. Two rounds hit near me, and I went down for the count. Splattered with my blood, Polar Bear stayed with me until I passed out from the pain. I don't remember anything else from that action. I have tried to recall what had happened many times since then, but the mind blocks out those things.

I never saw Polar Bear again. I was medevaced out the next morning.

Photo by the author, 1970

Fire Base Diana, Tay Ninh Province, 1970
I took this photo on January 26, while waiting to be medevaced out, after having been wounded by mortar fire the night before. I wanted my wife and children to see what hell looked like.

Polar Bear was killed in action two weeks later. He was buried with full military honors.

HEADQUARTERS
UNITED STATES MILITARY ASSISTANCE COMMAND, VIETNAM
APO San Francisco 96222

GENERAL ORDERS   16 April 1970
NUMBER   2082

AWARD OF THE BRONZE STAR MEDAL
(SECOND OAK LEAF CLUSTER)

1. TC 439. The following AWARD is announced.

MORGAN, PAUL B. 130-28-4404 MAJ INF USA Adv Tm 162 III CTZ APO 96307
  Awarded: Bronze Star Medal (Second Oak Leaf Cluster) with "V" Device
  Date of service: 25 January 1970
  Theater: Republic of Vietnam
  Authority: By direction of the President under the provisions of
              Executive Order 11046, 24 August 1962
  Reason: For heroism in connection with military operations against a
            hostile force: Major Morgan distinguished himself by heroic
            action on 25 January 1970 while serving as Senior Advisor to
            the 5th Airborne Battalion, Airborne Division, Army of the
            Republic of Vietnam. At 2330 hours on that night, the base
            camp received sixty rounds of incoming mortar fire. Alerted
            by the mortar fire, the defenders prepared for a possible
            ground attack, probe or sapper attack. Completely disregarding
            his personal safety during the mortar attack, Major Morgan
            moved around the perimeter of the fire base to check individual
            bunkers and fighting positions. A short time later the enemy
            attacked the western edge of the perimeter, and Major Morgan
            dashed through a hail of mortar, rocket and small arms fire to
            direct aerial rocket artillery gunships on the attacking North
            Vietnamese Army force. Major Morgan was knocked to the ground
            twice by mortar fire and was injured. Despite his injury, he
            moved from one exposed position to another on the berm to
            direct aerial rocket artillery gunship fire within twenty-five
            meters of the perimeter. The North Vietnamese Army force
            covered the fire base with CS gas, and Major Morgan continued
            to direct the gunships on the enemy soldiers in the wire until
            he was forced to leave his position because of the heavy
            concentration of CS gas in the forward bunker area. Major
            Morgan's inspired leadership and courageous action during the
            attack was the primary factor in the paratroopers being able to
            repel the enemy thrust. Major Morgan's heroic actions were in
            keeping with the highest traditions of the United States Army
            and reflect great credit upon himself and the military service.

FOR THE COMMANDER:

OFFICIAL: W. G. DOLVIN
                                        Major General, USA
                                        Chief of Staff

LOUIS J. PROST
Colonel, USA
Adjutant General   DISTRIBUTION:
                                        Special

Chapter 7

Back Home
1971

Matt Dillon

Flying High

After Vietnam, I was stationed at Fort Campbell, Kentucky, in 1971 and assigned to the personnel staff section, G1, where I supervised some military police operations. As a K-9 and prisoner of war specialist, I oversaw K-9 patrol, POW operations training, and drug interdiction operations. We inspected cars at roadblocks and searched barracks on an irregular schedule. We patrolled the training areas outside the garrison and troop billeting facilities, where personnel were not allowed, unless scheduled for combat training operations. The work was dull and boring most of the time.

One weekend, we got two tips about drugs being brought onto post. I was assigned to handle the mission of drug interdiction on the first tip.

The information was from a worried mother who was certain her son was dealing drugs at the high school on post. Because marijuana was at that time a leading cash crop in Kentucky, grown in the rural eastern part of the state, we took the information seriously. I interviewed the woman and her husband at a coffee shop on Sunday morning after church and received all the particulars. They didn't want their son arrested, but they wanted him stopped. The reason for suspecting their son, who was a football quarterback, class leader, and recipient of a college scholarship, were his long distance calls and trips to eastern Kentucky. They had no relatives there.

The calls had been made to a pay phone at a rest stop on Interstate 64 near Morehead, Kentucky. All had been made at 11 P.M. on Thursday nights. Kentucky State Police (KSP) gave us the location of the phone booth when we shared information with law enforcement authorities off post. KSP also confirmed that drug dealers in eastern Kentucky used rest stops to make contacts and sell drugs. They called them common-area traffic points because public facilities, not personal property, were used. If private property is used for drug trafficking, it can be seized under federal law.

We had no probable cause, no legal excuse, to search the student's home or locker at school because the student was not a suspect. His father gave us permission to search his room at home, his car, and the shed in his back yard that Sunday afternoon while their son was away on a camping trip in eastern Kentucky for the weekend. We conducted a K-9 training search with a drug-sniffing dog, with the parents' permission, but the results were negative. We put a plan into action for Monday morning that would stop the dealing at school, if indeed the boy was in the marijuana business.

On Monday mornings during the first period, the high school generally had assemblies. This Monday was no exception. While the students were in the gym, we went through the football locker room with our sniffer dog and hit pay dirt in the trash can in the shower room. There we found three shaving kits wrapped in clean towels full of marijuana and $160 cash. Since the contraband was in a common area, we confiscated the substance but made no arrests.

The school principal then introduced the military police and our drug dog to the assembly. We watched our suspect and some football teammates squirm in their seats in the gym. I took over with a presentation. It was a standard speech we made as part of the Drug Awareness and Resistance Education program, or D.A.R.E.

"Good morning," I said. "We have a great show for you today. Our drug dog, Matt Dillon, is here this morning to show you how he can detect marijuana. This dog is so smart that he can even detect clothing worn by people using drugs. If anybody here has been smoking marijuana, Matt Dillon can smell it on your clothes. We've got five shaving kits with us. Three contain marijuana and $160 cash. Two contain paper and plastic bags filled with brown sugar. We want to show you how Matt will find the contraband drugs during this assembly this morning. We need five volunteers to pick up the five shaving kits. Come on now, let's have some volunteers."

Three students came forward and picked up the two brown sugar kits and one of the marijuana kits. No other volunteers came forward. Even though it was a wet, chilly morning, some students quickly discarded their jackets, including football team jackets usually worn with great pride.

I walked over to our suspect and his buddies and gave them the other two kits we found in the football shower room trash can. From the expressions on their faces, we concluded they immediately recognized the shaving kits as their possessions. I directed our suspect to place one at his side and one five students from him. The boys were beginning to sweat as they began to realize we knew they were guilty of possession with intent to distribute marijuana.

Matt Dillon was told, "Seek," and he began to work his way through the student body, which was very excited but absolutely still. Every breath the dog breathed could be heard. The rhythmic tapping of his nails on the wooden floor as he trotted along sounded like a clock ticking on a time bomb. School busses leaving the parking lot outside the gym could be heard with the silence in the assembly. There was great suspense in the air.

Our football players were trying to be cool, but I could see they were very upset. I locked eyes with the suspect, and he faced away, then back, then away again. He finally dropped his head down to his knees, placing his face in his hands. His buddies all glared at him as I moved closer. I could feel that, if I snapped my fingers or uttered one word, they would have jumped and run. The tension was unbelievable.

As puppies, drug dogs are given used evidence wrapped as leather toys to play with. As adult dogs on the job, when they detect contraband substances in vehicles, structures, aircraft, and luggage, it's still a game for them. The dogs bark and get very excited, awaiting praise and a reward for their good work. They are rewarded with dog snacks while suspects are arrested and possessions are forfeited.

Matt Dillon walked past the first shaving kit but alerted on the second, barking and pawing it like a favorite toy. Several girls in the gym screamed. The German shepherd trotted over to the third shaving kit next to a football cheer-leader. She screamed when the dog sniffed her clothing and pawed her jacket. Shedding her jacket, she ran from the assembly in tears. She must have been smoking a marijuana joint with that jacket on, and the dog had picked up the scent. We found out later that she just happened to be our suspect's girlfriend. The cheerleaders and the football team were sitting quite close to each other in the assembly. The girls glared at their team. Our suspect almost passed out from the anxiety. Students began talking nervously.

Matt Dillon, passing by the other kit filled with brown sugar, moved in on shaving kit number four and became very excited, barking and tearing the kit away from a football player with curly red hair. The boy jumped out of the stands, shouting, "It's not my stuff, I swear it!" The dog worked his way across four students and jumped at kit number five next to our suspect. The stands were emptied as panic ensued and the dog tore open kit number five with the cash and marijuana in small plastic bags.

I called off the dog and tried to stop the panic. It didn't work. It took over twenty minutes to calm down the students who were all shouting and talking nervously. There were plenty of chances to get confessions, I'm sure, but safety was our main concern. The bell rang, and the assembly was over. Students rushed out of the gym. I noticed that not one student went down to the locker room as they usually did. They knew they had been found out.

At the start of the second period, the principal talked to the student body over the intercom speakers in the classrooms, thanking them for their participation in the D.A.R.E. program assembly. The D.A.R.E. program was the focus of attention during the entire second period throughout the school. According to teachers at a conference later in the day, there were heated discussions in the classrooms about drugs and problems caused by drugs. Our suspect's homeroom teacher reported the quarterback was silent for the rest of the day. He did not show up for football practice, according to the coach. Our suspect said he had a case of the flu. Not feeling well, he went home to bed, exhausted.

The suspect's mother called me on the phone about 6 P.M. on Monday night. She told me the phone had been ringing off the hook at her home all afternoon. Several worried-looking teammates stopped by after football practice. They were all very hush-hush, whispering about confidential matters in our suspect's room.

Father and son faced off about 9 P.M. that night. The boy expected the worst. News of the drug dog at the high school had spread rapidly throughout the community. The quarterback was certain he would be arrested. When his father asked, "Why?" the boy answered, "They found three bags of marijuana in the football shower room, and they probably think it's my stuff since I was in eastern Kentucky over the weekend."

"Who told you the stuff was found in the football shower room?" asked the father.

The boy's face turned flush. He may as well have confessed to drug dealing with this slip of confidential information. We had never mentioned where we found the marijuana at school. The boy began to sob and shake, stuttering, "There goes my scholarship. I'm going to jail!"

His father first warned and then consoled him, saying, "Don't tell the cops anything. Besides, you had nothing to do with it, right?"

Tuesday morning, the suspect's father was in my office. We had two cups of coffee and he nervously laughed about the problems we had caused the football team. "Drugs are no laughing matter," I told him.

His face drained, and he became deadly serious. "I didn't know how to handle this, sir. Thank you for all your help," he responded.

The quarterback went off to college the following fall. I'm not sure if he went back to drugs again. I never saw him after high school.

However, while I was teaching a K-9 class at Eastern Kentucky University some ten years later, I faced off with a police officer with curly red hair who was from western Kentucky. He looked familiar, but I couldn't place his face in my memory.

"Major Morgan, do you remember me?" he asked.

"No, I'm afraid not," I replied. As I spoke, I suddenly recognized this officer as the first student who denied the drugs were his.

"I played football at Fort Campbell High School about ten years ago. You brought in a drug dog. Boy, was he good!" the officer responded. "Is that Matt Dillon?" he added, looking at my patrol dog sitting on the desk facing the class.

"This guy is Teddy Bear," I answered. "It's funny you remembered that dog's name," I commented.

"It wasn't my stuff, I swear it!" he shouted, as officers in the class roared with laughter.

"That's what you told me ten years ago. I still don't believe you," I joked.

The officer was very nervous and stood up in front of the class. "It wasn't my stuff," he insisted.

"Sure, it wasn't your stuff!" the class roared back.

As the period ended, I asked the officer, "What are you doing at the police department now?"

"Drug interdiction with K-9s," he replied. The whole class started laughing again, and the man's face turned red as he stormed out of the room. In the hallway, he approached me with a serious look on his face, surrounded by his friends. "It wasn't my stuff, I swear it!" he repeated once again.

I said no more and walked away with a smile on my face. As I left the instruction area with my patrol dog, Bear turned around and stared at the red-headed officer with a curious look, as if he was telling him, "You've got to be kidding me."

The officer looked at Bear and told him, "You don't believe me either, damn it!"

Chapter 8

Morgan K-9 Security
1976–92

Teddy Bear, Wolfgang, Sampson, Danny Boy,
Kenny, Bonnie Bear, Simon

My Right Arm, Bear

When I retired from the U.S. Army in 1976, I brought my military skills to Lexington, Kentucky, organizing a small K-9 patrol service. Within six months, Morgan K-9 Security Service had three officers, three vehicles, six

Photo by Maureen Morgan, 1983

The author and Wilhelm von Entenfall, alias (Teddy) Bear

My favorite dog was Wilhelm von Entenfall from Erlangen, West Germany. I had bought him in Stuttgart when I was in the Military Police. His name on the street was Bear. Together with Bear, I started out my security patrol business with one K-9 patrol unit, a pickup truck with a camper top, a mobile phone, a shotgun, and a handful of small businesses under contract.

dogs, and more work answering alarms with man-dog teams than any business planner could have predicted. Most of my clients owned automobile dealerships or warehouses in industrial parks. Many of these business customers were referred to Morgan Security by officers of the Lexington Police Department.

My staff grew to five officers and seven German shepherds. It was about the size of a city police department K-9 squad. Most of my men were ex-military personnel who had served in the combat arms and military police. Each officer who joined my small security staff brought his own dog, usually a German shepherd, although some had Doberman pinschers or Rottweilers. We enjoyed the comradeship and the dangers of the job, working on K-9 patrol each night.

Staff photo courtesy of *Lexington Herald Leader,* Lexington, Kentucky, 1987

The author, Ron Hackerson, and John Shouse with their dogs, Bonnie Bear, Simon, Little Bear, and Max

Welcome to Holiday Inn!

It was early one hot, muggy August morning in Lexington, about 1:30 A.M., and the bars were closing. I was a self-employed, independent K-9 security officer on duty with my patrol dog, Teddy Bear, eighty-five pounds of high-speed, black-and-tan terror. Recently retired from the U.S. Army, I had plenty of K-9 experience and so had organized my own security business.

Bear and I were on a break at the Shell service station around the corner from the Holiday Inn. I was slowly sipping a cup of black coffee, halfway through my shift, while Bear was drinking down a few gallons of chilled water, making a mess out of the back seat of my GMC Blazer. On my police scanner, I heard an emergency call dispatched from headquarters.

"Armed robbery, Holiday Inn. Intoxicated subject, white T-shirt, jeans, male, white, twenties, 200 pounds, six feet, armed with a blue steel automatic, took off on foot. No vehicle or direction of travel. Is there a K-9 available?"

The K-9 supervisor responded, "Headquarters. We've got three units on calls at this time. We'll need a few minutes to clear. Will advise." The thief was going to get away in the blackness of the early morning hours because police K-9 units were unavailable for this call.

I knew the night auditor at the Holiday Inn. Her name was Cici. She was a part-time student in law enforcement at Eastern Kentucky University in Richmond, an hour away from Lexington. She was the mother of two young boys, and her husband was an army officer. I knew the family well. Cici wanted a career of her own. When Cici finished college, she was going to apply for a position as a patrol officer with the police department. I worried about her and wondered how she would survive this experience.

Dumping my coffee, I jumped in my unmarked patrol unit and with lights out moved towards the Holiday Inn at a slow rate of speed. Three marked police units converged on the front office as I arrived in the rear of the motel. Bear started barking viciously at movement in the shadows near room 118. I saw a light. A door was open. A man in a T-shirt looked at me, then the door slammed quickly. It was now 1:45 A.M. Three police officers with drawn weapons began searching the property.

I went to the front desk and asked Cici who was registered in room 118. She responded, "I can't tell you any information, you know that."

A sergeant at the front desk told me that the police department was handling this call. The sergeant added, "Thanks for your assistance, but our K-9 units are on the way."

"Bear spotted somebody near room 118. Just thought it might be the guy you were looking for," I answered. The sergeant checked the folios on file, and Cici told him a female was registered in 118. Just then the K-9s arrived, and more police patrol units were on the scene. I returned to my beat, patrolling three car dealerships, a travel trailer dealership, and two warehouses.

About thirty minutes later, I heard the sergeant calling headquarters. "We're clear at Holiday Inn. No arrests. Suspect has vanished, if there was one." I knew what that meant. The police suspected Cici had stolen some money from the cash drawer, reporting an armed robbery to cover her theft. Cici would be furious.

At 3 A.M. I returned to the Holiday Inn to check on Cici and have another cup of coffee. She was very angry and crying. Her boss was there, and $500 was missing. She shouldn't have had that much cash on hand. The general rule was to keep the cash drawer down to $50. Since most people pay with credit cards at night, having a large cash supply on hand was not necessary. Cici was not only a suspect but she was also about to lose her job for violating procedure.

At 3:20 A.M., the guests in room 120 called the desk, saying, "There's a couple fighting next door. It's been going on since the bar closed. Please send security."

Holiday Inn was not my contract at that point, so I had no authority to act on behalf of management, but I told the manager about my observations at 1:45 A.M. "The guy who robbed the front desk may be in room 118," I warned.

The manager was in a tough spot. He asked me to check the room with him. He promised he would notify his corporate headquarters that he needed security. He said, "If they approve, you've got a patrol contract, Mr. Morgan."

I went out to my GMC Blazer, produced a blank security contract, and handed it to him. Bear and I moved out to room 118 with the manager eager to get this problem resolved.

As we knocked on the door, an angry female voice was heard. "Leave me alone. What do you want?"

I responded, "This is maintenance, miss. Didn't you call the front desk?"

A terrified, hysterical woman who had been badly beaten opened the door. When she saw my blue SWAT uniform and Bear at my side, she clasped her hands as if praying. No man was seen in the room. I motioned her to move forward. Half naked, with a ripped night shirt and no underwear, she stepped outside. She had been beaten and was bleeding from injuries to her right eye and jaw.

The room was a total mess, with overturned furniture, broken lamps, and the TV set on the floor. It looked like a terrible fight had taken place. I carried on as if I were the maintenance man. "Your air conditioner is frozen up. We'll move you to another room."

The manager and Cici slammed the door behind me, escorting the woman away to the front desk where they called the police again. Bear and I waited for her roommate to reappear. He was hiding in the bathroom.

I took off Bear's collar and lead and told him, "Watch him." His back hair bristled, and his eyes were fixed on the bathroom door. A male voice was heard inside the bathroom. "Are you out there? Are they gone?"

Bear began to growl and flash his teeth. I whispered, "No, Bear. Watch him."

After many years in the military police, I still carried a .45 caliber Army-type Colt automatic. I drew it and aimed my pistol at the door. A heartbeat later the bathroom door opened and out stepped an angry, violent, giant, drunken, naked man with a 9mm automatic in his right hand.

"Drop it or you're a dead man!" I shouted.

Bear attacked the man, sinking his teeth into his right forearm, pulling him down to the floor, and shaking the man from side to side, tearing flesh from his right shoulder. The man dropped his weapon, placed his hands over his head, and begged for mercy. Ordering Bear, "Out," I pulled off the dog.

The police sergeant opened the door behind me and shouted, "I'll be damned!"

The female who occupied the room returned with Cici and the manager, identifying the suspect as the man who had forced his way into her room and had raped her and beaten her for over an hour. Cici identified him as the bandit who robbed her at gunpoint. In the man's trousers were $500 in twenties.

The police were embarrassed. They had not followed up on my lead two hours before.

The paramedics arrived, and the embarrassed rape victim refused any treatment. She just wanted to go home. "Get out of my room! I hate men!" she screamed.

We all walked to the front desk to write reports. I sat down at a typewriter to print up not only a report but also a patrol contract.

Cici returned to room 118 to express her concerns, helping the woman get cleaned up and dressed. She also returned the guest's credit card slip. The manager was soon at the scene, trying to set things straight with the guest and begging Cici's forgiveness for accusing her of stealing. Cici had also been a victim as well that night. The manager gave the female guest a letter, apologized to her, and guaranteed her another night's stay, "on the house."

"Get out of my room and leave me alone!" she ordered.

As the paddy wagon arrived to transport our violent suspect to the hospital and the county detention center, a red car drove out of the parking lot at a high rate of speed. It almost collided with three police units as it screeched to a halt in front of the motel. The angry female guest at the wheel threw some papers out the window and screamed words which can't be printed here.

As she burned rubber speeding out of the parking lot, the manager picked up the papers. I couldn't believe what I saw written on the Holiday Inn stationery. After all this woman had been through, the insensitive manager had given her only a form letter, welcoming her back for another "pleasant night's stay." The letter started out with the greeting, "Welcome to Holiday Inn!"

The manager called me on the phone two days later, informing me that Holiday Inn didn't need my services. They didn't even say thanks for the work I had done. The hotel was robbed three more times that summer.

Cici moved to Phoenix, Arizona, and joined the police department there.

A Ribeye for The Bear

The Ribeye was a popular steakhouse one mile from the beltway around Lexington, Kentucky, and five minutes from the interstate highway running north and south. It was always full on sports nights after University of Kentucky ball games and especially so on weekends, every weekend. The bar was packed, TV sets were blaring, and the restaurant was filled to capacity. Money filled the two cash registers at the door.

It was the perfect armed robbery target, always busy and always noisy. Security was lax. Two bouncers stood guard at the exit doors, flirting with college girls, checking IDs, and serving as valet parking attendants on many occasions. All that would soon change when four good old boys from eastern Kentucky decided to make a fast buck one Saturday night.

I was the security officer at a nearby mobile home and camper dealership, walking a beat with my German shepherd, Teddy Bear. Recently retired from the military police after two tours of duty in Vietnam and two years in Germany, I was feeling bored to death this evening on the job at Hall's, a huge dealership on the beltway with millions of dollars in inventory.

I had just recently started a K-9 security business to supplement my income. One other officer worked with me. His name was Mike Simpson and his dog was Bear's buddy, Kenny. Every two to three hours, Mike would come by and check on me. Mike brought me a cup of coffee at 11 P.M. to keep me awake for the next few hours. We had three other places to check besides Hall's Campers. Mike would check them while I worked at Hall's. I was like Mr. Magoo, the laughable TV cartoon character, unaware of what was going on two blocks away at the Ribeye.

The four good old boys had a simple plan. They would have dinner, watch the cash registers, use the men's room near the exit door several times, talk to the security guards, and make their move at closing time around 1 A.M. Two of the good old boys would start a fight in the men's room shortly after closing. While security was distracted with the fight, the other two would each take out a cash register and run into the parking lot. They had a truck parked near Hall's Campers at the Embers Inn. It belonged to one of those bad actors who would stage the bathroom fight. Those two planned to stop their shoving and pushing soon after it started, surrender to security, and walk away from the Ribeye, joining up with their two buddies with the cash. It was too simple a plan to be good.

When the bathroom brawl started at 1:05 A.M., Ribeye security called the police immediately and told the girls at the two cash registers to secure their drawers tight. One of the guards had experience at things like this. Tammy and Samantha Rogers followed orders well and locked down their registers. The two security officers had the two bad actors in custody in seconds, handcuffed and flat on the floor. The other two thieves made their moves, ordering Tammy and Samantha to open their registers and empty their cash drawers. Both said they were armed and flashed small blue steel revolvers, which it later turned out were starter pistols. The registers were opened, $3,000 was taken, and the two good old boys headed out according to plan. Just for safekeeping, they decided to take the girls with them so no alarm would be spread. They had just committed a federal offense, kidnapping.

Metro police rolled into the parking lot as Billy Latham and Joey Smith ran off with Samantha and Tammy. The armed robbery wasn't discovered until 1:15 A.M., when the girls were found to be missing and cash drawers were checked. One security officer in the restaurant put the plan together very quickly, implicating the two bad actors now in police custody. Threatened with armed robbery and kidnapping, the bathroom brawlers started crying and told all. Police rolled over to the Embers Inn, confiscating the get-away truck, a black Ford pickup. Three thousand dollars and two girls were still missing, and that's where I came in as Officer Magoo.

Feeling bored, about 1:45 A.M., I was just walking along with Bear when the dog got very serious about something in the grass near a railroad track. I flashed my light on what appeared to be two women. One got up and ran off, screaming and crying. The other lay there, motionless. I thought she was dead. Bear sniffed her face and ears, pawed her shoulder, and barked. She began to move and started crying.

I told her I was a security cop and asked her what she was doing on a railroad track at two in the morning. She had been beaten pretty badly, bleeding from her right eye, nose and mouth. Her jaw was discolored and her clothes were torn. The girls had been abused, tied with tape, and dumped near Hall's Campers by Latham and Smith. They threatened the girls that they would come back and finish them off if they talked.

Seconds later, Samantha Rogers returned with a police officer and two paramedics. She had thought I was one of the kidnappers coming back to kill them. Samantha flagged down the police who had been patrolling the beltway looking for the armed robbery suspects and led them back to Tammy and me.

If Bear hadn't been with me, I would have had some hard explaining to do, with this frightened woman in my arms. I wasn't wearing a police or security uniform, and in a blue work shirt and jeans, I didn't look like a security cop. Undercover at the dealership in this busy part of town, I dressed the part to look like a customer shopping for a camper, hoping to apprehend kids who vandalized Hall's Campers, stealing stereos and television sets. Bear was my only defense.

The policeman believed me and told me what had happened at the Ribeye. He cautioned me, "Watch your butt because some bad guys are in the area wanted for armed robbery and kidnapping these two women cashiers from the restaurant." The FBI would want these guys too, I was told.

I had an unmarked K-9 patrol truck near the Embers Inn loaded with police equipment, including my badge, a pistol belt, pistol, flashlight, and shotgun. I went to the truck, called Mike Simpson on my mobile phone, and told him to stop by and bring me a cup of coffee. I planned to use Kenny and Bear as a team to search Hall's Campers. Back in uniform and armed, I was no longer bored. I was out hunting men again, armed men.

Before Mike and Kenny arrived to help me, Bear alerted on a camper in the rear of the dealership. Its rear door was half open. Bear cocked his head, looked at me, and pawed the door. Four males in their early twenties were inside. Bear barked and growled, flashing his teeth, terrorizing the men. They began shouting, cursing, and scrambling for safety when I stepped in the camper and blinded them with my flashlight. Bear continued to bark and threaten the four as if he were going to attack at any second. When the men stopped talking, Bear suddenly became quiet.

Then Bear started to growl again. Ordering the four to crawl out of the camper towards me, I almost started laughing. Bear was playing the role of "Rin Tin Tin, K-9 Cop" better than I had seen it on TV. The men were terrified, but I was amused.

I asked them, "Why did you kidnap those girls?"

"I didn't do anything, officer, I swear," one replied. "I didn't know this was going on, I swear it. I was just smoking a joint with these guys, and they told me about it, I swear."

I didn't believe him, but at least I had a confession from one suspect and knew I had the armed robbers.

I had only one set of handcuffs and four prisoners, no radio, and no backup from Mike Simpson as yet. Searching the four men, I found two loaded 9mm automatics, two blank starter pistols, and two knives. It was a very dangerous situation, but Bear was of immense assistance. He strutted back and forth and walked over the men spread out on the ground, growling, sniffing them, pawing their heads, barking, and holding them in place.

There was no talking. I told all four to look straight down at the ground and eat dirt and the dog wouldn't harm them. Nervously trying to buy time, I began to talk into my pager as if it were a radio handset, requesting a paddy wagon to transport these clowns to jail. I had to make them believe I had a radio and my backup was only a short distance away.

Bear at full bark

Bear continued to bark and threaten the four men as if he were going to attack at any second.

File photo, U.S. Army Military Police, Fort Knox, Kentucky, 1981

As luck would have it, Mike Simpson arrived with a Metro K-9 officer seconds later. "What took you so long, Mike?" I inquired.

"You wanted some coffee, didn't you?" he laughed. Mike's dog, Kenny, joined Bear in terrorizing the good old boys until a prisoner transport arrived.

Every dollar stolen from the Ribeye was recovered. Bear got a ribeye steak as a reward for his efforts. I was the butt of jokes for months for not knowing what was going on when thirty cops around town were looking for the Ribeye bandits. I was nicknamed Officer Magoo. Bear got his picture in the paper. My security business flourished, and I still have Hall's Campers as a contract twenty years later.

Kentucky Justice

My newly organized K-9 patrol service was giving me plenty of work to do after retirement. My daughter, Maureen, helped me with the business, answering the phones and booking contract appointments.

In high school, she was given an assignment: Go to the office with Dad and report to the class what he does to support your family. My office was a K-9 patrol car, so Maureen went along on patrol one night and watched a sting operation. She quickly took up the pen and became a junior Joseph Wambaugh with a "Police Story" of her own.

There was an ambitious salesman from Columbus, Ohio, who had moved to Kentucky and was working at Plywood Plaza on Newtown Pike in Lexington. He could think fast, talk like a salesman, and satisfy almost any customer, making good money for himself. His problem was that the fifty-percent sales he bragged about, "strictly cash, no credit cards," were off the books and without his boss's knowledge. He generally gave special discounts on Friday nights.

Missing stock from the lumber yard was generally attributed to thefts which took place over the weekends when Kentucky Plywood Plaza was closed. The boss didn't know about the Friday night specials until a customer, who was sold some poor grade plywood, tried to return it on a Monday morning. He wanted his money back and complained bitterly when he was told, "You have no proof of purchase, and there was no fifty-percent sale on Friday night."

The boss called me in to find out what was going on. I contacted the customer and guaranteed him a fair exchange of plywood if he would exchange some information with me. Together we set up a sting operation.

The following Friday, the unhappy customer identified our ambitious salesman from Ohio as the employee who had sold him bad stock at fifty percent off. I accompanied the customer to the store as his brother. We made no mention of the poor quality plywood. We just told the salesman we needed more supplies.

He took down our order. "I'll get back with you the first of the week," he said. "I have to special order some of this stuff, you know."

On Monday night, the salesman called the customer to say the supplies would be in next Thursday, ready for a Friday night delivery. We informed the boss, who was unaware of any special orders. Thursday night rolled around, and the customer was asked to come in and check the order. "Plywood Plaza also needed a deposit of at least $300," he was told. That was not company policy.

Marked money was provided by management, and details of the delivery were coordinated. The marked money changed hands, and the salesman struck a cash deal for lumber worth over $2,000, on sale for half that price. Two of the salesman's brothers would pick up the order from Plywood Plaza and deliver it to the customer's home on Friday night after the lumber yard closed.

Maureen was thrilled to go along and observe this operation firsthand after having watched police stories on TV. To make sure nobody got away, we brought along our German shepherd, Teddy Bear, for security.

At 9:30 P.M. on Friday night, the customer walked into Plywood Plaza, meeting the Ohio salesman, who was closing the store. He had already told two other employees they could leave early, although they were still on the clock, saying he would cover for them. The remaining $700, marked money provided by management, was given to the salesman who promptly introduced his brothers to the customer. "The stuff is loaded out back, ready to roll. Just give us the directions to your house, and we'll be on the way," they told him.

Bear and I had slipped into the lumber yard while the deal went down inside. Finding the truck loaded with soon-to-be-stolen property, I put Bear in the front seat. The keys in the ignition went into my pocket. Then I gave them to the boss who accompanied Maureen and me into the store. A uniformed security officer also went in with us to make an arrest. Two other officers waited outside and locked the gate so no vehicles could leave the Plywood Plaza compound.

When the delivery brothers saw a uniformed officer coming into the store, they ran out the back door. The boss confronted the salesman, thanked the customer for coordinating the sting, and faced off with his employee. "How long have you been giving my stuff away at a fifty-percent discount, John?" inquired the boss. He stated that stock missing from the yard totaled at least $5,000 over a three-month period. This employee had been at Plywood Plaza just about four months, always eager to work those Friday nights.

Before he could reply, John broke down crying. Seconds later, his brothers ran back into the store and said, "There's a German shepherd running loose in the yard. He was in our truck."

"That's my truck now," said the boss. "Great customizing job. Must be worth at least $5,000," he added.

Bear had rounded up the two brothers who admitted their part in the thefts from Plywood Plaza over a two-month period. No arrest was made. Instead, we all sat down in the front office, working out a deal.

The boss, with a big smile on his face, gave the three brothers a chance, saying, "You know what the judge will do, boys. A $500 fine and ninety days of community service, plus restitution. Y'all will have convictions, and I'll be out the money, since you won't have jobs. Now you just sell me that truck for one dollar." He turned to his employee John and continued. "I'll keep your paycheck for the last two weeks, and it's all forgotten."

"What about our shotguns and tools in the truck?" the brothers inquired.

"The truck is mine, boys, and everything in it!" he snapped back, with a gunfighter's look on his face. A former Navy fighter pilot with a personalized license plate on his pick-up truck that read Top Gun, the boss was deadly serious. "You boys from Ohio will have to understand that's how things are done in Kentucky."

The three brothers left the store on foot, leaving behind their possessions.

"Not everybody goes to jail," the boss told me. "It's better this way."

Maureen had some story to write. She called it "Kentucky Justice."

The Hills Street Blues

It was the night before Christmas, and my patrol dog, Teddy Bear, and I were out on the north side of town on routine patrol from 9 P.M. Christmas Eve until 6 A.M. on Christmas morning. The stores and restaurants had all closed early, the radio was quiet, and all was peaceful in town.

The weather was cold, wet, and nasty. No new snow had fallen for ten days. Dirty ice and snow were piled up in parking lots and on the sides of roads all over town. It had turned into rock-hard ice, with the temperature hovering around the twenties in the daytime and in the teens at night. Teddy Bear rode up front with me, head on my lap, snoring away with the heater on full blast.

The only place to get a cup of coffee was at the Shell station on Newtown Pike. It would be closing at midnight this Christmas Eve. It was going to be lonely out there from midnight until 6 A.M.

Just as I was about to get that cup of coffee, a call came in: "Unit 100, proceed to the Marriott Resort, Newtown Pike. DWI in the parking lot, no operator's license. Animal control officer also on the way. Vehicle is blocking the hotel entrance." By the time I got there, the DWI had driven off, according to the doorman. I asked for the particulars and began to write my report. The doorman couldn't keep a straight face. I didn't know what was going on.

The manager came out and told me what happened. "This drunk rolled up to the front door and blocked the fire lane. He was about five feet, four inches tall, had a white beard, and appeared to be in his sixties or older. He was wearing a red suit and a ski hat. His eyes were bloodshot, his speech was slurred, and he wouldn't identify himself. He said he never had a driver's license and wouldn't move his vehicle, and then his animal bit me."

The manager didn't have a scratch on him. I asked the man if a dog had bitten him. He began to pull up his trouser leg, but I couldn't see any marks. "What kind of a vehicle did he have?" I asked.

"It was a sled. He had eight reindeer pulling a sled."

The doorman started laughing, as did the manager. I had fallen for the old Santa Claus call on Christmas Eve ploy.

"Would you like some coffee, officer?" said the manager. "We've got some cake, too. We're open all night, so stop by any time."

How could I be mad? It was Christmas Eve.

Halfway through the cup of coffee at the Marriott, I got a second call. It was just about midnight. The dispatcher reported, "Hills Department Store, North-park Shopping Center, banging and smashing noises. Sonitrol can hear voices."

Hills had lots of cash, with no credit card purchases. I suspected thieves were breaking open the safe in the manager's office. The department store had thirty sound-activated alarm sensors monitored by Sonitrol's central station.

Three other officers arrived along with the manager. Four of us and my Teddy Bear rushed into the store. With weapons drawn, we proceeded to the manager's office. All was secure. The safe was closed. The manager opened it and counted out all the cash. Not a dollar was missing. Nothing was out of place.

We phoned Sonitrol and asked if there were any different sounds being heard. With four officers, a K-9 patrol dog, and the store manager present, the banging and smashing sounds had stopped. The three other officers soon left the store, officially reporting a false alarm. I remained with the manager to check out all doors and windows while finishing my cup of coffee. We made it a point to be silent for ten minutes before calling Sonitrol again.

After we called the central station, the Sonitrol manager told us there were scraping noises again and voices could be heard. "Maybe Santa Claus and his elves are on the roof loading up toys for needy children," he added.

The Hills store manager locked himself in his office and stayed on the phone with the police department. Teddy Bear and I began checking out the entire premises. All doors were locked and nobody was in the store. Suddenly the dog stopped, looking up at the ceiling. That's where they were. Sonitrol was right. Somebody was on the roof, but they weren't elves.

The store manager led me to the attic entrance where a pull-down ladder provided me a way up to the ceiling storage area, which was used for storing stock, mostly boxed items like TV sets and kitchen appliances. My dog wouldn't climb up the ladder so I carried all eighty-five pounds of German shepherd up there on my back. "This is why they make you carry sand bags up a stairwell in police training," I whispered to the store manager. I was very embarrassed that the dog wouldn't climb up the ladder.

Bear searched the storage area from one end to the other, alerting at the end of the loft. I could hear voices. Was a radio on? It sounded like music and talk. Yes, it was a radio. The radio sounds were coming from the outside. Then I heard voices which sounded like three teenagers joking around. They were laughing about the police, commenting on their ability to successfully win their game of hide and seek. After climbing back down the ladder with Bear hanging on to me for dear life, I called in to the police department on the manager's phone, just in case the kids had a police scanner for monitoring calls.

We secured the building and walked outside into the cold, wet night. I had become overheated carrying my partner and felt the cold outside with temperature readings well below freezing. In the back of the building, we found a small sled loaded with four cartons containing seventeen inch, black-and-white TV sets. The elves on the roof were lowering TV sets and small kitchen appliances by rope to the ground.

"How did they get up there?" the manager asked me. I had no idea.

Down came another TV set, and when it hit the ground, I pulled hard on the rope. The kids at the other end fell down on the roof, slid on the ice, and let the rope go. Unable to figure out what had happened, there was all sorts of cursing and arguing among the three boys fifty feet above me. They were now stranded, or so I thought. Teddy Bear and I hid in the shadows, waiting for their next move.

Then I heard the scraping noises Sonitrol had reported. These enterprizing youths had an aluminum ladder with them. They pushed it over the side and began to descend into the parking lot one at a time. When the first of Santa's helpers touched down on the ground, Teddy Bear greeted him with flashing teeth and a bark that could be heard all over town.

The teenager stumbled and slipped on the ice, trying to get away. Teddy Bear pulled him down on the ground, and the boy lay still, hoping the dog would go away. The shepherd didn't, and the teen said nothing, didn't warn his friends, didn't utter a word. With their radio blasting away with rock music on the roof, the teenagers hadn't heard the dog down below.

The second youth climbed down, and I told him to spread out next to his buddy on the ice.

"'Zat dog bite?" he asked me.

"Yes," I assured him, and he flattened out next to his friend. My Teddy Bear laid out on the ice, breathing in their faces, flashing his teeth, and growling. The radio on the roof was suddenly silent.

The remaining teenager called down to his buddies. When there was no response, he cursed them and slid down the ladder quickly, like a fire fighter. He hit the ground, slipping on the ice. As he fell, I told him, "You're under arrest. Merry Christmas!" The youth was in a state of shock as he faced me, Teddy Bear, and the store manager.

The manager knew the third teenager, a straight-A student and star athlete from a good family. He was also a store employee, a stockman who worked in the storage area after school. The appliance department had reported TV sets disappearing from inventory for several weeks, but no one could figure out how they had been taken. It was clear now. They had been taken and stored on the roof outside. The plan was to stay behind on Christmas Eve and then sell all the stolen merchandise, over twenty TV sets and some kitchen appliances, to pay for some holiday expenses.

The TV sets and appliances had been ordered two weeks before Christmas by the teenagers' accomplices and partially paid for with cash and food stamps. Their new owners would be in for a surprise the day after Christmas because Santa's helpers provided detectives with their names and addresses in hopes of cutting a deal with the commonwealth attorney. If the TV sets had been delivered, the new owners would have been in for a different surprise.

The manager recovered the aluminum ladder, which belonged to the store. However, not one TV set ever worked again after being left on the roof in the snow, ice, and extreme cold for an extended period of time.

After the prisoner transport arrived, the shivering youths went off to a nice, warm jail cell at 2 A.M. Christmas morning. As the paddy wagon driver cleared the parking lot on the way to the detention center, the police dispatcher asked for a situation report. The officer reported his status to headquarters. "We're enroute with three elves. They don't want any more Teddy Bear surprises. Merry Christmas to all and to Hills a good night! Clear."

You Can't Burglarize a Tent

Each year at the end of summer, several merchants near the University of Kentucky organized a sidewalk sale to allow students to stock up on T-shirts, jeans, casual clothes, and jackets at fifty percent off. The sale was a once-a-year event, and a very popular one, held outdoors under a big-top tent.

I was asked to provide security at night, and I brought along my wife for company on this simple job. My official partner, of course, was Teddy Bear, my German shepherd patrol dog.

At 10 P.M., the cash drawers were emptied, clothes were covered with plastic, and the blue and white big-top tent was zippered shut for the night. Bear and I were required to make rounds once an hour. My partner, Mike Simpson, and his dog, Kenny, would relieve me every two hours. We would be on duty until 8 A.M. the next morning. Mike and I had a regular beat to patrol in addition to this big-top security job. The blue and white tent was next to Howard Johnson's Motel, a great place for coffee breaks during the night.

About 2 A.M., my wife and I left the area for our coffee break when Mike and Kenny were scheduled to take up their posts. Mike got hung up on a burglary call, and the tent area was left unsecured. A car full of teenagers had checked out the tent several times between 10 P.M. and 2 A.M. When my wife and I left the area and Mike and Kenny didn't take our places, the teenagers made their move. Within seconds after our departure, they unzipped the tent and started loading up clothes.

I checked in with Mike on the radio, and he told me he was unable to watch the tent until 3 A.M. My wife and I went back to the area, finding the teenagers' car fifty feet from the tent and loaded with stolen property. The kids were inside trying on clothes while we were outside with their vehicle.

My wife called in on the telephone at Howard Johnson's, telling the police dispatcher a tent burglary was in progress. "You can't burglarize a tent!" she was informed. My wife told the dispatcher, "You'd better get someone here soon before somebody gets shot."

I knew the teens were committing a felony and were brazen about it, but I decided not only to arrest them but also to play a game with them. The keys to the teens' car were in the ignition so I removed them, preventing any escape by vehicle from the scene of the crime. Next I secured the trunk, in which several hundred dollars' worth of stolen property had been stashed. I also found a wallet in the auto that identified the vehicle operator and his home address.

While my wife was calling the police on the phone from Howard Johnson's, Bear and I moved in on the tent, listening to the youths joking about their new threads. I found the side zipper that the kids used to gain entry, and Bear entered the tent in a heartbeat. I reclosed the zipper and listened to the confusion inside.

Bear slowly walked up to the four thieves, lowering his head as does a quarter horse about to herd cattle. All the joking stopped. "Is that a police dog?" one teen asked.

Outside the tent I answered, "Sure is! Come on out. You're under arrest."

The kids made a run for it. Bear barked as the teens scrambled under the sides of the tent running in four separate directions. Most had no sneakers on since they had removed their footware to try on clothes. Three of the teenagers left their own clothing at the scene. Wallets, drivers' licenses, other identification, and paychecks from McDonald's supplied us the names of all the individuals in the group.

It didn't take a rocket scientist to identify this gang of incompetent thieves. Police units went to all addresses listed on the identification and waited for the culprits to return to their homes, a few miles away from Howard Johnson's Motel. While detectives photographed the crime scene, I put Bear in the front seat of the teenagers' car to ensure it didn't leave the area.

Streaking across Lexington, Kentucky, at 3 A.M., barefoot and half-clothed in stolen jeans, shorts, and underwear, the gang was soon rounded up and brought into the detective bureau at police headquarters. The stories the kids told detectives were amusing. I thought I was going to die laughing.

Story number one: Somebody stole my car, and I had to walk home from work.

Story number two: A guy held me up, told me to take off my clothes, and left me without any clothes or identification. I had to walk home in my shorts.

Story number three: I was out with my new girlfriend in the backseat of her car, making out, with my clothes off, you know. Then her old boyfriend showed up and told me to get out and start walking. He took off with my girlfriend, driving her car. We were at Howard Johnson's Motel in the parking lot. I can't tell you her name because it would embarrass her family.

Story number four: I don't know what happened. I had a few beers, passed out, and woke up walking in my sleep. I don't know what happened to my clothes.

The next day in police court, all the teenagers pleaded guilty to criminal trespass. They were ordered to pay a fine of $750 to the court and also to purchase the clothes worth $750 they had taken in their attempted burglary.

I faced off with the bandits in court and later at school in a D.A.R.E. program class. The kids were terribly embarrassed and red-faced, holding their heads in their hands while I spoke about drugs, alcohol, crime, and stupidity. I told the story about this group of teenagers who tried to burglarize a tent and steal some jeans. The class was hard to control, as all the students knew the story firsthand.

"Can you really burglarize a tent, officer?" one student asked.

"Sure you can. It's like Hotel California. You can check in, but you can't ever leave." I replied.

Just Another Day at JFK

It was a Saturday afternoon, and Customs Officer Don Kent was at home with his family, working in his basement carpenter shop. His drug dog, Wolfgang, a black and tan German shepherd, was sacked out on an old couch in the shop. The TV was on, and Don watched a western while he worked on some lawn furniture.

They had worked a long, tough week at John F. Kennedy (JFK) Airport outside of New York City. There was a shortage of drug dogs and handlers due to retirements, vacations, special assignments, and government cutbacks in personnel. Mandatory overtime forced officers to work sixty hours a week on many occasions. Six nights on the 10 P.M. to 8 A.M. shift can wear out any man-dog team.

Don Kent was not an ordinary K-9 cop. He was soft spoken, only five-feet, eight-inches tall, and weighed just 160 pounds. Most K-9 officers were over six feet tall, over 200 pounds, and very aggressive. They were like their huge German shepherds, big, rough, and tough. Wolfgang was not a tough street dog who snapped at anything or anybody. Wolf was only sixty pounds. Yet both were perfectly suited for their job. Don and Wolf crawled in and out of aircraft, cargo compartments, and small places looking for drugs at JFK Airport.

Don had been what we called a tunnel rat in Vietnam, spending four months of his one-year combat tour of duty underground, searching for Viet Cong in caves and tunnels with Labrador retrievers.

They were in public contact a great deal and could pass for just a man and his dog out for a walk had Don not worn his blue uniform and duty belt with radio, pistol, handcuffs, nightstick, flashlight, and keys to gates. Don and Wolf were the perfect pair for the mission they were about to be assigned.

The phone rang, and they were asked to report in civilian clothes to Penn Station, Thirty-fourth Street and Eight Avenue, New York City. The Drug Enforcement Administration (DEA) needed Don and Wolf for a special mission.

The fastest way to get into Penn Station was the subway. Don dressed as an unsighted person with a black raincoat, sunglasses, and rain hat. Wolf had a guide dog harness. Don also carried a red and white cane. Don and Wolf had worked in the subways on many occasions, training new K-9 cops for the New York Police Department. He could always get through the subways with that outfit while still managing to get his dog to work. Nobody asked questions. Nobody knew they were customs personnel, armed and part of the drug enforcement team. Crime was down on the subways because of K-9 man-dog teams.

When they arrived at Penn Station, they reported in to the police desk. The desk sergeant asked Don, "May I help you, sir?"

Just then, a DEA agent popped his head out of the conference room and asked, "Is customs here yet?"

The desk sergeant said, "Not yet."

Don answered, "Yes, sir!"

The desk sergeant laughed and said, "Could have fooled me."

Don replied, "We did."

A tip had been received that a drug courier was coming in on the train from Florida with a great deal of cocaine in personal baggage. Drug dogs would have discovered the load of cocaine if it came through an airport, so the Florida–New York train was being used to deliver this contraband to New York distributors. The description of the suspect was quite vague, specifying only an old guy with gray hair and mustache with a green suit jacket and a silver attaché case. No height or weight or age description had been provided.

The FBI and DEA moved quickly on the tip, organizing a joint task force of nine agents from three departments to work in teams of three. Don, as the customs K-9 officer, was to float the area and be directed at probable targets by agents working the gates in civilian clothes. Don wore a hearing aid device to receive instructions from the officers, whom he did not know.

The planning was flawed from the beginning. Operations like these require intimate knowledge of partners, with code names, distinct clothing and mannerisms, special answers to simple questions, and back-up plans. None of these task force officers had worked with K-9 teams before. Coordination was poor, and communications were worse. Somebody could get hurt if the drug courier decided to resist arrest with a gun. Civilians could be in great danger if caught in the middle of a violent situation. Murphy's Law, if anything can go wrong, it will go wrong, was the order of the day.

A first suspect was approached by one team of three drug enforcement agents moving towards Seventh Avenue. Kent was directed to have Wolf check out the suspect's silver attaché case. Don bumped into the man and asked him directions to the post office on Thirty-third Street. Wolf did not alert on the silver attaché case, which meant no drugs.

The man with the green jacket was very cordial and almost accompanied Don all the way to the post office before Don Kent excused himself and said he was waiting for his sister. Don was out of radio range or could not hear signals clearly, with all the taxi and truck traffic on the street. None of the officers followed him out of the terminal to maintain radio or visual contact. Another unsighted person with a German shepherd entered the terminal, and the team thought this man was Don Kent.

A second suspect was located in the terminal near Thirty-third Street. Don could not be found, and special agents directed this unsighted civilian to follow them. Frightened by these three giants in civilian clothes, the blind man walked away and went to a newsstand to ask for police assistance. The Long Island Railroad Police officers who responded, unaware of the special operation, got into a confrontation with the plainclothes federal agents.

The second suspect was signalling for a taxi to pick him up on Thirty-third Street when Kent spotted the agents in pursuit arguing with a uniformed police officer. Don signalled the agents to back off and bumped into the second suspect on the street. Wolfgang did not alert on the suspect's silver attaché case. No drugs again. Don excused himself for bumping into the suspect and walked away. This second suspect in a green jacket insisted this blind man take the taxi he had summoned until the cab driver told him, "Sorry, no dogs allowed, sir."

No radio communications could be heard in all the confusion on the street. Finally, an FBI agent approached Don and said, "Excuse me, sir, are you Don King?" Don told him he was waiting for his sister, his name was Don Kent, and everything was OK at JFK. "I'm waiting for my sister" was an identification code for this K-9 operation, as was "OK at JFK."

Two other agents approached. Kent knew only one of them. Don was really upset the FBI didn't even have his name right, didn't know his identification codes, and got him mixed up with another disabled person. He told them he was going off duty unless they got their act together.

The agents had failed miserably in their efforts to coordinate this arrest thus far. Don was ready to get back on the subway and go home. His ear receiver still did not work, and that only frustrated the situation more than one could imagine. As Kent was getting ready to pack it in as a lost cause, another team of agents was tracking a third man in a green jacket with a silver attaché case.

Kent knew what to do even though not directed by any agents. He bumped into the man, asking for directions. Wolfgang alerted on the attaché case, and the suspect began to draw an automatic from under his coat. Wolf jumped up on the suspect's chest and dropped him to the ground. Don told him, "You're under arrest!"

The suspect, who looked like an elderly man in his sixties, was obviously much younger and in excellent physical condition. He kicked Officer Kent in the groin as three other agents joined in on the arrest. Wolf scratched the suspect in the face and mauled him, tearing a piece of flesh out of his neck. One FBI agent trying to take the man in custody pushed Don Kent aside, and Wolfgang attacked him also. Kent had lost control of the dog, and a crowd gathered, along with six uniformed New York City policemen who had been alerted by people in the crowded station that there was a man with a gun.

Staggering to his feet, Don called Wolfgang back and regained control of his partner. Two cops tried to assist the blind man until Kent notified them he was a customs K-9 officer working under cover. No coordination with the New York City Police Department had been made.

The cops were not about to allow these federal officers to take anybody into custody. While one FBI agent explained to the New York City cops that they were a special operating task force on a special operation, a police lieutenant arrived and had to be briefed all over again. The suspect almost got away in all the confusion while paramedics treated him for his injuries.

The lieutenant opened the attaché case and found only an automatic weapon and some ammunition. The drugs had already been dropped, and the dog had alerted on drug residue alone. New York City police took jurisdiction and arrested the third suspect on a gun possession violation.

Don Kent decided to leave the area and call his supervisor. He was not too complimentary about the plan of coordination in this operation. His supervisor directed him to stay on station until he arrived and to search all the trash recepticals he could find, to look for the stash.

When Kent returned to the police desk for a coffee break, the suspect was being booked and fingerprinted. One of his possessions was a locker key. Kent asked for the key and told the desk sergeant he would check out the locker for drugs. "Not without a search warrant!" the sergeant shouted. They refused to give him the key.

Don wrote down the number and went searching for large storage lockers in the terminal. The key belonged to a bottom locker on the main level. Wolfgang alerted on the baggage locker area immediately. Kent called the desk sergeant and informed him his dog had identified drugs. A judge was contacted, and the search was authorized. In the locker, they found two large duffel bags, one stuffed with cash and the other packed with cocaine. Despite all the confusion, miscoordination, and chaos, the drugs had been identified and recovered. Wolfgang and Officer Don Kent rode home on the subway that night unaware their work had probably destroyed a major drug operation.

The suspect, held without bail for two days until properly identified, turned out to be the number three man on the FBI's Ten Most Wanted list of criminals. It seems the suspect had decided to act as a courier on this drug shipment, not trusting his lieutenants who were cutting down on his profits by making deals on their own in New York City. It was they who had turned him in, hoping to take over his area of operations for themselves. Aware his career was over, the suspect went into the federal witness protection program after identifying major crime-family drug connections in the northeast.

When Kent and Wolfgang arrived home about 10 P.M. that night, his wife asked him how things went at work. Unable to tell her about this special operation, he calmly answered, "Just another day at JFK, Honey."

The late-night news on TV told a different story. Mary Ann Kent clearly saw videotape of Wolfgang at Penn Station, working on a search of storage lockers. The duffel bags were photographed as Wolfgang pawed them. Media reporters had made a circus out of the arrest of suspect number three. Passengers were interviewed, and every person interviewed claimed to know exactly what had happened.

Wolfgang went to sleep on the couch not at all impressed with the news. Mary Ann looked at Don again and asked him if the dog on TV was Wolfgang.

Don replied, "You know, Honey, all those German shepherds look alike."

It Was My Bust, Dad!

My daughter, Maureen, received another one of those school assignments in the spring semester of her junior year in high school. Go to work with your father one day and write about it, then bring your report into class and tell us what your father does at the office all day.

My office, of course, was a K-9 patrol car. My partner was Wilhelm von Entenfall, from Erlangen, West Germany. We called him Teddy Bear. He was a three-year-old German shepherd and very intelligent, but not exactly a Gentle Ben.

Maureen went to work with me one Saturday afternoon and quickly became a top cop.

A construction site on my security patrol beat had been vandalized the previous two weekends. Thousands of dollars worth of copper tubing had been stolen shortly after it was delivered. Two thousand dollars worth of the copper had been taken on one day. It looked like an inside job, an internal theft by employees. The deliveries and the thefts took place on Saturdays. The site was in an industrial park.

Maureen and I dressed in civilian clothes and went out in my unmarked pickup truck with a shotgun under the seat. We carried no radio and let Teddy Bear sit between us. We didn't look like cops. Many unmarked units are easy to spot if you know what to look for. Professional thieves watch for unmarked units, usually two detectives in a four-door white car, most with spotlights on the left side and a radio antenna on the roof. The pros also monitor the police radio, listening for detective or patrol traffic. If you are going to catch a criminal, you can't look like cops or operate like cops. No unmarked cars with spotlights or radios are allowed.

About 4 P.M., we passed by the construction site for the third time, looking for anything out of place. No employees were on the job on Saturdays when the thefts took place, and none were on the job this day either. Yet there was a truck on the site. It was a flatbed, and nobody was at the wheel.

I was sure something was going on and recorded the license plate number. I dropped Maureen off at a truck dealership and told her to call 911. She used the standard reporting format of who, what, when, and where. The police dispatcher received the following information from this 17-year-old professional:

> My dad is a K-9 security officer, and he wants a police patrol unit to check out two warehouses under construction on Nandino Boulevard, now! A truck is out there, a red flatbed, license number AHG-777. No employees are supposed to be on the site, which has been burglarized the past two Saturdays. My dad is wearing a black T-shirt, Levi's, and combat boots. He has his patrol dog with him. My dad has his shotgun but no radio. He is standing by. Thank you.

Two police units were immediately on the way, and Maureen watched the whole operation from across the street.

While Maureen was on the 911 call, I dismounted with Teddy Bear and the shotgun and approached the truck. The windows were rolled down. The vehicle was empty, but the keys were in the ignition. I opened the door and let Teddy Bear jump in the cab. I put the keys in my pocket, told Bear to stay, and then went around the warehouse with my shotgun, searching for thieves.

As I got to the rear door, I saw two large construction workers, 250-pound men with beards, gathering up coils of copper wire. They were getting ready to leave the construction site as I confronted them. I told them to halt and identified myself.

They laughed at me when they saw my badge and shotgun and scoffed, "You're just a security guard. Go to hell!" They took off running. They knew I couldn't handle both of them. I couldn't shoot them either, but the shotgun rattled their cages.

They ran to their truck and opened the door. As they tried to jump in and make their escape, Bear introduced himself with a loud bark and let these guys know who was in charge of their truck. And, it wasn't their truck, either. They had borrowed it from their boss just as they had borrowed the copper tubing.

The police units arrived, and the two men gave up without a fight. It was pretty comical, watching these two thieves trying to talk their way out of the situation. "Due to the rain, this job is behind schedule, and so we were trying to catch up on our work after hours. We don't know who this security guard is, the one with the dog. You should haul him away. He's aiming that shotgun barrel around like he's crazy. That's why we ran."

Bear and I got credit for the arrest, and I began to write my report. I was so proud of myself, taking my daughter to work and conducting the perfect arrest with my Teddy Bear.

The patrol officers didn't see it that way. "Your daughter did a great job, Mr. Morgan," they said. "She explained everything. This was a piece of cake for us."

I showed my report to Maureen, and she read it for accuracy since we would be in court on Monday morning.

"You left out one thing," she commented. "It was my bust, Dad!"

The Outlaw

Trooper William Smith had been following an outlaw biker, a so-called Iron Horseman, for twelve miles after he crossed over into Kentucky on Interstate 64 from West Virginia. The Kentucky State Police had a tip that bikers were carrying drugs and selling them at rest stops in the eastern part of the state, between the hours of 9 P.M. and 6 A.M., usually on weekends. It was a Friday night, and the Iron Horseman knew he was being followed by a marked police unit several hundred yards back.

Six more bikers zipped past the KSP trooper's unit at high speeds in excess of 80 miles per hour, hoping to get him away from the lone outlaw by chasing them for speeding. It didn't work. Smith knew the game and stayed behind the lone rider. Two minutes later he called in to headquarters, "Traffic stop, Iron Horseman, I-64 west, 175-mile marker, license tag is covered with mud."

The trooper's blue overhead lights flashed brightly in the darkness on the deserted interstate, and his spotlight beam blinded the outlaw as it bounced off his left rear-view mirror. The Iron Horseman pulled over and dismounted, shielding his eyes from the glare of the high beams and the spotlight on the trooper's unit. The biker reached into his saddlebag and pulled out a .44 bulldog magnum, aimed it at the lights, and fired four times.

Trooper Smith never made another report. One of the rounds hit him in the throat; another bullet struck him in the chest. He bled to death in his cruiser, trying to unbuckle his seat belt. In the last moments of his short life, the twenty-five-year-old officer wrote down two numbers, 35, believed to be from the motorcycle's license tag. He was found slumped over the wheel by fellow officers five minutes later.

A statewide alert was sent out over the air within minutes, and every motorcycle on the interstate from Grayson to Lexington was stopped by state police, local officers, and off-duty law enforcement personnel looking for a cop killer.

I went on duty in Lexington at 10 P.M. with my patrol dog, Sampson, a 100-pound Doberman pinscher. The statewide call had gone out thirty minutes before, and I was unaware of Trooper Smith's death. About 11 P.M., I headed down New Circle Road en route to Taco Tico where the girls at the counter always wanted me to be there at closing while they counted out their money. The night manager, Tammy, a pretty girl and always smiling, was ever ready for me with a cup of regular coffee with cream and sugar.

This night, I came upon a strange scene. Tammy didn't greet me and looked away as I rolled up to the take-out window. Something was wrong, so I waved my hand, rolling out of the place as fast as I could. I didn't want to get shot in the back, but I needed to get out to find out what was happening. I could see an Iron Horseman was in the place, and he gave me a mean look. His bike was outside. I figured he was getting ready to rob the place. Two other males were inside with him. The three girls at Taco Tico were not counting out their money nor cleaning up the place.

After driving down the street and parking across from the Embers Inn, I dismounted with Sampson at my side. With my shotgun in my right hand, I cut through the brush back towards Taco Tico. The three men were outside now. Two of the men had guns drawn on the Iron Horseman, who was laughing and walking towards his motorcycle.

I called in, "Headquarters, it looks like the showdown at the OK Corral at Taco Tico. There are three white males in some sort of a standoff, one Iron Horseman and two guys with beards, guns drawn. I'm watching from the gas station next door. Better send a back-up quick, but tell them to watch out for their safety. Somebody is gonna get killed soon."

The two guys with beards were Kentucky State Police detectives who had failed to notify Lexington police that they were on the trail of a suspect believed to be Trooper Smith's killer. They had shields on their belts and gave standard orders. They were even reading this Iron Horseman his rights as they tried to take him into custody. He was reaching for his saddlebag and his .44 bulldog revolver as I stepped silently up behind him.

Both officers raised their service revolvers and told the outlaw I was there with a deadly Remington 870 shotgun. He laughed, until I jacked a round into the chamber. The Iron Horseman stood straight up but didn't turn around. He told me in a clear voice, "If you think you can take me, try it. I got nothing to loose! You can't shoot me, I'm unarmed. Besides, I got a flak jacket on."

Under his leather vest, this 300-pound giant had an Army bullet-proof jacket. He also had a U.S. Marine Corps knife on his belt. He outweighed me by one hundred pounds. Sampson and I together weighed as much as he did, but we were no match for this six-foot-six mountain man from eastern Kentucky.

The outlaw didn't know Sampson was with me. The two detectives told him about my dog. One of them said, "That's a big Doberman. About a hundred pounds, isn't he, officer?"

"What's his name?" asked the other detective.

Sampson growled and barked. The outlaw became unnerved.

We were playing head games with this killer, trying to stay alive, waiting for more cops to show up. This guy wouldn't give us an excuse to drop him.

Sampson and I had always played a game while on patrol. I would talk like Humphrey Bogart in the classic film, *Casablanca* and would tell him, "Play it again, Sam!" Sampson couldn't play the piano, but he would flash his teeth and bark for a minute or so.

I told the detectives, "Sampson is his name, and he plays the piano, too. Play it again, Sam!"

Sampson barked and flashed his teeth for thirty seconds. When the outlaw turned around to see my dog, Sampson attacked, landing on his chest with his front paws. The dog's head smashed into the biker's face like a sledge hammer.

The outlaw collapsed over his motorcycle as if he had been shot in the chest at close range by a powerful handgun.

I aimed my shotgun at his head. I was going to give him the Clint Eastwood special, "Go ahead, punk, make my day!" But I was too professional to do that. I said nothing, hoping this guy wouldn't kick me as he struggled to get back on his feet.

Out of the woods behind me came three Lexington Metro Police officers, and this killer gave up, like most criminals do when faced with overwhelming force, quickly and without a struggle. The detectives searched the outlaw and his saddlebags. When they pulled out his .44 magnum is when I found out about Trooper Smith. That officer never had a chance.

Tammy came out of the Taco Tico and offered us some coffee. It was from the bottom of the pot and had been sitting there since 10 P.M. "Got any Scotch?" "How about some sour mash?" "What about Jim Beam?" were the responses she got.

Tammy answered, "I don't drink, but I guess you all do with stuff like this happening all the time."

I was shaking so much I couldn't safely hold a cup of hot coffee. I didn't need it anyway, after that brush with death. I stayed wide awake the rest of the night without any of the stuff.

After the prisoner transport arrived to haul away the Iron Horseman and a truck came to take his motorcycle to the evidence compound, I climbed back into my K-9 truck and rolled back on routine patrol. On my radio, I could hear the dispatcher ask for the status of the prisoner, and the paddy wagon driver respond, "En route with one Iron Horseman from Rick's Place. Play it again, Sam!"

Sampson, listening to the radio, barked and snarled for a minute or so. Then he settled down with his head on my lap for the rest of the night.

Danny Boy, the Vicious Dog

Danny Boy was a two-year-old, black and tan, eighty-pound German shepherd when he was sent to the humane society for adoption. He had a vicious snarl and growled at anybody who approached him. Nobody felt safe with him, and he was designated a vicious dog.

Raised on a construction site with a litter of puppies who became guard dogs for a large excavating company, the dog was abandoned when the company moved on to another job. The poor animal had never been socialized, never lived with a family, and never was trained to do anything but guard work, living behind a chain link fence. Desperate for food, he raided garbage cans and prowled his old guard post as he had been trained to do. The problem was that this construction site was now a subdivision, no longer a fenced vehicle park for construction materials and machinery. Danny Boy terrorized the new home owners in the neighborhood.

I met him on day thirty at the animal shelter. Most dogs don't make it to day thirty-one, unless adopted. He sat alone in his cage in a defensive posture, looking like the Great Sphinx at Giza, Egypt, dignified, wise, noble, and distant. He had not eaten in two days. The dog was in a rare mood indeed.

He flashed his teeth at me as I entered his cage. Instinctively I knew he was not going to attack. Sitting down next to him, I maintained eye contact with him, showing the dog I was not afraid. I stroked his head and spoke to him softly. The animal stretched out his paws, rolling over on his right side and breathing deeply. He was going to sleep. I sat with him for twenty minutes stroking his head and sides, talking softly, telling the dog, "Everything is alright. You're going home with me today."

During the entire time I spent with the dog, I called out names I thought he would understand, names which German shepherds are often given. Luger, Rommel, Bear, Prince, King. I soon realized the dog probably didn't have a name. Being an Irish-American, I called out names of shepherd dogs I had seen working in Ireland: Brandy, Buddy, Jack. He seemed to like the name Buddy but only responded slightly to it. Then I called him Boy, and he alerted quickly. Buddy Boy, then Danny Boy came to mind. He jumped up into a sitting position at the sound of Danny Boy. He didn't wag his tail, but he looked at me with great eye contact. I called him Danny Boy once again, and he yawned and made sounds like he was trying to speak to me. He sat down and leaned against me in the cage. We were bonding. After feeding him two large milk bones, I hooked my lead to his collar. He seemed ready to go out of the cage with me.

We walked out of the cage area into the adoption office. He hadn't had a bath, and Danny smelled very bad, growling at anybody who came near him. I thought he would bite somebody, but he didn't. I pulled him closer, and he staggered out the door with me. Once outside he was very calm, looking at me as if to say, "Well, let's go for a walk." Then he collapsed.

I almost had to drag him, for he had not been exercised in thirty days. I led him back to my K-9 truck in the parking lot. Opening the right door, I had to help him in. His entire attitude changed once inside the truck. He was ready to go on patrol. I assumed Danny Boy was accustomed to riding in pickup trucks or sleeping in them on the construction site.

My wife, Eileen, was in the truck. He greeted her with a relaxed look, began to breath quickly, and lay down on her lap, ready for the ride home. The dog fell asleep almost immediately in Eileen's arms. He was exhausted and very hungry.

When we arrived home, we introduced him to my three other patrol dogs, other German shepherds we had adopted. Danny Boy went off by himself and went to sleep again. The animal was absolutely worn out. I placed a bowl of dog chow next to him, stroking his head. He gave me a pleasant look as if to say, "Thanks, but I'm so tired. I'll eat later."

That night, I went to work at 9 P.M. as usual, with two patrol dogs, Kenny and Bear. Returning home at 5 A.M. the next morning, I found Danny still sleeping, but he had eaten all of his food and drank two bowls of water. He didn't pay attention to the other dogs, chewing on rawhide bones on the back porch before they all settled down for some rest.

That afternoon, Danny was out in the yard walking around by himself, watched by Bear, Kenny, and my white shepherd, Polar Bear. He didn't associate with those dogs but kept to himself. The following night, I took Danny Boy out on patrol with Polar Bear. The white shepherd could take care of me if I had some difficulty on patrol. I brought Danny along to get him accustomed to riding on patrol and possibly to do a building search if I had to answer a burglary alarm.

I had to respond to three alarms before midnight. As soon as Polar Bear jumped out of the truck on the first alarm call at a construction site, Danny Boy was ready to go to work, too. He barked until we returned from an area perimeter search after checking out two office trailers. As usual, the call was a false alarm, set off by adverse weather conditions. When Polar Bear got back into the truck, the two dogs had a conference. It seems that Danny was interviewing Polar Bear, getting all the news about what to do on this job.

The next two alarms were on the same five-acre construction site. Copper tubing for plumbing had been stolen from this site previously, and I used both dogs to search the property on each call. The dogs worked well together as a team. Danny Boy knew how to search construction sites quite well, walking out front like an Army scout dog on patrol looking for signs of an ambush. Polar Bear walked to Danny's left rear. Danny was suddenly in charge.

On the first call we found nothing out of place. It was another false alarm, activated by rain and wind. At the edge of the construction site, there was a swollen stream, and Danny plunged in and took a much needed bath. Polar Bear went for a swim with him. Then they raced back to the K-9 patrol truck, jumped in, and crashed down on each other, playing together. What a difference one day had made. Danny ate all the dog chow I had carried along on patrol that night, and he drank almost all of the water in a two-gallon bucket.

The second call was at midnight. This time we found a pickup truck with the driver's door open parked near a construction trailer. Polar Bear charged into the trailer and caught an employee stealing cash from the company manager's desk. Polar Bear barked, and I heard screams from inside the trailer. Danny Boy stayed glued to my left leg as if to tell me, "I'll protect you."

Knowing the thief may be armed, I wouldn't enter a dark trailer. Waiting outside, Danny and I closed in on the intruder's vehicle to cut off his escape. I approached the truck cautiously, and Danny jumped in behind the steering wheel. He waited in ambush with the door still open. I told him to stay.

Without a dog at my side, I called Polar Bear back from the trailer. He appeared at the door and returned to me as directed. The intruder was still inside. I called my partner, Mike Simpson, on the radio, requesting a police backup.

Polar Bear had a reputation at the police station. One officer, Carl Tuttle, called him the Great White Shark. Officer Kent Piatt called him Jaws. Polar Bear weighed almost 100 pounds and could tackle a man like a linebacker, brutally fast and hard, and then hold him in place.

As the police backup units were responding to my call for assistance, a barefoot intruder dashed out of the trailer and jumped into his truck, meeting Danny Boy nose-to-nose. Danny snarled at him, holding him in place. Looking straight forward, hands gripping his steering wheel, the burglar was ashen gray, frozen in horror with the dog breathing in his face and snarling the entire time. He must have thought he was going to die.

The paddy wagon took the intruder away but only after the paramedics had treated him for shock. Polar Bear had removed both of the the burglar's shoes, but Danny Boy hadn't touched the man. Danny Boy never did bite anybody in the four years I worked with him.

We recovered almost a thousand dollars in cash and many stolen checks that night. The intruder was a company employee who worked in the trailer office as a payroll clerk. He had already stolen about twelve checks made out to recently discharged employees, cashing them by using several different forms of false identification. His thefts had never been discovered since the payroll clerk generally cashed a stolen check made out to a former employee the week follow-ing that employee's dismissal. He had padded the company payroll to the tune of $4,000 a month for several months when caught by my patrol dogs.

When the construction site manager arrived on the scene and saw my two shepherds, he told me, "I'd like to reward them with something special, like milk bones or a steak. That white dog looks friendly enough, but that black and tan one looks bad."

I quickly answered, "They call Polar Bear, Jaws, but Danny Boy wouldn't harm a fly. He's a real Gentle Ben, but don't tell anybody. Most people think he's a vicious dog!"

The Worthless Dog

Kenny was not your regular German shepherd. He was pure bred, but he was short and stocky, not tall and slender. His nose was shorter than most police dogs, but his black and tan coloring and aggressive nature convinced everyone he was definitely a German shepherd. Kenny was extremely intelligent and very friendly, snuggling whoever fed him. He loved to go on patrol. His previous owner gave him up as a worthless dog because this two-year-old, sixty-pound beast was a fence climber.

Kenny now earned his keep working as a patrol dog four nights a week, ten hours per shift, with my K-9 security company. His handler was Mike Simpson.

My three-year-old patrol dog was Bear. Tall and slender with a large head, Bear dominated and controlled Kenny. They played together in the back yard all the time. On one occasion, while I was asleep in the house after a night shift, they watched two cable-TV installers climb over our fence and up a telephone pole. The cablevision technicians sat up there for six hours while Kenny and Bear watched them, holding the workers in place until I woke up. Those dogs would let somebody in, but it was another thing when somebody wanted to get out.

We had a patrol contract with Hall's Campers, a travel trailer, camper, and recreational vehicle (RV) dealership in Lexington. It was vandalized frequently because of its location on the beltway next to a budget motel which featured a country western band in the bar six nights a week. The parking lot was often full of red-necks and motorcycle bums. Thieves often watched the dealership from the motel parking lot and burglarized Hall's Campers between security patrol checks. Kenny and Mike Simpson patrolled this dealership and numerous other businesses four nights a week. When Mike was off, I patrolled the same beat the other three nights a week.

Kenny often went home with Mike Simpson when Mike was off duty, but when Mike went on vacation one June, the dog was left with me and Bear. They played all the time. They were the dynamic duo, and K-9 patrol was just a game for them.

While Mike was on vacation, I worked in his place. It was a seven-day work schedule for me. Seventy hours a week would exhaust anybody, especially on the night shift, 8 P.M. to 6 A.M. On Saturday night, day seven of Mike's vacation, I was worn out. I wasn't able to do all my work efficiently due to lack of rest. When the midnight check of the RV dealership was due, I had to have a break. I didn't walk the perimeter, check the locks, or patrol the inside of the lot that was surrounded by a six-foot chain-link fence. I just put Kenny and Bear inside the gates and went on a break. I needed some coffee and a rest for at least thirty minutes.

About 12:45 A.M., Sunday morning, I was ready to go back to work and drove back to the RV dealership. I didn't know it, but when I had left the property around midnight, my departure was watched by two thieves, one of them a dealership employee. They jumped the fence and broke into the office, stealing a cash box with $1,600. They were unaware that Kenny and Bear were inside the fence until they left the office and tried to return to their car in the motel parking lot.

When I arrived at the dealership, a large crowd had gathered. An ambulance was on the scene and Lexington Metro Police officers were just arriving. Inside the fence, Bear had stopped the RV dealership employee cold, removing his right shoe, tearing his trousers, and mauling his right leg as he struggled to fight off the German shepherd. A cash box lay open on the ground next to the suspect. Dollar bills blew across the gravel inside the fence as the wind picked up that hot, humid night.

Outside the fence, Kenny had the second thief flat on his face. When pursued by the two dogs, the second thief had jumped the fence when his buddy was tackled by Bear. The thief outside thought he had gotten away and was free to run when Kenny climbed over the fence after him, taking him to the ground instantly. Somebody at the motel watched the drama unfolding and dialed 911. Kenny was sitting on suspect number two, with his paw holding the man's head on the ground, snarling at the crowd nearby. He was telling them, "I'm in charge here!"

I approached Kenny and told him, "Good dog!" I tried to place Kenny in my patrol car, asking him where Bear was. Kenny broke away from me, scattered the crowd, and ran to the fence again, helping me find Bear and suspect number one. The police arrested the number two man, who babbled on about not being involved with the burglary. They repeatedly told him to remain silent but he carried on, insisting "that dog just attacked me!"

People in the crowd told me the true story. They were amazed at Kenny's ability to scale the fence, apprehending a thief without being ordered to do so. I informed them that Bear had probably signaled Kenny to catch the thief. They were unaware how well German shepherds can communicate with their handlers and each other. Both dogs knew I would return to the RV dealership shortly.

I opened the gates, and the paramedics drove into the dealership to take custody of the RV employee moaning from his wounds and his fight with an eighty-pound German shepherd.

The police dispatcher called the officers on the scene. "Four-eleven, are you clear yet?"

"Headquarters, we'll be clear shortly," answered one officer. "We just watched a tag team wrestling match at Hall's Campers. The winners were half the size of the losers. The score was German shepherds two and bad guys a flat zero. We'll take a report at Central Baptist Hospital. That's where these two fellers are heading. Four-eleven clear."

I had no trouble staying awake the rest of my shift that night. That worthless dog who climbed fences had earned himself a reputation. I was proud of him, and thinking about what had happened kept me wide awake.

A freelance photographer had taken a picture of Kenny with his paw on the number two suspect's head while he snarled at the crowd. The photo was on page one of the metro section in the Sunday newspaper the next day.

When Mike Simpson came off vacation on Sunday and tried to take Kenny out on patrol by himself, the dog refused to go to work. Mike and I had to make some changes in our work schedule so that I could send Bear out with Kenny. Those two dogs worked as a team seven nights a week for several years. Mike worked with them four nights, and Kenny and Bear were my partners the rest of the time. We tried to figure out a way to teach them how to drive, too, so Mike and I could just stay home.

Little Orphan Annie

It was a frosty Saturday morning, November 10, 1979, and the temperature readings were in the twenties. No snow had fallen yet, but winter was definitely here. I was on patrol with my K-9 partner, Bear.

About 5 A.M., I was just finishing up my shift, getting ready to go home to a nice, warm bed and much needed rest. I had just completed my work week and was looking forward to a weekend off with my family. Bear was part of the family, and he was glad to be going off duty, too.

As I rolled through the parking lot of a local food mart and gas station, a frequent armed robbery target, I noticed three police units there. They weren't at that location for coffee, and there had not been an armed robbery call on the police radio. When I stopped to inquire, the officers told me a man was missing from a nursing home half a mile away. An elderly patient, Mr. Thomas Ward, had walked away from the home at 2 A.M., wearing nothing but light pajamas and slippers. At 5 A.M., he had not been found and was presumed dead.

For three hours the police had searched for this patient on the grounds of the nursing home complex and in two parks nearby. Street people in the parks were of no assistance at all. Huddled in their cardboard boxes and blankets to fend off the cold, most wouldn't even talk to police officers or volunteers searching for Mr. Ward. His daughter suggested a check of the food mart since it was a warm place and an especially favorite one of her father's.

The man loved ice cream and visited this food mart with his daughter who bought him ice-cream sandwiches twice a week, winter, spring, summer, and fall. Since he suffered from Alzheimer's disease, he seldom recognized his family, but for some reason he always remembered the ice-cream sandwiches at this store. It was now a focal point in the search for him.

A homeless person I had seen before was standing in the food mart parking lot, shivering from the cold in a dirty Army field jacket and a grimy wool hat, carrying a sleeping bag. Her name was Annette, or Little Orphan Annie to those who knew her. Married for twenty years, the mother of four, Annie had a drinking problem, and her husband had forced her out of the house because of her drinking. An alcoholic, weighing less than a hundred pounds, she grubbed cigarettes and scrounged for food from trash cans at the food mart. At forty-five years old, she appeared to be in her seventies.

Annie had been a registered nurse but lost one job after another and her license due to her drinking. Educated and charming, she could carry on a conversation with most people on almost any topic. She was strong willed and street tough. She was also very gentle and blamed nobody but herself for the life-style she was forced to lead. I bought Annie a cup of coffee and some donuts, sat her down in the front seat of my K-9 truck, and asked her if she knew Mr. Ward. Unlike many of the other street people, Annie was usually willing to talk.

Annie didn't know Mr. Ward by name, but she remembered a patient about 75 years old who often sat on the small concrete bridge near the gas station. Annie told me she had begged for food from Mr. Ward's daughter on several occasions. In the middle of the conversation, Annie dozed off to sleep in my patrol unit once the heater warmed her frozen parts and she could relax. The woman was exhausted.

The police were talking to Mr. Ward's daughter inside the food mart. I asked the daughter if Mr. Ward had a favorite place to walk or sit on his trips to the store for ice cream.

"We sat on some park benches, mostly," she replied.

"Did he ever sit on a bridge near this store?" I inquired.

"On sunny days we sat down on the grass and sometimes on the bridge over there," she said, pointing past the end of the parking lot.

After dismounting Bear, who had been watching everything with great interest from the back of my truck, I approached the bridge and looked down over the edge. I could hear the trickle of a stream down below, but everything was dark until I lit up the area with my portable spotlight. Overgrown with weeds and scrub brush, the place was filthy with garbage, broken glass, papers, and trash thrown over the side by passing motorists.

When I had been at the bridge for only a few minutes, Annie appeared at my side, asking me what was going on. Although exhausted and hungry, she was ready to help in the effort to find Mr. Ward.

I told the three police officers and Annie that I was going down to take a look under the bridge with Bear. Using my rear bumper as an anchor, I threw down a sixty-foot nylon rappelling rope over the side and began a descent down into the blackness. Bear scrambled through the brush and slid down the muddy slope into the streambed to join me. It was brutally cold and damp under the bridge. Sweating from all the excitement, I began to chill as I started my search for Mr. Ward. Using my spotlight, I was alert for any sign of movement, but all I saw were rats in the streambed eating garbage thrown from above.

Suddenly I heard a thrashing sound and then a call for help. Annie had followed Bear down the slippery slope, fallen into the black murky water, and was in trouble. Soaked to the skin, she was chilled very badly. Shivering from the cold, she told me she was ready to help if I needed her assistance. I ordered her to climb out of the streambed and go back to the parking lot.

"You need a partner!" she shouted at me.

An ambulance was now on the two-lane bridge directly above us. I begged her to get into the ambulance and report to paramedics. She refused.

"I'm here to help. I don't want your pity," she told me in no uncertain terms.

Defiantly, Annie began to walk ahead of me, up to her ankles in icy water, stumbling every few seconds, slipping on rocks and garbage under the bridge. Bear gave me a backward glance, walking with her as if she were in charge. She hung on to Bear's collar searching for Mr. Ward.

Moments later, Bear began to bark halfway under the bridge. I threw my spotlight beam forward and found Mr. Ward, curled up in a fetal position with only blue-striped pajamas as protection from the dampness and cold. Still carrying her sleeping bag, Annie rushed forward and wrapped him in it. If anybody needed the warmth of the sleeping bag, it was Annie. It was hard to believe she would give this man her only possession at the risk of her own life.

Coordinating with paramedics on the roadway thirty feet above me, I requested more assistance while spotlighting Annie and her patient. It was a scene one only sees in *Time*, *Life*, or *Newsweek* magazine. Two wet, cold, miserable human beings were motionless, huddling together, trying to stay alive, waiting for help. I felt guilty being dry and protected from the cold by my tall rubber boots, waterproof cold-weather gear, hat, and gloves.

Two emergency service officers immediately came over the side of the bridge with blankets, first-aid packs, and an aluminum litter lowered by nylon ropes from above.

Annie told the officers she was a nurse and took charge, wrapping Mr. Ward in survival blankets. Loaded into the litter, he was raised up to the road surface. Annie supervised the extraction, standing there shivering in the cold as daylight began to light up the streambed and the filth under the bridge. Refusing any assistance, she climbed up to the roadway on her own. Calmly walking over to the ambulance, Annie told the paramedics she was a nurse. They brought her inside to warm up and gave her a cup of coffee.

I left the scene moments later. It was now 6:30 A.M., and I knew my wife would be worrying about me and Bear out there on patrol. I hadn't called home and knew she would begin to think the worst had happened. I phoned her right away, telling her that I would be home shortly, that we had just completed a search and rescue mission, and that everything was OK.

On the way home, Bear sat in my lap. The poor dog was wet and cold, covered with ice and mud, shivering from his exposure to the elements, never complaining about anything. What devotion and love he had shown serving humanity, I thought. Then I began to think about Little Orphan Annie. I knew where she had once lived and stopped by her home on the way off duty.

Her husband came to the door. When he saw my uniform, he expected the worst. "Is Annie OK?" he inquired, dead seriously.

"Do you still love that woman?" I asked him.

"You might not think so, officer, but I do. Is she OK?"

"Yes, she is," I responded, adding, "She's waiting for you at Good Samaritan Hospital. She saved a man's life this morning. Annie is quite a nurse. She needs some dry clothes, a hot meal, and some love."

"Thank you," he whispered, tears in his eyes, as he closed the door.

I walked back to my patrol car. Bear was snoring away, stretched out on the front seat, enjoying the blast of the car heater. By the time I woke Bear up and pushed him over to the passenger side of the front seat so I could get behind the wheel, Annie's husband was backing his car out of the driveway.

It's my guess he picked her up at Good Samaritan Hospital and took her home. Some months later, Annie received an award for life saving from the American Red Cross, although Mr. Ward had died. Her husband was standing beside her in the photo on page one of the *Herald Leader*.

I hardly recognized her in the photo. She was wearing a white uniform with an American Red Cross nursing pin and a name tag. She had gained thirty pounds and looked well nourished. Only when I read that she had saved Mr. Ward, a man missing and presumed dead, did I realize she was the same homeless creature who stood with me in that frigid streambed that cold November day.

I never saw her again on the street.

General Patton

In central Kentucky we had a thug who called himself General Patton. He had a military appearance, wearing Army field uniforms with combat boots and a patrol cap. He drove a dull brown, four-wheel-drive Chevy Blazer, with a front license plate with four white stars centered on a red background. He had a high-pitched voice and stood well over six-feet tall, as did George S. Patton, Third Army commander in World War II.

This thug had robbed Wendy's, McDonald's, and Burger King and had broken into change boxes at a car wash on Richmond Road in Lexington. One night, I observed him through powerful binoculars at the car wash cleaning up his Blazer. I suspected he would break into the change box, but he didn't. At midnight, the owner told me he had cleaned out the change box at 10 P.M. when he saw Patton cruising the neighborhood. The owner was certain Patton had ripped him off at least twice, taking well over $100 each time. I told the owner the police were looking for Patton as a suspect in a series of strong-arm robberies.

Patton's method of operation was very simple. He would enter an almost deserted fast-food restaurant just before closing and jump the counter after ordering some food. When a cash drawer was opened, he would take what was there and run off. He always attacked female counter attendants. It was rumored he had a .45 caliber pistol that he flashed to some victims who moved too slowly when he demanded cash during a robbery.

Not one victim could remember what his face looked like. It was always the clothing description that identified him in police reports. "He was just big and mean," one attendant told me at Wendy's on Richmond Road across from the car wash. He was hard to catch when on the move. He drove like a wild man in his Blazer, generally across open fields and construction sites. Police cruisers could not box him in.

Only a K-9 unit with four-wheel drive could catch him, I told myself. I was in the K-9 security patrol business and had a Chevy Blazer. I also had an excellent patrol dog, Teddy Bear. With the car wash under contract, I could pursue Patton if he broke into their cash box, but I had no authority to apprehend him if he hit a fast-food restaurant unless I was there at the time.

Patton disappeared every so often, completely dropping out of sight. After sixty days, he would be back, smashing and grabbing again. I wanted to know who he was, so I always watched for his Blazer to get a rear tag number.

My persistence paid off one December evening about 11 P.M. while patrolling a contract, Conrad Chevrolet, on Richmond Road two blocks from Wendy's. Patton's Blazer was parked next to a furniture warehouse one block from the fast-food restaurant. The red license plate up front with the four stars was bent and badly scratched. The rear tag was missing, but a cardboard temporary tag was taped to the back of the truck. It read, "LOST TAG." It was so well printed that it could have been mistaken for a personalized license plate.

I notified a police officer within ten minutes, but the vehicle was moved almost immediately. Patton must have been watching me. At least Metro Police had been alerted, and the information went out over the air. The cops were looking for him on Richmond Road too.

I rolled up to Wendy's drive-in window, ordered a double cheese plain and a frosty, and asked if Patton had been there. The girl at the window didn't know who I was talking about. The manager came outside and told me to stop asking questions and frightening his help.

I drove back to the Conrad dealership and then checked the car wash, looking for the dull brown Blazer with the lost tag. Listening to the police scanner all the time, I heard a double beep, then the call went out: "Armed robbery, McDonald's, Richmond Road. Male, white, six-feet, twenties, bald head, Army fatigues, .45 blue steel automatic, left on foot, no direction of travel."

Patton was in the area. I knew it. Now, I wondered, where is his truck? Police cars began cruising Richmond Road in great numbers, checking out parking lots, fast-food restaurants, and Conrad Chevrolet.

One of the officers rolled up to me and thanked me for the tip I had given the police just minutes before this call was dispatched. The lieutenant was very pleased and told me to keep alert. He said, "Signal us with your spotlight if you see Patton."

Patton had disappeared as usual. He had taken $500 from McDonald's at gunpoint. He would have taken out Wendy's if I had not been so close. I was sure he knew where I was, so I watched myself.

It began raining a few minutes later, and visibility was dismal. Another officer drove up, and we discussed the scenario. Patton was a master at escape and evasion, this state trooper told me. "He must be one of those Special Forces guys," he commented.

"I don't think so! I was one of those Special Forces guys. This guy is a thug, a wannabe," I answered back with anger. The state trooper drove off slowly, feeling like a jerk, not saying another word.

My security business had a good reputation in Lexington. Police often asked us for assistance, and our coordination with the Metro cops was very good. My officers were just as tough as any cops on the street. There were four of us on duty this night, and we all had K-9s and unmarked trucks. Two of my fellow officers called me on our radio net and told me they were en route to assist me. I assigned one to Conrad Chevrolet and the other to the car wash. I went looking for Patton.

We had several car dealerships, apartment complexes, and RV dealerships to patrol on the east end of Lexington, as well as one construction site and a Christmas tree lot. I checked out all the contracts, keeping my partners aware of my location.

As luck would have it, I found Patton's truck on the construction site where a shopping center was being built on Richmond Road. It was submerged up to the front hood in mud. Without lights, while escaping cross-country from the McDonald's robbery, he had driven into a newly dug foundation. I scanned the area with my spotlight but saw no movement. My buddies notified Metro Police who surrounded the site in two minutes.

The rain was heavy now, and with the temperature in the forties, I knew nobody in his right mind would be out walking. Patton was a master at escape and evasion, they had said. We would soon find out, I thought.

The wind was blowing so hard that the rain was coming down at a forty-five degree angle. Visibility was terrible. Patton was out there somewhere, and I knew he was on foot. I looked for him for three hours, but he was nowhere to be found. I figured the cops were right.

By 3 A.M., the police traffic had died down on the radio and on Richmond Road. Patton's truck was still on the construction site, but he would be back before dawn to get his truck, I was sure.

I let my fellow security officers go off duty at 4 A.M., but I decided to stay out until 5 A.M., confident I would find this guy. One of the officers, Mike Simpson, told me he wouldn't leave me out there alone, so I told him to stay at Conrad Chevrolet and act as my backup. He would call the police by phone if I signaled him on the radio that I had found my target.

At 5 A.M., Mike went off duty but stayed on the radio and wouldn't go off the air or to sleep until I told him I was home. Meanwhile, I went to check Conrad Chevrolet one last time.

Next to the dealership was a Gulf gas station that opened at 6 A.M. I noticed somebody walking around the station. No vehicles were at the station, so I knew it wasn't an employee who had come to work early. It had to be somebody on foot. I dismounted with Bear and approached the rear of the station on foot. By radio I told Mike, "Bear alerted on the men's rest room." I drew my shotgun from my truck and approached the door with Bear glued to my left leg.

I kicked open the door and rushed in with my shotgun and flashlight. Bear barked and growled, pinning a man against the urinal just inside the door. There he stood, Patton, soaked to the skin, drying himself off, stripped down to his underwear, all six-feet, 200 pounds of him glaring at me like a wounded cougar about to charge. He had used part of the roll of cloth towels in the rest room cleaning himself up. His .45 was in the sink, as clean as a good soldier's weapon should be. It was unloaded. He had no ammunition or even a clip. The money from the McDonald's robbery was also in the sink, in a McDonald's sandwich bag.

Patton looked down at Bear who barked viciously, holding him in place. I commanded Bear, "Out!" Bear stopped barking, continuing to flash his teeth. Patton slid down to the grimy, wet, cold floor, putting his wrists together, and began crying. Keeping my shotgun aimed at his chest, I put my flashlight on the floor and grabbed my handcuffs. I threw them at Patton, ordering him to put them on. While Bear watched, Patton put the handcuffs on both of his wrists. Bear then guarded against any other movements he might make. I took a few steps back, picked up my flashlight, and called Mike Simpson on the radio.

"Mike, call Metro. Got my man at the Gulf Station, in the men's room on the floor. Got his gun. Bear's holding him against the wall for the paddy wagon."

The man began glaring at me again and started to move. I got very nervous, but Bear held his ground, barked twice, and the man stopped. The paddy wagon arrived about ten minutes later, along with two other police units, and Patton was taken into custody.

Patton confessed to several strong-arm robberies and the McDonald's robbery. He also confessed to destroying the car wash cash boxes several times. His confessions also closed out many other investigations in Lexington of business break-ins, gas station robberies, and construction trailer thefts.

Patton's real name was Gerard Pettit. His mother called him George after George S. Patton. His grandfather had served in the Third Army with Patton in 1945, but this poor man had served in the military for only a few months. Pettit had been discharged unfit for duty due to psychological problems. He had spent several months at private psychiatric facilities because of his drug dependency, which accounted for his regular disappearances. In his small trailer in a mobile home park, police detectives found numerous military uniforms, medals, weapons, military magazines, and countless paperback books about military adventures. His vehicle had been put together from scrap parts and never had been registered.

Bear and I got the credit for taking Patton off the street. Bear and I had terminated Patton's career, but I felt sorry for the man.

The Smoking Bandit

July 21 was a hot, sticky day. At 4 A.M., it was almost eighty degrees, and the humidity was a hundred percent. I was on K-9 patrol, and we were answering an alarm at Paul Miller Ford in Lexington. My partner was Wilhelm von Entenfall, affectionately known as Bear. I dismounted in the rear of the dealership and worked my way along with Bear to the service department where the alarm company had detected scratching noises and two voices. I couldn't see a thing, but Bear did.

Two teenagers had used a coat-hanger wire to retrieve the keys out of the early-bird service drop box. A customer had left his vehicle for maintenance, placing his keys in an envelope in the box, along with instructions for the service department. The kids decided to steal the car before Paul Miller Ford knew the car was in for service. The owner would not have known his car was stolen until after the kids had taken it for a joy ride and, possibly, destroyed it.

Bear spoiled their plans and saved the owner and the dealership hundreds, if not thousands, of dollars. The dog detected the teenagers under the car and let me know where they were hiding. We recovered the keys, notified the teenagers' parents, and arrested the youths for attempted auto theft. At 5 A.M., we went off duty, hot, sweaty, and dirty from the game of hide and seek with the thieves under the car they had planned to steal.

When we arrived home thirty minutes later, Bear was breathing heavily, and I was afraid he would suffer heat exhaustion. My wife, a nurse who worked the day shift, was just getting out of bed. She suggested we let Bear stay in our air-conditioned house because there was no way he could get rest outside in the hot weather. He usually slept outside under the trees next to our back porch. When my wife left for work, Bear crawled onto her side of the bed and slept like a baby for six hours in air-conditioned comfort.

He woke me up exactly at 12 noon wanting to go for a walk. I had a better idea and asked Bear if he wanted to go for a swim that hot day. He went crazy, jumped all over the house, scratched at the front door, and barked like a wild animal. "Yes!" he was telling me.

In the sixteen years I did K-9 work, I never had a dog better than Bear. A black and tan, highly intelligent, high-speed police dog, Bear never worked on a leash. He understood complete sentences. Out on the street he anticipated moves a criminal would make. He was the first of many dogs to work with me in my K-9 security business. All other dogs were compared to Bear. He was the bravest of the brave, the most loyal dog I've ever known, and by far the best partner I ever had.

It was the start of my weekend off, so I didn't care that I hadn't had enough sleep that day. Back in the vehicle with Bear at 1 P.M., I headed out for Richmond Road where there was a local park that had a beautiful lake.

On the way to the lake and a good swim for my partner, I monitored a 911 call. "Armed robbery, Bank of Lexington, Richmond Road. Subject wearing a gray sweat suit with a hood and a ski mask. Six-feet, 200 pounds. Undetermined amount of cash taken. Subject activated a blue dye pack when exiting the bank. Subject armed with a .45 caliber blue steel automatic."

We had a real Smokey and the Bandit that day. Dye packs explode when an electric circuit is broken as thieves leave the bank area after a robbery. The smoke trails out the door behind the thief as he runs. Blue dye packs are usually given out to armed robbers mixed in with marked money to identify them, their clothes, their stolen money, and everything else they have in their possession.

I couldn't help thinking how stupid this man must have been, robbing a bank in a sweat suit and ski mask on a hot, humid day. He would stand out like a sore thumb on Richmond Road where most persons would be in business clothing or shorts and T-shirts. Then I thought, "Maybe he's not so stupid. He could get out of the sweat suit and be in shorts and a T-shirt and blend in with everybody else in the area." In a T-shirt and Levi's myself, I was off duty, and since it wasn't my call, I just moved on to the park with Bear. I was going to keep my promise and take my partner for that swim.

As I prepared to turn into the park, police cars were racing back and forth on Richmond Road, checking side streets, parking lots, and shopping centers for the suspect. I couldn't help pulling alongside of a Metro Police unit watching one shopping center. I asked the officer, "Anything new on the Bank of Lexington smoking bandit?"

He quickly answered, "Headquarters has three calls placing him on Richmond Road heading for the Interstate. He probably has a car out here someplace. He'll change clothes and be gone in all the traffic."

"I'll be at the park with Bear if you need a K-9 team," I told him and moved on to the parkside lake.

Since he never worked on a lead, I didn't bring his leash, so Bear was out in a flash and headed for the cool water as soon as I stopped my truck. Police cars rolled through the park and raced back and forth, to and from Interstate 75 a few miles away. They must have been closing in on the bandit, probably having found an abandoned car with blue dye stains on the front seat.

While in the lake, Bear began acting strange. He splashed out of the water and started watching a man who looked like a camper, with a bag, washing his clothes and taking a bath. He was wading along in shorts and a blue-stained T-shirt. I stared at him, and he glared back with a terrified look on his face. Then he turned around, saw my marked K-9 patrol unit, and took off running as fast as he could.

It was too hot for me to run but not for Bear. The dog closed in on the man and, without a command, Bear pulled him to the ground in a matter of seconds. The man was carrying a sports bag, and it was stained with blue dye. We had the bandit — or rather Bear did.

Since I was unarmed, I walked slowly towards the man, who placed his hands on top of his head like a prisoner of war. Bear guarded him until I got close. I looked at the man's belongings, which included a blue-stained sweat shirt with a hood. I told him he was under arrest for armed robbery. But without a portable radio, handcuffs, or a duty weapon, I was at a serious disadvantage. This guy was armed, according to the first police radio call.

"Where is your gun?" I shouted.

"I don't have a gun, man!" he whimpered back.

"You have a gun according to the witnesses at the Bank of Lexington. I have every right to shoot you, or the dog can tear you to pieces, if you make a move. Where's the gun?" I shouted again. I reached behind my back as if I had my duty weapon in my belt. "Take him, Bear!" I ordered.

With his head low, Bear moved forward at a slow pace like he was stalking game. The dog's teeth flashed, and he barked viciously. The dog would only attack if the man made an offensive move. The bandit didn't know that.

"Is that dog gonna bite me?" the man cried out.

"No, just going to shake you up for a few minutes," I replied. "Where's the gun?" I shouted again.

The man buried his face down in the ground, pulling his hands and arms under him, prepared for the worst. Bear, not knowing what to do, walked over to the man, sniffing him, then placing his left front paw on the man's shoulder. The bandit screamed out in agony as if he had been dismembered.

I opened up the bag and found a .45 caliber automatic, a bunch of blue money, car keys, sweat pants, a ski mask, and the suspect's wallet. I emptied his pistol. It had a round in the chamber and five rounds in the magazine.

A Metro Police unit rolled by, and I signaled the car to stop. "Got the bandit!" I shouted.

Six police cars were on the scene in two minutes, along with prisoner transport, detectives, and two women from the bank that had been robbed. A few minutes later, the FBI had two agents on the scene. They had located the suspect's car and were closing in when Bear spotted the man.

One of the agents was a neighbor of mine who knew my dog quite well. "Did Bear tear him up, Paul?" the agent asked.

"Not Bear, you know that," I shot back with a smile on my face. Bear had a reputation in Lexington for managing things well. He terrorized people with his stalking, barking, and flashing teeth. His reputation was much worse than his bite.

The suspect was taken into custody, and I turned over all the evidence, including his .45 caliber automatic. "Thanks very much, Paul," the FBI agents told me as they escorted the Smoking Bandit away for identification by the ladies from the Bank of Lexington.

Bear went back into the lake for another swim, and we stayed in the park for about twenty minutes while the prisoner was identified and interrogated. I was talking to a bunch of other officers, then started to leave the park just as the press began to converge on the scene. Along with the press came two Kentucky State Police troopers.

As I headed back to my truck, out of uniform, in T-shirt and jeans, with Bear off lead, one of the troopers shouted out to me, "Sir, you can't have your dog in this park without a leash!"

Members of the press who had monitored the arrest on the police radio told the trooper that Bear had captured the Smoking Bandit. The officer's face turned red, he began to laugh at himself, placed his hands over his ears, and shouted, "I don't wanna hear it!"

On the radio and TV news that night, the FBI gave a good account of their quick and professional work capturing an armed robber without having to fire a shot. There was no mention of the dog off the leash in the park.

Caveman

Caveman was a professional thief in Lexington, Kentucky, who scouted out his targets and broke into businesses at night or burglarized unoccupied homes and self-service storage facilities. He carted off a small fortune in personal possessions, generally selling them at flea markets in Kentucky, Indiana, Ohio, and West Virginia. Radios, stereos, televisions, office equipment, tables, and lamps were on display at his booths. His friends and family were in this very profitable business with him.

This thief could not be mistaken for anybody else. He was unique in personal appearance and behavior. He was very hairy and looked like a caveman one sees in a museum. Short, stocky, bearded, and with shoulder-length hair, he always wore farmer's coveralls, generally without a T-shirt in the summer. During winter months, he wore a black hooded sweatshirt with his coveralls. His personal hygiene was poor. His clothes were generally filthy, and he frightened people in public with his appearance and unusual behavior. He could run like a deer and ride a bicycle faster than a Frenchman in the Tour de France, and police on foot could not catch him. Caveman would hide stolen goods in any number of places. He had taken a locksmith's course and could open almost any lock in a matter of seconds.

Rumor had it that this master thief was a genius who played the poor soul game when stopped by police or when taken into court after being charged with theft. He had no known address or phone number. He always told police or the judge he was homeless and unemployed, thrown out on the street by his family because he couldn't hold down a job. Investigations revealed that he lived above a garage in a residential neighborhood on the east side of town. An old, unmaintained home adjacent to the garage was paid for and owned by Emile Mathis of Paintsville, Kentucky. James Mathis was the name Caveman used to identify himself in court.

Informants told officers Caveman had access to a series of self-service storage lockers in town in which he sometimes slept and stashed stolen goods. None were registered to his name or names which he used. He had no automobile operator's license or social security number.

The storage units were registered to persons who were not aware Caveman was using their facilities. Most lockers were half full of household goods registered to persons who had moved away from Lexington, planning to retrieve their possessions at a later date. Some lockers were filled with household goods belonging to owners who did not pay their rent. It is a mystery how he knew which lockers were full of unattended goods at any given location.

Once caught getting into a locker registered to a police sergeant, Caveman was arrested. Nothing had been stolen, and he was released. He claimed the sergeant's unit was next to his sister's storage facility, and since there was no lock on the sergeant's locker door, he opened it by mistake. The policeman told me he had two locks on the unit and both had been picked open or cut off and thrown away. The locker next to the police officer's unit, allegedly Caveman's sister's locker, was empty and had been unoccupied for three months. Caveman was arrested on a Wednesday night and then released from jail on Thursday afternoon.

Caveman was generally seen at self-storage facilities on Wednesday nights. One informant told me that Caveman would burglarize units on Thursdays and Fridays, selling his stolen property on Saturdays and Sundays.

I chanced onto Caveman on a Wednesday night, about 11 P.M., August 13, 1979, while patrolling the east end of Lexington with two German shepherd patrol dogs, Danny Boy and Bear. The Caveman was checking out self-storage facilities near the Embers Inn. I watched him for twenty minutes from the parking lot of the motel in an unmarked GMC Jimmy. He tried every door in a 200-unit warehouse. None was open. Next, Caveman disappeared into the wooded area behind the motel. He was unaware of my surveillance. I discussed my observations with two other officers, and they told me, "He'll be back with bolt cutters later tonight."

At 3 A.M., on August 14, Caveman returned to the motel area. I had been looking for him for three hours while on patrol and spotted him on his bicycle with an orange flag. He was in coveralls, without a shirt, and barefoot. I followed him and watched him.

In front of the Embers Inn motel, a large Harley-Davidson motorcycle was parked at the door. The owner had left it there with two helmets and two leather jackets while he spent the night with his lady friend. They had been drinking and dancing to country-western music from 10 P.M. until 1 A.M., according to the security guard who said he was "watching the bike."

Caveman told the security guard that somebody was fighting in the parking lot. While the guard went to investigate the nonexistent disturbance, Caveman stole both helmets and both jackets and disappeared into the woods behind the motel. I called in the theft on my mobile telephone, knowing Caveman monitored police radio traffic. I didn't want him to know I was watching him.

On foot with Bear and Danny, I set out after him. He was unaware we were on his trail, and we caught up with him 200 yards from the motel by 4 A.M. He had already hidden his stolen property. As he was returning to his bicycle, we surprised him.

Danny knocked him to the ground off the bicycle and I ordered him to halt. Caveman disregarded my command and disappeared into the darkness across a stream. Danny and Bear remained with me, and we confiscated the Caveman's bicycle, which was also stolen property. We searched the area for an hour but could not find Caveman or the stolen helmets and jackets. I assumed they were stashed in a self-serve storage locker, but I was wrong.

After some rest the next day, I returned to the motel, hoping to get some information from the bike owner about his stolen property. He had checked out after filing a theft report with the police at 9 A.M. Caveman also stole an automatic pistol and some drugs from the saddlebags, according to the security guard, who refused to name his source of information.

I went to the storage warehouse manager and reported my observations and actions the night before. The manager told me that owners of property in twenty lockers were behind in their rent. We began to check each locker. Fourteen of the twenty lockers were empty. Every locker was secured. All locks had been opened and resecured after contents had been removed.

One thing was missing from the crime scene since I had worked it early that morning. A Ryder truck had been parked at the warehouse complex, but it was gone now. I hadn't taken down the license tag number and doubted if I would be able to find it again. Yet I began watching for Ryder trucks at self-service storage warehouses the next night.

On the next Sunday, August 17, I decided to go shopping at the flea market in Georgetown, Kentucky, near Lexington. I found a Ryder truck and Caveman's display tables. I wrote down the vehicle tag number this time and then went looking for helmets, jackets, and pistols. I photographed Caveman's wares from several angles. The tables were not attended by anyone. When I asked the owner of the flea market who had rented these tables in this display area, he told me I would need a court order to get that information and said, "Client identification is confidential, mister." The owner was very nervous as I photographed every table again. "What are you doing that for?" he inquired.

I replied, "It's very confidential." I also photographed the Ryder truck. I got some angry looks from dealers and left the area.

The Ryder truck manager in Lexington was a friend of mine. I had done some private security work for him during a truckers' strike and often used his truck wash to clean my K-9 truck on hot nights since two German shepherds can smell up a truck very quickly in the summer. On Monday, the manager checked on the Ryder truck information I gave him. It had been taken off his lot without being rented that Sunday or Monday. He would watch for it when it was returned and file a stolen vehicle report in the interim.

The truck was returned Monday night by an employee. It was loaded with flea market goods. The employee was arrested, as was his companion in the front seat next to him, who was — you guessed it — Caveman. Caveman went to jail again. He was out on the street again by Wednesday morning, August 20.

The Ryder manager dropped charges when his employee paid for the truck rental but fired him for unauthorized use of company property. I later found out the truck had been used to store the goods stolen from the self-service storage warehouse next to the Embers Inn on August 13. Caveman also stashed the motorcycle helmets and jackets in the truck. They were among the articles still in the back of the vehicle when it was returned on Monday. Many of the household goods, radios, stereos, tools, clothing, and boots in the truck had been on display at Caveman's flea market tables in Georgetown.

Getting owners to identify and reclaim their goods was most difficult because most owners were out of town or had already collected insurance money for their stolen property. Charging Caveman or the Ryder employee with possession of stolen property was not worth the trouble as all the items were well worn, used up, and nearly worthless. We had to catch Caveman in the act of burglarizing property to put him away for any period of time. He was temporarily out of business now, however, with his transportation cut off, his flea market operation discovered, and cops watching for him all over Lexington and Georgetown. Caveman dropped out of sight or just crawled back into his cave for the fall and winter.

Six months later, in February 1980, while on patrol in the parking lot of a Holiday Inn on the north side of town, I saw the Caveman again. He ran from me as soon as he saw my K-9 patrol unit.

Television sets had been stolen from this motel, and the manager suspected it was internal theft. He requested extra patrol. It was a great place to work with my two patrol dogs, Danny and Bear. The weather in February was quite bad and the motel was only half booked most nights. We could do building searches and get free coffee while on breaks from patrol in the frigid weather.

Somebody knew which rooms were unoccupied. These were entered at night and TV sets removed. All TVs were clearly marked Property of Holiday Inn, so they couldn't be sold at flea markets. We figured the thief had a list of customers in private homes. I immediately jumped to the conclusion that Caveman was in business again and started looking for Ryder trucks or commercial vans in the parking lots.

Out on foot patrol with Danny and Bear, I found one blue van without a license tag. It was filthy, covered with salt and road grime, and the tires were bald. It was obviously not a guest vehicle. I pulled open the back door, and it looked like a homeless person's hideout, with trash, newspapers, dirty clothes, and food wrappers scattered throughout. I removed the keys from the ignition and took them to the front desk.

The Holiday Inn security guard at the front desk just happened to be the same man who had worked at the Embers Inn the previous August, the man who had watched the motorcycle on August 14. Our eyes met, and he knew I suspected he was the guy who worked with Caveman. He told me the van belonged to him and that the missing license plate was easily explained. "I lost it in the snow and couldn't find it." As the vehicle was not registered or insured, he received a citation.

The next morning, I spoke to the manager and told him I suspected his security guard was the thief. I also told him about the van. The manager gave me an address and a phone number for the security guard's home. I decided to pay the man a visit. He lived in a trailer park two miles from the Holiday Inn.

I got some hard looks from people in the trailer park when I rolled in with my K-9 unit about 4 P.M. that afternoon. It was cold and wet and nasty that day. All residents were inside their mobile homes. When I saw the blue van which belonged to the security guard, I started asking neighbors about him. Nobody knew his name, but they knew he worked at night. Two residents told me they thought he was a drug dealer. I also found out he had a strange friend, the Caveman.

One elderly female resident asked me to come in and sit down, offering me a cup of coffee. She was watching a movie on a TV set marked Property of Holiday

Inn. I asked her where she had gotten the set. She told me the boys next door gave it to her since her set was in need of a new picture tube. "They are the nicest boys. They shop for me once in a while when I can't get out in all this bad weather." I didn't want to tell the woman the property was stolen. I called the Holiday Inn manager on the phone, and he paid the woman a visit. The serial number on the set matched one listed in a stolen property report filed in January 1980. The value of the set was over $300.

The manager went next door to the security officer's trailer and knocked on the door while I remained with the neighbor. The guard let his manager in, and Caveman was on the way out the door a few minutes later. Inside the trailer in plain view were two TV sets on the stolen property list from January. As the manager began to leave the trailer, he got into a fight with the security guard. I stepped in and placed the man under arrest for assault. A search warrant was issued, and a trailer full of stolen property was recovered.

After three hours at the detective bureau, the security guard gave an account of his business dealings with the Caveman. The blue van was Caveman's transportation when his Ryder truck dealership connection shut down. It had been taken off an impound lot in January 1980. Records revealed the van had been stolen from Paintsville, Kentucky, on Christmas Eve, 1979.

The guard gave us three locations for Caveman's major residences. Search warrants were issued for all three, and more stolen property was recovered. Although property from numerous burglaries was recovered, Caveman could not be found or connected to the properties or stolen goods. The security guard was not considered a credible witness against the Caveman. Caveman had evaded police once again.

A month later, on patrol near the Paul Miller Ford dealership on the east side of town, I spotted Caveman looking at used vans about 3 A.M. one Thursday morning. I drove past the dealership and parked behind a gas station two blocks away. Dismounting my best patrol dog, Bear, I worked my way back to the Ford dealership, looking for the thief. There he was, trying to open doors, soaking wet in a black hooded sweatshirt, overalls, and sneakers. The man was exhausted and a frightening site to behold. It was one of those nights in the forties and raining, pure misery to be out in the weather.

I approached him from the rear with Bear at my side. If he came at me, Bear would make sure I wouldn't get hurt. I asked Caveman if he wanted to go to the Salvation Army for a place to stay, a hot meal, and a change of clothes.

There were no warrants on the man, and he wasn't doing anything now which could be listed as a criminal offense. We were in an open parking lot with no fences and no gates to keep anybody out. I felt sorry for the man. It was like the end of a fox hunt. The game was over. I had wanted to put this man out of business, and I had.

He spoke to me in a clear and loud voice, "You and that dog have given me a lot of grief. Just leave me alone, please!" He stumbled off the lot and started to trot out onto Winchester Road, heading for Interstate 75. I never saw Caveman in Lexington again.

Some years later, I was talking to a police officer who asked me how Bear was doing. That good dog had died a year before. I told the officer Bear was dead.

"Did Caveman kill him?" he asked.

"No, he died of cancer. Why?" I replied.

Caveman hated that dog, Bear, the officer said. Caveman told all his friends that Bear and I had stalked him for a year. Everywhere he turned we were there, day and night, watching him drive down New Circle Road, eating at McDonald's, walking through the park. We even watched him while he was fishing at the lake. We put his friends in jail. He couldn't hold down a job he was so nervous because we were watching him. He lives up in eastern Kentucky now, in the mountains. He won't come back to Lexington ever!

File photo, Maryland State Police, Salisbury, Maryland, 1985

The author with Bonnie Bear
When Teddy Bear died in 1983, Bonnie Bear started her career as my patrol dog. She worked with me until her death in 1992. I bought her from a retired U.S. Air Force Security Policeman because she looked so much like Suzie, my K-9 partner in Vietnam in 1965.

Bonnie was a real crowd pleaser when I took her to schools to teach kids about personal safety and drug prevention.

Not Too Simple Simon

Simon was a big, beautiful, strong, black and tan German shepherd and my patrol dog from 1987 to 1992. He weighed in at seventy-five pounds. Fast as lightening and very intelligent, Simon had a stare that would stop movement of any kind. When he barked, everybody listened. When he flashed his teeth and growled, suspects would kneel down on the ground and be still.

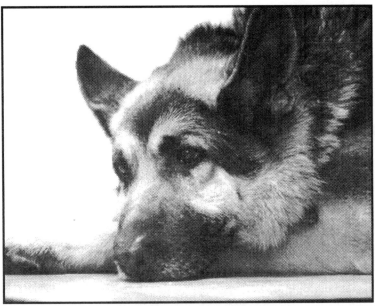

Simon

Photo by LaFayette High School newspaper staff, Lexington, Kentucky, 1988

A local woman was Simon's first owner. She brought him from the pound where he had been dropped off at six months old. Simon's mother had worked on a construction site for two years, guarding earth-moving equipment. He was born on the site and abandoned when the contractors moved on to another job. Simon needed a lot of love, and his new owner adored him.

When the woman's husband came home one day upset about a personal matter, the man and his wife got into a very heated argument. Simon took the man to task for abusing his wife, and the man took Simon back to the pound to be destroyed. However, the woman happened to be a member of the board of directors of the humane society, and so she saw to it that Simon got a good home, not the needle.

Simon was given to me for K-9 patrol work in Lexington. He was a fine dog from the start. He didn't like men much, but he did like me for some reason. All he wanted was love. I gave him plenty of hugs, groomed him daily, shared scraps of food with him, and fed him every day on time. In my patrol truck, he sat up front with me on cold nights, head in my lap, snoring away, sprawled out on the front seat. Simon loved my wife and just about any woman who approached him. He was a ladies' man.

Simon's partner was Bonnie, a classic female German shepherd, about sixty pounds. Also a black and tan, Bonnie looked like the perfect mate for Simon, who protected her from harm while out on patrol. They both appeared on TV on the Eleven O'Clock News one night after they apprehended a thief at Paul Miller Ford in April 1987.

The thief was an employee who had come back after hours to steal some truck tires. The man had parked his truck on a back street near a telephone pole adjacent to the fence at the rear of the auto dealership. After climbing up the telephone pole, he jumped over the fence into the service lot. He loaded four tires and some expensive tools into his truck bed by throwing them over the fence.

Before I arrived on the scene, Simon surprised the employee and held him in place for me. He had approached the man from the rear, growled once, barked once, and sat down to watch the suspect. The thief was so glad to see me as I made my rounds of the property that at first I had no idea what was going on.

"Put me in jail please! Anything is OK if you'll just call off that dog," he pleaded with me through the fence. He thought he was going to die. Then I saw Simon, the truck, and the stolen property.

Two burglary detectives commented in their report that they believed Simon was very smart to stop the man only after the thefts had taken place. He behaved as a seasoned detective on a stake-out, watching the crime in progress, then holding the suspect, and preserving the crime scene after the felony had been committed. He seemed to understand the law. They called him Not Too Simple Simon.

When it was my turn to give K-9 orientations and D.A.R.E. classes at local high schools, I brought Simon along to the classroom. He was impressive, sitting next to me, chained to a table, looking individual students in the eye. There was no doubt he demonstrated how smart police dogs are as he watched the classes, the students, and me at the blackboard. He seemed to know what was going on and was very alert and involved.

The girls in the classes patted him on the head and hugged him. The boys got the message to stay away from him. When photos were taken of Simon in the classroom, he posed for every shot, ears up and classic in appearance. He even appeared in the high school yearbook, identified as a special guest instructor.

File photo, Maryland State Police, Salisbury, Maryland, 1985

Bonnie Bear and the author on duty for D.A.R.E.

Simon Takes a Bite out of Crime

In the summer of 1987, several complaints had been filed by video stores on the last end of Lexington, charging that two teenagers were hassling employees, stealing video cassettes, and taking small amounts of money. The teenagers usually took off on skate boards or roller blades. No manager could catch them on foot. As a result, police K-9 patrol units going on duty were asked to provide extra patrol to video stores in their sector from 10 P.M. until closing. Man-dog teams could outrun kids on skate boards or roller blades, but more importantly, they served as a deterrent to crime.

Since I owned a K-9 security company at the time, one manager of an east end video store asked me to come inside on occasion to have a cup of coffee while his staff counted out their money and closed down. I had a great, ninety-pound patrol dog, Simon, who remained outside in my K-9 unit. Simon barked at anybody who came near his truck and sent a strong message to teenagers on skate boards and roller blades, as if to say, "Nobody can outrun a German shepherd."

As luck would have it one hot Sunday night in July, two suspects were robbing the east end Movie Warehouse when Simon and I just happened to be on duty. They had stolen one X-rated cassette and were on the way out when I appeared with Simon. I was not aware that the suspects were inside.

As I walked into the store, they bolted out the back door with a cash bag and two more movies. They knew I couldn't catch them. The thieves were wearing sneakers, and they could run like the wind. They disappeared into an apartment complex nearby.

Four hours later, the duo appeared at a Shell service station three blocks from the Movie Warehouse. This time they were hassling a girl at the cash register, stealing cigarettes, and threatening to kill her if she reported them to the police. They demanded cash from the register and fled on foot with $300. The night manager immediately dialed 911, and an armed robbery call was dispatched to all police units in the area.

I drove quickly to the general area of the gas station in an unmarked unit. First on the scene, I spotted the boys immediately, following them down a side street. An accurate description of the teenagers on the police radio confirmed my suspicions that I was following the right suspects. I dismounted on foot with Simon.

Police cars reporting to the Shell station to take reports gave these two thieves a sense of security. They had no idea I was on their trail with a German shepherd. The teens were laughing and strutting along the walkways in the apartment complex where they had some lady friends. Marked police units streaked past with sirens screaming and overhead lights flashing. Soon the laughing stopped, and the boys hid in the shadows.

I stopped with Simon thirty feet from the suspects and listened to them talk about their exploits. They had robbed four businesses that night, the video store, a Gulf station, a Dairy Queen, and the Shell station. They had stolen over a thousand dollars, beaten up three girls behind cash registers, and outrun the police every time. The boys then began to fight between themselves with the taller youth telling his shorter companion, "You wanted in. You can't get out, that's the rules. You don't get none of this bread, man." This was a rite of initiation for a gang of teens.

I was very close to them, but I knew I couldn't catch both boys if they decided to run. I also worried about my safety in the event the youths were armed. It so happened that they both had knives. Backing off was impossible, and going forward would give my position away. I decided to be cool and wait things out.

A police K-9 unit and two other patrol units approached the apartment complex. The two teenagers panicked. A marked police unit was coming our way, and the boys decided to split up. The younger one ran across the field, and the other boy ran back towards Simon and me.

I had just released Simon to move off lead while I drew my automatic, got ready to use my flashlight to reveal my position, and to command "halt." The tall youth, a high school football tackle, was two-hundred-fifteen pounds of lightning. Simon hit him in the chest and pulled him to the ground in a flash. The boy was terrified and quickly surrendered. I had him rolled over, faced down, and handcuffed in two minutes, recovering the stolen video cassettes and the thousand dollars in cash from the four robberies.

The younger boy, only fourteen, ran as fast as he could, but police units using spotlights found him without much difficulty. Another K-9 unit was on the scene, and when the dog started barking, the boy stopped in his tracks, throwing up his hands. We couldn't stop him from telling all.

We told the younger boy we had been watching the two teens since they robbed the Movie Warehouse at 10:15 P.M. We mentioned the Gulf station and Dairy Queen. The boy admitted he had been to all those places with the one he called The Boss. This was his first time out with his newfound friends.

Simon had taken a bite out of crime that night, solving four strong-arm robberies without drawing a drop of blood. No officers were injured, no weapons were fired, and no youths were injured in the two arrests. After a lengthy interrogation, four more strong-arm robberies were cleared from the books, and a gang of high school football stars was put out of the stealing business.

One of Simon's great demonstrations was alerting on dropped evidence. I had recently been in court testifying against a youth who dropped drugs behind him when confronted in an apartment complex. No witnesses would testify against this bully, a high school football tackle who was a successful drug dealer at age seventeen. When he dropped a packet of heroin which he was trying to sell, Simon alerted on the bag as it hit the ground. I arrested the man for possession of a controlled substance.

In court, the dealer's attorney alleged his client was unfortunate to have been at the wrong place at the wrong time when I encountered him at 3 A.M. in his neighborhood. "The drugs could have belonged to anybody," the attorney argued in court.

"I saw the man drop the drugs, and Simon alerted on the plastic baggie full of heroin," I replied.

"You're sure of that, officer?" the defense attorney said, challenging me. "Would your dog be willing to testify too?" he asked, smiling.

The judge requested I bring Simon into court. I positioned myself with Simon at my left side facing the jury. A court officer faced me with his back to the jury and with the evidence in his right hand. I ordered the court officer to place his hands on his head and interlock his fingers as I was about to search him. The court officer dropped the drug evidence packet as he placed his hands on his head, just as the suspect had done when I arrested him.

When the packet hit the floor in plain view of the twelve members in the jury box, Simon moved forward, alerted on the packet, and pushed the court officer back, jumping on his chest. I picked up the heroin packet and said, "You're under arrest for possession of a controlled substance." The jury believed Simon. The street dealer was found guilty.

Simon, the guest instructor

Photo by LaFayette High School newspaper staff, 1988

Simon demonstrated his ability to identify drugs not only in court but also in the classroom during D.A.R.E. classes. This made some students very uncomfortable. For instance, Simon didn't like people who smoked. He barked at them. If they had been smoking pot, he unleashed horrific growls and snarled at them. The woman who was his first owner said, "As a puppy he must have been abused by construction workers who smoked cigarettes and possibly marijuana."

One day in December 1990 when I was teaching a class to high school seniors, a student came into the class late. Simon almost turned over the table he was chained to, trying to go after the boy. I had a terrible time trying to teach the class while keeping Simon quiet. I knew the kid must have been smoking cigarettes or pot. The student looked dazed and expressionless. Simon was almost uncontrollable. The class was disrupted, and the teacher asked me to take the dog out of the classroom for safety reasons.

As I left the school to place Simon in my K-9 unit, two school security officers approached me, inquiring, "What's wrong with that dog? Is he crazy?"

I quickly answered back, "Nothing is wrong with my dog. You've got a drug dealer in a senior class."

The school principal was very upset at my comments. "We're drug free here!" he boasted.

"Not according to my dog," I replied.

After a few minutes, I returned to the classroom. The senior students were upset that I had returned. The teacher hoped I would just go away. They had started on a new subject, and the D.A.R.E. class was over. "Thank you very much, officer. Goodbye," he told me.

I looked at the class seating chart, wrote down the student's name, and left the classroom. The school security officers had called the narcotics detectives at police headquarters, and they were on the way.

The school principal said, "You have no right or probable cause to search any student's locker just because of that dog."

He was wrong. A dog's ability to smell substances combined with his training and experience in the field are sufficient for probable cause, according to a 1903 U.S. Supreme Court decision. Drug detection dogs working with handlers in the U.S. Customs Service had uncovered millions of dollars worth of drugs over the past thirty years. I had been certified as a U.S. Customs K-9 Specialist in 1981.

I gave the student's name to the detectives. They searched his locker after receiving authority from a district court judge. In the locker they found several hundred dollars worth of street drugs including marijuana. When the student left the classroom a short time later, he came face-to-face with detectives at his locker.

"What's the name of your dog, officer?" some students asked as we were getting ready to leave the school grounds.

"Simon," I replied.

"Simple Simon," they chuckled.

"I'm afraid not. He just busted one of your classmates for possession at this drug-free school. I call him Not Too Simple Simon."

The Courtyard

A ladies' man in his early twenties, Joe Spencer made it a game to play with older women, especially the recently divorced or widows who were vulnerable and looking for companionship. He often used the same line, "You remind me so much of my mom," or "my older sister who died last month."

Joe was a good-looking man with a silver tongue who always dressed like a gentleman. He always complimented women on their personal appearance or mannerisms after studying his potential victims for a few days at grocery stores, in shopping malls, or at gas stations. He would tell them, "My mom always looked at fruit that way when we went to the grocery store back in Idaho" or "Sis wore a dress like that when she worked for a lawyer in Texas."

He would stalk his victims for several days, finding out where they worked, lived, and went to church. Sitting near them in church or bumping into a woman in a church parking lot was his favorite way to start a relationship. He never asked any woman to go to bed. They usually invited him first.

One December, a Mrs. Thomas called the police and asked them to get rid of Joe, who she said had basically, "moved into my Courtyard town house for the duration." In response, Joe told a female police officer, Mary Ann Davis, "Mom is an Alzheimer's patient. Everything is OK." He also asked Davis for her home phone number.

Mrs. Thomas was found by her daughter two days later, bound and gagged in bed, suffering from dehydration. Joe was later seen on a bank video tape closing out Mrs. Thomas' three bank accounts. She lost over forty thousand dollars. Mrs. Thomas sold her Courtyard town house and moved in with her daughter on the other side of town. Spencer left town but returned three months later after a vacation in Florida where he victimized another older woman.

After the December incident, the owner of the Courtyard hired my security company to patrol the twenty town house residences there. Their gates were closed at night, and residents could gain access only by using an electronic device similar to a garage door opener. I patrolled the property four times a night with my dogs, Bonnie and Simon.

Back in town in March at a local cafeteria, Joe ran into another victim dining by herself. She was forty, and her husband had left her for a young woman half his age. Sitting at the table next to her, Joe used the older sister routine, and it worked beautifully. Sarah Lee was from a rural area and was not street wise in the city where hustlers like Joe Spencer abound. They went out to dinner, to country western places, and on walks in the country. Spencer told the woman that he owned a series of fast-food stores, traveled a great deal, and was lonely and that he just had to settle down but had never met the right woman.

Sarah Lee liked Joe Spencer whom she called "a fine lookin' man who treated me good." They moved in together when Sarah Lee insisted he stop running all over the state on business. She rented a town house in the Courtyard. Joe Spencer thought she owned the place and had money. All went well for three weeks, and then Joe found out Sarah had more bills, credit cards, and debts than he had. Joe Spencer had been had.

When Sarah Lee caught Joe reading her mail, she was outraged, pointing a .38 caliber pistol at him. Then she fired a shot. The slug parted his hair and became embedded in the beam at the doorway to his room. Spencer fled the property in his T-shirt and jeans without his car keys or wallet. It was a cold, wet night in April, and Joe Spencer was in trouble.

Sarah Lee called the police and reported an intruder. Then she went through Joe's wallet which was full of credit cards and several hundred dollars in cash. She kept the cash and placed his wallet in his Lincoln Towne Car in the parking lot. When the police arrived, the same officer who had responded to Mrs. Thomas' call in December, Mary Ann Davis, interviewed Sarah Lee. She showed Officer Davis a picture of Joe Spencer. Officer Davis had been taken once but not this time. She had been chewed out by her commander for believing Joe Spencer three months before.

Davis asked Sarah Lee if the Towne Car out front was her vehicle. When she said no, a records check was made, and the vehicle turned out to be stolen from Joe's victim in Florida. The car was searched, and Joe's wallet was recovered. He had over forty credit cards in his name or registered to Spencer's BBQ in Louisville, Kentucky. There was no such business, although there was a post office box and a telephone registered to Spencer's BBQ, and Spencer's BBQ had an ad in the Yellow Pages. An answering service took his calls while Joe was supposedly on business trips.

Joe Spencer was a first-class crook. He had negotiated loans from banks as the owner of Spencer's BBQ. This business also received credit card applications in the mail daily. Spencer had over a million dollars due out to major banks. He would use one credit card to pay off a loan or another credit card. Money from his victims also paid off credit cards.

Officer Davis swore to Sarah Lee that Joe Spencer's luck had run out. She was not aware then that Joe had worked his way into the Salvation Army shelter for the night, saying he was a victim of a robbery, left on the street to die, shot by his assailant for the leather jacket he wore. The paramedics were called to the Salvation Army.

Davis was dispatched to take the call at the shelter regarding a gunshot wound since the Salvation Army was only two blocks from the Courtyard.

Davis left Sarah Lee and reported to the Salvation Army to take a report. When Officer Davis encountered Joe, she asked him how his poor, sick mother was. "You know, the woman you tied up and robbed last Christmas." Spencer took off out of there, and Officer Davis got chewed out again for not requesting a backup on this call.

I was unaware of all that was going on at this time, just rolling along on K-9 patrol, trying to stay dry and warm on this nasty spring night. My dog, Simon, was in the front seat with me, head on my lap, snoring away. I saw Officer Davis and pulled up alongside her police cruiser to say hello. She was so angry she couldn't tell me the whole story, but I got the picture quickly. I headed for the Courtyard to look for Joe Spencer. That was the only place he could go.

As I pulled into the front gate of the town house complex, all was quiet. Only one light was on, and it was at Sarah Lee's place. I knocked on the door, and there he was, soaking wet, cold, and shivering, talking his way back into Sarah Lee's arms. Spencer took one look at me and headed upstairs. I didn't want to get shot on a domestic disturbance call, so I retreated outside to get Simon.

This dog could be just mean and nasty. Give Simon an excuse and he would put you in the hospital in a heartbeat. He could scare anybody to death. He didn't even have to grab hold of body parts. Simon was also very nasty if aroused from a deep sleep. He was snoring in my K-9 unit when I opened the door and called him.

Just as Simon dismounted, Joe Spencer jumped down from the second floor of Sara Lee's town house and started running. He disappeared in the darkness behind some bushes at the main gate to the complex. Since he didn't have his security gate opener, he was trapped inside the gates.

Simon heard Joe cursing. He had hurt his leg in the drop from the second floor window. It was all over in three seconds. Simon attacked Joe head on, barking and growling, flushing Spencer from the bushes. Officer Davis drove up at the same time, and Joe Spencer quickly surrendered to her, requesting transport in the safety of the back seat of her police cruiser.

As you might expect in a domestic disturbance call, Sarah Lee came out of her home and offered Joe Spencer another place by her side. "All is forgiven," she cried. I was cursed out for turning loose my vicious dog on the poor man. If it hadn't been for the outstanding warrants on Joe Spencer, he might still be in her arms.

I told Simon, "Load up," and we left the Courtyard to go get a cup of coffee after saying good night to Officer Davis.

I dropped the security contract at the Courtyard because it was gaining a reputation for too many crazy calls. Whenever I see hotels or motels with the name Courtyard, I try to stay away from them, always remembering good-looking Joe Spencer standing there soaking wet in the rain.

A Chance to Be the Good Samaritan

At 2 A.M. one cold, wet, miserable night in April 1992, I was on K-9 security patrol in Lexington with my two dogs, Bonnie and Simon. While parked at one of my contracts, Conrad Chevrolet on Richmond Road, I was taking a break when I was approached by a dirty, disheveled, bearded street person who had been drinking. He had no coat. Blood was on his shirt collar and right sleeve. A tall, dark-skinned man with a soft voice, he had a kind face and great eye contact.

As he approached my patrol vehicle, neither of my dogs alerted or even took notice of him. It was as if he did not exist. Except for this man, not a single person has ever come near me nor my vehicle without my dogs alerting, flashing their teeth, and growling. There was something different about Walter Peartree.

Mr. Peartree asked me, "Officer, can I hitch a ride on the interstate?"

The answer, of course, was no. "It's too dangerous out there. Sorry," was my reply.

"Sir, my unmarried sister, Anne, in Charlotte has died, and I need to get home. There's a bus to Charlotte from Knoxville. I need to get a ride down there. How can I do that?"

Knoxville is a three-hour drive south on Interstate 75 from Lexington. I told him I would try to get him a ride from the Greyhound Bus station. I invited him to get in the car and warm up. On the way across town, my dogs ignored Mr. Peartree while normally they would have been very inquisitive about any stranger, sniffing, pawing him, and perhaps barking. I always kept the back window open in my truck cab so the dogs in the rear cage could assist me in the event I had trouble with any prisoner or passenger.

I asked Mr. Peartree why he had blood on his collar and right sleeve, also inquiring if he had been drinking.

"I've been drinking ever since the word came that my sister died. I've been drunk for two days," he answered.

"Were you in a fight?" I persisted.

"Yes, sir, I got into a fight on the interstate at a rest stop. Two young fellas rolled me and took my coat, money, and back pack," he said. He explained that he had hitched a ride from Columbus, Ohio, to Lexington that day then had walked the three miles into town looking for shelter when he spotted me.

I turned into the bus station about 2:45 A.M. A Greyhound cruiser was about to depart the area. About twenty passengers were loading up as I parked my vehicle. Since my patrol dog, Simon, needed a stretch and a walk, I dismounted with this ninety-pound German shepherd. Suddenly, the passenger sitting behind the bus driver's seat darted from the bus and disappeared into the darkness. Five other people ran from the bus station. They must have thought I was a police officer getting ready to make an arrest with my K-9 partner.

Both Bonnie and Simon were barking viciously. Simon was ready to pursue the man who ran from the bus. Two paper bags full of drugs were left behind in the terminal. The man who was seated behind the driver also left a grimy sheepskin coat on the bus.

"That's the kind of coat I had, officer," Mr. Peartree whispered to me.

The bus driver gave me the coat. It fit Mr. Peartree perfectly. There were a few twenty dollar bills in the right pocket, enough money to buy a bus ticket to Charlotte.

"How much money did you lose out there on the interstate when you were robbed?" I inquired.

"Only twelve dollars; I didn't have all this money, but I'm sure this is my coat," he said. He put it on and buttoned it up, warding off the chill in the air.

Mr. Peartree was very hungry. I had given him about four dollars in change when I picked him up at Conrad Chevrolet. He spent every dime of it buying cakes, candy, peanuts, crackers, and milk from the bus station vending machines.

The bus driver told me he had to move out to keep up with his schedule. "Knoxville by 6 A.M.!" he said.

I explained that Mr. Peartree was a victim of an assault who needed a ride south. I asked him if he would sell Mr. Peartree a ticket.

"Can't do that," he said, "but he can ride with me. I've got space." Tickets could not be purchased after 9 P.M. at the bus station, nor were bus drivers allowed to sell tickets or make change for passengers for reasons of personal safety. "Load up, sir. Gotta go," the driver shouted as he began to close the door. Mr. Peartree ran into the bus, never looking back, never saying a word to the driver or me.

I told the driver I would pay for Mr. Peartree's fare to Knoxville. "Just send me the bill," I said and handed him my business card from Morgan K-9 Security Service.

"Don't worry about it," the driver commented as the bus departed the Lexington terminal right on time. I mounted up with Simon to go back on patrol.

I never heard from Mr. Peartree again. I called the phone number he had given me when he first identified himself at Conrad Chevrolet. It belonged to a small funeral home in Charlotte. They had never heard of Anne Peartree, and they had no funerals that week. I called the Charlotte Police Department and asked if they could locate Mr. Peartree at the address he had given me. The desk sergeant told me, "We don't have a street by that name."

Being a spiritual person, I thought of the story about the centurion who gave a beggar half his cloak on a bitterly cold night. I also thought about the good samaritan who had stopped on the side of the road to help a man who was beaten and robbed and left for dead. I began to wonder why Simon and Bonnie had not alerted on Mr. Peartree. They almost went crazy with the people running away from the bus station.

I spoke to the same bus driver from the Greyhound station two weeks later, thanking him for his kindness, inquiring about Mr. Peartree. He could not recall the incident. When I asked him about paying for Mr. Peartree's fare, he replied, "We wouldn't let anybody on the bus without a ticket."

I often reflect on that night. I remember the words of the hymn, "Whatever you do to the least of mine, that you do unto me." My encounter with that man was a unique experience. It also changed my attitude about street people. Had I been tested as a good samaritan? Had I seen Christ face-to-face?

Chapter 9

At the Wall

1994-97

Duke, Cody

Tom Mulvey

Tom Mulvey was born June 6, 1940, on a small farm in southern New Jersey where his grandfather raised hunting dogs. Tom's grandfather had served with an Irish regiment in the trenches of France in World War I. In July 1916 at the Battle of the Somme River, his grandfather's left foot was crushed and amputated after his bomb shelter was destroyed by German artillery.

When Tom was two years old, his father, Jim, was drafted into the infantry, serving in eight campaigns of World War II in the European theater of operations. On Tom's fourth birthday, D day, June 6, 1944, Jim Mulvey lost his left foot after stepping on a land mine at Normandy. This unfortunate family history would soon repeat itself after Tom joined the military.

I met Tom and his father at the Vietnam Wall, officially called the Vietnam Veterans' Memorial, in Washington, D.C., one recent Veterans' Day. Both father and son looked very relaxed, telling me they were glad to be there with so many other combat soldiers. They looked like brothers, both wearing Army field jackets with First Infantry Division patches and combat infantry badges, both walking with slight limps. There were a good many World War II and Korean War veterans at the Wall that day, and if one was interested in learning history from veterans who had experienced the horrors of war, that was the place to take notes.

In 1962, Tom enlisted in the service at age twenty-two. After basic training at Fort Dix, New Jersey, a short distance from home, he was assigned to Fort

Benning, Georgia, for advanced infantry training (AIT). "After watching a scout dog demonstration at AIT at Benning, I volunteered for duty as a dog handler," he said proudly.

I, too, had been trained as a dog handler at Benning. We had many things in common, and the war stories started. We both had been dog handlers working with Army ranger students at Fort Benning. We had also been to NCO school there and had graduated from ranger school, officially known as the U.S. Army Ranger Course. When things heated up in Vietnam in 1965, we shipped out to southeast Asia. I went with the U.S. Military Assistance Command, assigned to the 30th Ranger Battalion (ARVN). Tom went as an NCO with the First Infantry Division, The Big Red One.

In Vietnam, Tom Mulvey and I both worked with dogs. My dog's name was Suzie. Tom's dog was Duke. We had operated in the same area about six months apart. I was there from June to December 1965. He was in that area from April to July 1966, until he was wounded. He lost his left leg at a place called the sugar mill on the border of Gia Dinh and Hau Nghia Provinces almost fifty years to the date after his grandfather had been wounded in World War I. Tom had been wounded by a mine, just as his father had been in Normandy.

"My son has never served in the military," Tom told me, "otherwise, he would be walking on one leg made out of plastic like we do." He and his father laughed about it as GIs who have endured pain, hardship, and suffering so often do.

As we shared stories about dogs, getting shot at, and getting hit, three other combat vets from The Big Red One joined us at the massive flag pole near the Vietnam Memorial. A newsman from a local TV station was watching us intently. He approached with a video cameraman at his side, and we were interviewed, telling him our names and hometowns. Every one of the vets he interviewed had a combat infantryman's badge, a Purple Heart, and a story to tell about dogs in Vietnam.

One of the vets told us he was a platoon leader in the Bolo Woods and that a K-9 had alerted just seconds before his platoon walked into an ambush. "We did not lose a man, thanks to that scout dog. The gunships were on station in seconds, and when they were finished, we lit the place up with napalm courtesy of the U.S. Air Force."

A second vet told us about an ambush patrol he was on in the Iron Triangle. "We were dead tired after weeks in the bush and just didn't care if we lived or died. We all went to sleep, except for a scout dog handler and a beautiful German shepherd he called Honey. The dog alerted on a Viet Cong patrol, claymores were popped, and we got back the next morning without any losses."

The newsman placed a small tape recorder near Tom as he told his story. "There were about thirty of us on one of those long, hot walks in the sun. Vietnam was a beautiful place — too bad they had a war there. I was walking point as we approached an east-west road which ran from Saigon to Cambodia. We took a break on the side of the road. Vehicles used this route all the time, so we felt as if we were relatively safe. When the lieutenant stood up to give us some orders, a sniper shot him dead center. He never knew what hit him. The whole platoon scrambled for what cover we could find in the rice paddies. I dashed across the road with my dog, Duke, and a squad of guys. Then a command detonated mine got triggered. My left leg was blown off at the knee. Duke got hit but never complained a bit."

Tom's eyes filled with tears. Jim Mulvey was glassy eyed, too. They embraced each other, and we all stood silent for several minutes. The war stories stopped. The video camera was turned off. The newsman was at a complete loss for words. I had a dog with me, a golden retriever. Self-consciously, we all began to pay attention to my dog, talking to him as if he were a child. All six of us drifted away from the flag pole.

After about twenty minutes, Tom and his father returned to the flag pole, and we started to talk some more. "Duke died under my cot at the base camp the next day," Tom confided in me. "The captain brought me his ashes in an ammo box. I still have them today in a German shepherd statue at home. Some people have urns for ashes. I have a ceramic Goebel statue of a German shepherd, from West Germany. Duke is still with us," he added before choking up again.

Another dog handler came up to me wearing a bush hat from Vietnam. His dog's picture was pinned up on the left side of the hat band where we used to display hand grenade pins in Vietnam. The newsman joined us again as his video cameraman panned the scene near the three soldiers statue at the Vietnam Memorial.

"Did you all serve in Vietnam?" he inquired.

"Yes, except for Jim Mulvey. He was in World War II, wounded at Normandy," I answered.

"Was this a reunion for you?" the newsman asked.

"No, we just met for the first time this morning," I informed him.

"You seem like old friends. I can hardly believe it, that you just met this morning," he commented.

The video cameraman joined the newsman and explained, "Combat veterans are very close. They all wear pins and patches to identify themselves. All these guys have that blue rifle badge. They're infantrymen."

The newsman asked me to explain all the pins and patches. I did my best to give him a short course on awards and decorations, unit crests, and division patches. He asked me why GIs wear those things. I told him, "Doctors and lawyers and teachers and newsmen display their achievements in framed documents on the walls in their offices. GIs don't have offices. They wear their awards on their jackets and hats."

"I was born in 1970 and don't know much about Vietnam or Korea or World War II, for that matter. I've got a lot to learn, I guess," the newsman commented as he scribbled down some notes getting ready to make a tape for the evening news.

No Dogs at the Wall!

On Veterans Day in 1994, my wife and I went to the Vietnam Veterans' Memorial in Washington, D.C., something we have done several times since 1983. I was dressed in Levi's and a camouflage field jacket with combat insignia, including my combat infantry badge and Army Ranger tab.

The comradeship was great. It was a privilege to be there with hundreds of other combat veterans. I had my ninety-pound German shepherd with me. Cody Bear was solid black, just like the Wall. He wore a yellow cavalry neckerchief and strutted next to me.

As we started to descend down the path to the black granite monument, we were stopped by a U.S. Park Service Ranger. "No dogs at the Wall!" he told me.

"Why?" I asked.

"Too many people. He's too big," was the response.

"I'm a Vietnam vet, and I was a handler in 1965. This dog will be part of the ceremony today," I answered back.

Suddenly there were four police officers around me, my wife, and Cody Bear. I became very uncomfortable as I was taken away from the Wall and the thousands of visitors who were there to pay respects to our honored dead. I thought I was going to be arrested.

In the open field by ourselves, Cody and I were suddenly surrounded by some fifty veterans. Many were members of the Vietnam Dog Handler Association (VDHA). Some wore combat fatigues while others were in khakis and civilian clothing. Others wore VDHA sweat shirts with air-brushed photos of German shepherds and names of dogs imprinted on them. Some wore VDHA baseball caps. The cops disappeared.

"Welcome home," I heard over and over again. The veterans patted Cody Bear on the head and started talking about their dogs in Vietnam. Photos came out of wallets, Vietnam battlefield locations were mentioned, combat outfits were identified, and the stories started. What a great feeling!

Cody and the author

Photo by Patrick Hughes, 1994

At noon, the ceremony started with a salute to Hispanic veterans by the Veterans' Band of Corpus Christie. Colors were presented by massed color guards from the 1st Infantry Division, the 1st Cavalry Division, the 25th Infantry Division, and the 82d Airborne Division. Our national anthem was played, and the speeches began. On the dais was a member of the VDHA, Mike Quinlivan, and his dog, Brandy. They represented all Vietnam veteran dog handlers. Then came the presentation of the wreaths at the Wall.

I stood in the crowd with combat infantrymen, Marines, Security Policemen from the U.S. Air Force, three Army rangers, and six paratroopers from the 82d Airborne.

Two members of the Vietnam Dog Handler Association, Mike Cagle and Bruce Fleming, walked up to me and asked if I would accompany them to the

Wall with Cody at my side. With a select group of veterans from many units, we walked down the same path from which we had been ejected an hour earlier. The VDHA veterans carried a wreath made by Bruce Fleming's wife, Judy. It memorialized all the dogs, some 3,800 of them, and their handlers who served in Vietnam, America's longest war.

Cody sat at the foot of the wreath, once the procession halted, and faced a crowd of thousands of spectators. My dog with the shining black coat would have been hard to find at this shining black Wall, except for his yellow scarf and the colorful VDHA wreath.

When the band finished playing and the ceremony was completed, Cody and I were surrounded by hundreds of Vietnam vets. Cody was photographed at least fifty times, and then it was all over.

The law may dictate no dogs at the Wall, but he was an exception to the law that day.

Photo by Wanda Lou McInturff, 1994

Cody and author at the Wall
·Vietnam Veterans' Memorial, Washington, D.C., Veterans' Day, 1994

My Buddy, Cody

Cody was my last patrol dog. After Simon died in 1992, I received Cody from a German shepherd rescue group. He had belonged to a police officer who could not keep him at home any longer. Cody was just about perfect, very intelligent, devoted, and beautiful to look at. He was also very sick. He had a brain tumor and died in my arms at age five.

I had to retire from K-9 patrol work after sixteen years on the job because of back problems. After Cody died, I could not go back on the street anyway. My wife had told me many times, "You've got to give up the K-9 work. Those dogs just break your heart!"

Painting by Patricia Olds, 1997

Index

WELCOME TO

Hellgate Press

Hellgate Press is named after the historic and rugged Hellgate Canyon on southern Oregon's scenic Rogue River. The raging river that flows below the canyon's towering jagged cliffs has always attracted a special sort of individual — someone who seeks adventure. From the pioneers who bravely pursued the lush valleys beyond, to the anglers and rafters who take on its roaring challenges today — Hellgate Press publishes books that personify this adventurous spirit. Our books are about military history, adventure travel, and outdoor recreation. On the following pages, we would like to introduce you to some of our latest titles and encourage you to join in the celebration of this unique spirit.

Our books are in your favorite bookstore or you can order them direct at *1-800-228-2275 or visit our Website at http://www.psi-research.com/hellgate.htm*

ARMY MUSEUMS
West of the Mississippi
by Fred L. Bell, SFC Retired

ISBN: 1-55571-395-5
Paperback: $17.95

A guide book for travelers to the army museums of the west, as well as a source of information about the history of the site where the museum is located. Contains detailed information about the contents of the museum and interesting information about famous soldiers stationed at the location or specific events associated with the facility. These twenty-three museums are in forts and military reservations which represent the colorful heritage in the settling of the American West.

BYRON'S WAR
I Never Will Be Young Again...
by Byron Lane

ISBN: 1-55571-402-1
Hardcover: $21.95

Based on letters that were mailed home and a personal journal written more than fifty years ago during World War II, Byron's War brings the war life through the eyes of a very young air crew officer. It depicts how the life of this young American changed through cadet training, the experiences as a crew member flying across the North Atlantic under wartime hazards to the awesome responsibility assigned to a nineteen year-old when leading hundreds of men and aircraft where success or failure could seriously impact the outcome of the war.

GULF WAR DEBRIEFING BOOK

An After Action Report   ISBN: 1-55571-396-3
by Andrew Leyden   Paperback: $18.95

Whereas most books on the Persian Gulf War tell an "inside story" based on someone else's opinion, this book lets you draw your own conclusions about the war by providing you with a meticulous review of events and documentation all at your fingertips. Includes lists of all military units deployed, a detailed account of the primary weapons used during the war, and a look at the people and politics behind the military maneuvering.

FROM HIROSHIMA WITH LOVE

     ISBN: 1-55571-404-8
by Raymond A. Higgins   Paperback: $18.95

This remarkable story is written from actual detailed notes and diary entries kept by Lieutenant Commander Wallace Higgins. Because of his industrial experience back in the United States and with the reserve commission in the Navy, he was an excellent choice for military governor of Hiroshima. Higgins was responsible for helping rebuild a ravaged nation of war. He developed an unforeseen respect for the Japanese, the culture, and one special woman.

NIGHT LANDING

A Short History of West Coast Smuggling   ISBN: 1-55571-449-8
by David W. Heron   Paperback: $13.95

Night Landing reveals the true stories of smuggling off the shores of California from the early 1800s to the present. It is a provocative account of the many attempts to illegally trade items such as freon, drugs, sea otters, and diamonds. This unusual chronicle also profiles each of these ingenious, but over-optimistic criminals and their eventual apprehension.

ORDER OF BATTLE

Allied Ground Forces of Operation Desert Storm   ISBN: 1-55571-493-5
by Thomas D. Dinackus   Paperback: $17.95

Based on extensive research, and containing information not previously available to the public, *Order of Battle: Allied Ground Forces of Operation Desert Storm*, is a detailed study of the Allied ground combat units that served in Operation Desert Storm. In addition to showing unit assignments, it includes the insignia and equipment used by the various units in one of the largest military operations since the end of WWII.

PILOTS, MAN YOUR PLANES!

A History of Naval Aviation   ISBN: 1-55571- 466-8
by Wilbur H. Morrison   Hardbound: $ 33.95

An account of naval aviation from Kitty Hawk to the Gulf War, *Pilots, Man Your Planes!* tells the story of naval air growth from a time when planes were launched from battleships to the major strategic element of naval warfare it is today. Full of detailed maps and photographs. Great for anyone with an interest in aviation.

REBIRTH OF FREEDOM

From Nazis and Communists to a New Life in America   ISBN: 1-55571-492-7
by Michael Sumichrast   Paperback: $ 16.95

"...a fascinating account of how the skill, ingenuity and work ethics of an individual, when freed from the yoke of tyranny and oppression, can make a lasting contribution to Western society. Michael Sumichrast's autobiography tells of his first loss of freedom to the Nazis, only to have his native country subjected to the tyranny of the Communists. He shares his experiences of life in a manner that makes us Americans, and others, thankful to live in a country where individual freedom is protected."

— *General Alexander M. Haig, Former Secretary of State*

THE WAR THAT WOULD NOT END

U.S. Marines in Vietnam, 1971-1973   ISBN: 1-55571-420-X
by Major Charles D. Melson, USMC (Ret)   Paperback: $19.95

When South Vietnamese troops proved unable to "take over" the war from their American counterparts, the Marines had to resume responsibility. Covering the period 1971-1973, Major Charles D. Melson, who served in Vietnam, describes all the strategies, battles, and units that broke a huge 1972 enemy offensive. The book contains a detailed look at this often ignored period of America's longest war.

WORDS OF WAR

From Antiquity to Modern Times   ISBN: 1-55571-491-9
by Gerald Weland   Paperback: $ 13.95

Words of War is a delightful romp through military history. Lively writing leads the reader to an under- standing of a number of soldierly quotes. The result of years of haunting dusty dungeons in libraries, obscure journals and microfilm files, this unique approach promises to inspire many casual readers to delve further into the circumstances surrounding the birth of many quoted words.

WORLD TRAVEL GUIDE

A Resource for Travel and Information   ISBN: 1-55571- 494-3
by Barry Mowell   Paperback: $ 19.95

The resource for the modern traveler, *World Travel Guide: A Resource for Travel and Information* is both informative and enlightening. It contains maps, social and economic information, concise information concerning entry requirements, availability of healthcare, transportation and crime. Numerous Website and embassy listings are provided for additional free information. A one-page summary contains general references to the history, culture and other characteristics of interest to the traveler or those needing a reference atlas.

K-9 SOLDIERS
Vietnam and After

ISBN: **1-55571-495-1**

by Paul B. Morgan

Paperback: $13.95

A retired US Army officer, former Green Beret, Customs K-9 and Security Specialist, Paul B. Morgan has written *K-9 Soldiers*. In his book, Morgan relates twenty-four brave stories from his lifetime of working with man's best friend in combat and on the streets. They are the stories of dogs and their handlers who work behind the scenes when a disaster strikes, a child is lost or some bad guy tries to outrun the cops.

AFTER THE STORM
A Vietnam Veteran's Reflection

ISBN: **1-55571-500-1**

by Paul Drew

Paperback: $14.95

Even after twenty-five years, the scars of the Vietnam War are still felt by those who were involved. *After the Storm: A Vietnam Veteran's Reflection* is more than a war story. Although it contains episodes of combat, it does not dwell on them. It concerns itself more on the mood of the nation during the war years, and covers the author's intellectual and psychological evolution as he questions the political and military decisions that resulted in nearly 60,000 American deaths.

GREEN HELL
The Battle for Guadalcanal

ISBN: **1-55571-498-6**

by William J. Owens

Paperback: $18.95

This is the story of thousands of Melanesian, Australian, New Zealand, Japanese, and American men who fought for a poor insignificant island is a faraway corner of the South Pacific Ocean. For the men who participated, the real battle was man against jungle. This is the account of land, sea and air units covering the entire six-month battle. Stories of ordinary privates and seamen, admirals and generals who survive to claim the victory that was the turning point of the Pacific War.

OH, WHAT A LOVELY WAR

ISBN: **1-55571-502-8**

by Evelyn A. Luscher

Paperback: $14.95

This book tells you what history books do not. It is war with a human face. It is the unforgettable memoir of British soldier Gunner Stanley Swift through five years of war. Intensely personal and moving, it documents the innermost thoughts and feelings of a young man as he moves from civilian to battle-hardened warrior under the duress of fire.

THROUGH MY EYES
91st Infantry Division, Italian Campaign 1942-1945

ISBN: **1-55571-497-8**

by Leon Weckstein

Paperback: $14.95

Through My Eyes is the true account of an Average Joe's infantry days before, during and shortly after the furiously fought battle for Italy. The author's front row seat allows him to report the shocking account of casualties and the rest-time shenanigans during the six weeks of the occupation of the city of Trieste. He also recounts in detail his personal roll in saving the historic Leaning Tower of Pisa.

Order Directly From Hellgate Press

You can purchase any of these Hellgate Press titles directly by sending us this completed order form.

To order call, 1-800-228-2275
Fax 1-541-476-1479

Hellgate Press

P.O. Box 3727
Central Point, OR 97502

For inquiries and international orders,
call 1-541-479-9464

TITLE	PRICE	QUANTITY	COST
Army Museums: West of the Mississippi	$13.95		
Byron's War	$21.95		
From Hiroshima With Love	$18.95		
Gulf War Debriefing Book	$18.95		
Night Landing	$13.95		
Order of Battle	$17.95		
Pilots, Man Your Planes!	$33.95		
Rebirth of Freedom	$16.95		
The War That Would Not End	$19.95		
Words of War	$13.95		
World Travel Guide	$19.95		
Memories Series			
After The Storm	$14.95		
Green Hell	$18.95		
Oh, What A Lovely War!	$14.95		
Through My Eyes	$14.95		

SHIPPING INFORMATION

If your purchase is:	your shipping is:
up to $25	$5.00
$25.01–$50.00	$6.00
$50.01–$100	$7.00
$100.01–$175	$9.00
over $175	call

Subtotal	$
Shipping	$
Grand Total	$

Thank You For Your Order!

Shipping Information
Name:
Address:
City, State, Zip:
Daytime Phone: Email:

Ship To: (If Different Than Above)
Name:
Address:
City, State, Zip
Daytime Phone:

Payment Method:
For rush orders, Canadian and overseas orders please call for details at (541) 479-9464
☐ Check   ☐ American Express   ☐ MasterCard   ☐ Visa
Card Number: Expiration Date:
Signature: Exact Name on Card:

For more adventure and military history information visit our Website

Hellgate Press Online

http://www.psi-research.com/hellgate.htm

With information about our latest titles, as well as links to related subject matter.

Hellgate Press Reader Survey

Did you enjoy this Hellgate Press title?
☐ Yes   ☐ No
If no, how would you improve it:

_____
_____
_____

Would you be interested in other titles from Hellgate Press?
☐ Yes   ☐ No

How do you feel about the price?
☐ Too high   ☐ Fair   ☐ Lower than expected

Where did you purchase this book?
☐ Bookstore
☐ Online (Internet)
☐ Catalog
☐ Association/Club
☐ It was a gift
☐ Other: _____

Do you use a personal computer?
☐ Yes   ☐ No

Have you ever purchased anything on the Internet?
☐ Yes   ☐ No

Do you use a personal computer?
☐ Yes   ☐ No

Would you like to receive a Hellgate catalog?
☐ Yes   ☐ No
If yes, please fill out the information below:

Name: _____

Address: _____

City, State, Zip: _____

Email Address (optional): _____

K-9 Soldiers
Vietnam and After

Please send this survey to:
PSI Research
c/o Hellgate Press
P.O. Box 3727
Central Point, OR 97526

or fax it: (541) 476-1479
or email your responses to:
info@psi-research.com

Thank You!